Albert Murray

and the Aesthetic Imagination of a Nation

Albert Murray

and the Aesthetic Imagination of a Nation

Edited by Barbara A. Baker

A Pebble Hill Book • The University of Alabama Press

Published by Pebble Hill, an imprint of the Caroline Marshall
Draughon Center for the Arts & Humanities, College of Liberal
Arts, Auburn University, and The University of Alabama Press

Typeface: Corbel
Designer: Michele Myatt Quinn

∞
The paper on which this book is printed meets the minimum
requirements of American National Standard for Information
Science—Permanence of Paper for Printed Library Materials, ANSI
Z39.48-1984.

Library of Congress Cataloging-in-Publication Data

Albert Murray and the aesthetic imagination of a nation / edited
by Barbara A. Baker.
      p. cm.
    "A Pebble Hill book."
    Includes bibliographical references and index.
    ISBN 978-0-8173-1697-6 (cloth : alk. paper) — ISBN 978-0-8173-
5593-7 (pbk. : alk. paper) — ISBN 978-0-8173-8488-3 (electronic)
    1. Murray, Albert. I. Baker, Barbara A.
    PS3563.U764Z53 2010
    813'.54—dc22

                                                    2009044306

Cover Photo: Albert Murray. Photograph by Carol Friedman.
Title page spread: Harlem cityscape taken from Murray's Lenox
Terrace apartment. Photograph by Carol Friedman.

This book is a project of the Caroline Marshall Draughon Center for the Arts & Humanities, the outreach and engagement center for the College of Liberal Arts at Auburn University. The center developed the symposium "Albert Murray and the Aesthetic Imagination of a Nation," held in January 2008, which brought together many of the scholars represented here. The resulting book, *Albert Murray and the Aesthetic Imagination of a Nation,* is part of the Pebble Hill Imprint Series. Books in the series grow out of or contribute to the center's outreach and engagement programs.

Contents

Reminiscences and Appreciations

Foreword

ANNE-KATRIN GRAMBERG

Someone told me once that Albert Murray said he would rather be judged on a basketball court than anywhere else because when it comes to sports, people always look for the best player. He has always striven to be the best player in whatever arena he plays, and in all his omni-American perfectionism, he has succeeded. This is the ideal that he shares with my concept of Auburn's College of Liberal Arts, and that is why we have chosen to honor him in this volume. His outstanding contribution to American letters, one that speaks to and for the state of Alabama in a musical, elegant, and sophisticated language, captures the rich heritage as well as the ageless complexities of our home state. And his theories of American culture illustrate the manner in which the triumphs and failures of our coming-of-age have contributed to American culture and art in, perhaps, a unique and more fluid way than have those of many other places.

But Mr. Murray would not want us to say that Alabama is unique; he would want us to recognize that in the possibilities presented to us, we are all the same. To him, it is a matter of procedure or how one chooses to address the adversity ever present in the world.

The College of Liberal Arts was honored and delighted to bring together the protégés and scholars who have absorbed Mr. Murray's procedures and theories and who have made it part of their life's work to spread the word about this outstanding Alabamian. It is our hope that this volume will be but a starting place for generations of scholarship to come that will explore the cultural critiques, novels, poetry, lectures, interviews, artistic relationships, friendships, and conversations—the outpouring of words, both spoken and written—by our Most Valuable Player, Albert Murray.

Acknowledgments

I am grateful to the National Endowment for the Humanities for the Extending the Reach Faculty Research Award (2002–3) that afforded me the opportunity to begin work on this volume. Thank you to Tuskegee University, particularly to Dr. Benjamin Benford, dean, and Dr. Luther Williams, provost, for granting me a sabbatical leave (2007–8) during which I was able to complete much of the work on this book. Thanks to Dr. Anne-Katrin Gramberg, dean of the College of Liberal Arts at Auburn University, who supported this project in its entirety, especially the symposium "Albert Murray and the Aesthetic Imagination of a Nation," which enabled the contributors to this book to meet and share their work in order to prepare it for publication. Special thanks to Dr. Mark Wilson of the Caroline Marshall Draughon Center for the Arts & Humanities for his hard work and attention to the details of the symposium. Special thanks also to Team Murray, especially Paul Devlin, who served as point man in networking Mr. Murray's colleagues, associates, and friends, and to Dr. Caroline Gebhard, my "coconspirator."

Introduction

BARBARA A. BAKER

No one has more eloquently and thoroughly represented Alabama's influence on the art and culture of the United States than Albert Murray. The lush landscapes of Murray's Alabama have always fed his astonishingly imaginative creative capacity and provided a spyglass tree from which he formulates both his poetic vision and his insightful cultural critiques. As a journeyman who made his way from Mobile County Training School to Jazz at Lincoln Center by way of Tuskegee Institute he all the while conspired with the most critically acclaimed artists of the century, changing the "fakelore" of white supremacy into a new folklore that conclusively illustrates that the blues idiom statement most completely reflects the elegant grace of the southern and black vernacular maneuvers at the core of what is truly American about our art.

Whether writing stories that embalm the spirit of the Deep South and Tuskegee in the 1930s or poems that jam on Armstrong, Ellington, Faulkner, Freud, and Hemingway or unique aesthetic observations of the twentieth century, he has always refined, extended, and elaborated on the riffs he learned in the southern briarpatch of his youth. It is most fitting that his lifetime of achievement in expressing the aesthetics of a nation through the lens of his Alabama upbringing be celebrated in a volume that collects critiques and criticism as well as expressions of appreciation from a broad range of scholars, friends, and protégés who have been forever changed by knowing Albert Murray.

The contributors to *Albert Murray and the Aesthetic Imagination of a Nation* share the special experience of having been personally as well as intellectually touched by the life and works of Albert Murray. This volume grows out of our deep appreciation for that experience as well as years of discussion and long conversations both among the contributors and between each contributor and Murray himself.

My own initiation into the world of Albert Murray began years ago when my dissertation director asked me if I would assist Jay Lamar and the folks at what is now the Caroline Marshall Draughon Center for the Arts & Humanities in their efforts to bring Albert Murray to Auburn University. I was given the opportunity to meet and spend time with the delightful Murray family, with whom I have shared stories and laughter ever since. From the beginning, Mr. Murray opened his heart, mind, and home to me, and as was the case for most of the contributors to this book, in his uniquely inviting openness he taught me many lessons, among them how to teach. For Albert Murray teaching is not a profession; it is a lifelong commitment to read, learn, synthesize, debate, and discuss with anyone at any time the defining issues of American culture and art.

Murray had graduated from and taught at Alabama's Tuskegee Institute (University), and so after I graduated, I followed my passion for his blues theories and him to Tuskegee, where I taught for eleven years. Over the course of those years I was given the opportunity to share the world of Albert Murray with a new generation of Tuskegeans, and I continued to collaborate with Jay Lamar at Auburn University. Together we brought Mr. Murray back to Alabama two more times: once to deliver the Ralph Ellison Lecture at Tuskegee University in 1999 (during which he read for the first time from his preface to *Trading Twelves: The Selected Letters of Ralph Ellison and Albert Murray*) and again in 2003, when Mr. Murray was awarded the Distinguished Artist Award by the Alabama State Council on the Arts. In his acceptance speech, "In Response to Being Awarded a Citation for Distinguished Literary Achievement by an Alabamian" (chapter 1 in this volume), he sums up his literary intentions to make his Alabama-bred perspectives speak to and for the American literary and cultural scene. That he succeeded in this is demonstrated by the caliber of writers and thinkers who pay homage to him here.

When the time came to bring together the people who contributed to this book (a group that proudly referred to ourselves as "Team Murray"), it was only natural that I would return to the Caroline Marshall Draughon Center and ask for its help in preparing the symposium that allowed us time to come together in January 2008 to share our thoughts on Mr. Murray and to collect the papers that make up this volume.

In preparation for the symposium, I traveled in June 2007 to New York City to visit Mr. Murray at his home on Lenox Terrace in Harlem and attend the celebration of his receiving the Du Bois Medal from Harvard University, an extraordinary event hosted by Henry Louis Gates Jr. and Wynton Marsalis and attended by over one hundred of Murray's closest friends, including members of Team Murray. Both Dr. Gates and Mr. Marsalis, along with many of the other guests, enthusiastically supported the idea of a symposium and book to further honor this American cultural pioneer. Marsalis says that Murray is like a grandfather who not only gives him information but helps him understand it. In his citation delivered to Mr. Murray that day (reprinted in this volume), Dr. Gates elaborated on the profound influence that Murray's breathtaking acts of cultural chutzpah had on him and so many other scholars of American literature and culture by saying, "He spurred Ralph Ellison's thinking for decades (and sparred with him as well), and sharpened the 'narrative' of Romare Bearden's gorgeous art. Today, Stanley Crouch and Wynton Marsalis still labor under his dictates, and I do, too."

In "King of Cats" (reprinted here)—perhaps the definitive statement on Albert Murray's contributions to American letters—Dr. Gates argues that one of Murray's most stunning dictates is his insistence that American culture is fundamentally black, as demonstrated by the far-reaching implications of the blues idiom statement for American music. As Gates says, "For generations, the word 'American' had tacitly connoted 'white.' Murray inverted the cultural assumption and the verbal conventions: in his discourse, 'American,' roughly speaking, means 'black.'" Gates goes on to point out that Murray expects from all American fine artists the same complexity and craft that he expects from himself. And he completely rejects the assumption that black art can be seen as something separate from mainstream American art. As Murray told the students at Tuskegee in 1999, "I don't want to be read during black history month. I want to be read every month of the year." For an artist, says Murray, only discipline and talent will gain one entry into the pantheon of great literature. He will accept nothing less.

He shared this ardent belief with Ralph Ellison, his lifelong coconspirator. So it was most fitting that we invited the literary executor of Ellison's estate and coeditor with Albert Murray of *Trading Twelves* to Auburn to deliver the keynote address for the Albert Murray symposium. In his keynote address (adapted here), John F. Callahan shows the intensity and tenderness of Ellison and Murray's friendship. Dr. Callahan calls on future Murray biographers to study the decade of correspondence, "which accelerates into a succession of rolling call-and-response jazz riffs" as "the steel-cut grist for an intense, evolving friendship." While the nature of Ellison and Murray's friendship continues to be debated among scholars, Callahan argues that the letters show that theirs was *not* a competitive rivalry but rather a "symbiosis of friendship—a mutually beneficial connection between two men unmarred by competitiveness, perhaps because they are thoroughly formed in style and personality when they commence their literary journey."

Mr. Murray has shown time and again that he values friendships. Just as he cultivated friendships with Ellison, Bearden, Gates, Marsalis, Crouch, and Callahan, he also often reaches out to budding writers and interested scholars, inviting all who will listen to join him in his travels through Cosmos Murray.

In "Cosmos Murray and the Aesthetic Imagination of a Nation," I discuss the main principles that guide Murray's aesthetic theories and apply them to his blues poem "Aubades: Epic Exits and Other Twelve Bar Riffs." Because Mr. Murray read the poem to me, commenting in asides about the significance of the images to his personal life, I am able to suggest in the essay how the journey of his life is told through this blues song, just as the great folk blues musicians re-create the depth and reality of experience in their music. As Murray explained to me, writers need a metaphor, and his is the blues. Thus a blues song is the ideal vehicle for conveying most fully the pragmatic utility of the key concepts in the Murray aesthetic.

The next two essays are by current Murray pupils Paul Devlin and Lauren Walsh, who both enjoyed a thorough extracurricular education in the Murray studio while taking doctoral degrees in the New York City area. Paul Devlin has an especially close relationship to Mr. Murray, who has shared with him surprising details of his forays into visual arts and their relationship to literature and music. In "Albert Murray and Visual Art," Devlin illustrates, through an anecdote that Murray told him about meeting Matisse, that the artist must function in the context of heroic action. Matisse was for Murray an example of "the heroic artist, the culture hero, not unlike Bearden or Duke Ellington or Louis Armstrong."

Through Paul Devlin's eyes we are also made witness to the art that surrounds Murray in his apartment. He describes sculptures that Murray created years ago that still line his shelves and the enormous (and valuable) paintings by famous artists that grace the walls of his Harlem dwelling. For example, Devlin describes *Wynton*, a Resika charcoal of a "trumpet player blowing the blues away," which hangs "perpendicular to and hugging the large window in Murray's apartment that faces out onto 132nd Street. Directly across the room is a Bearden sketch of Duke Ellington, in which Duke's arm is raised, as if conducting a band. In Murray's arrangement, it is as if Bearden's Duke is conducting Resika's Wynton from across the room."

In that same room, Murray urged Lauren Walsh to the immense wall of bookshelves to retrieve a copy of Thomas Mann's *Joseph and His Brothers*, and there he taught her that in Mann, Murray found the kernels of his aesthetic philosophy and his signature use of the "Once upon a time" idiom as a signifier for the universal, which is "inextricably linked to the narrative function of mythologies." In "Murray and Mann: Variations on a Theme," Walsh argues that Murray's first novel, *Train Whistle Guitar*, serves as a "model for exploration of the universal, the mythic, and the epic hero." According to Walsh, Murray playfully extends what he learned from Mann, applying the mythology of Brer Rabbit to his main character's (Scooter's) real-life experiences and extending them into universally relevant lessons.

Roberta S. Maguire also spent a good bit of time on Lenox Terrace while she edited a collection of interviews with Murray, *Conversations with Albert Murray* and, like Lauren Walsh, she finds within *Train Whistle Guitar* strains from the masters after whom Murray modeled his artistic approach. In "Dewey's Pragmatism Extended: Education and Aesthetic Practice in *Train Whistle Guitar*," Maguire shows that while Murray was an undergraduate at Tuskegee, his encounters with the writings of John Dewey were to have a "lasting effect on his thinking" and are illustrated in two ways in Murray's first novel. The themes in *Train Whistle Guitar* reflect Dewey's pragmatism by showing, first, that "black U.S. culture is the quintessential American culture," and second, that "[t]hose who claim the culture and are shaped by it possess a heightened openness to change." According to Maguire, adaptability "just happens to be the human trait on which Dewey's pragmatism is based." Maguire argues further that "Murray should himself be seen as a contributor to and shaper of the intellectual tradition of pragmatism, a distinctively American mode of thought and arguably our country's major addition to philosophy."

Caroline Gebhard also illustrates the manner in which Murray's time at Tuskegee affected his thinking and influenced his writing. In "Albert Murray and Tuskegee Institute: Art as the Measure of Place," Gebhard says that in the case of *The Spyglass Tree,* a novel that both resonates with and counters Ellison's *Invisible Man,* "[i]t seems clear that Albert Murray cannot conceive of his hero's development without Tuskegee." Of Murray's travelogue *South to a Very Old Place* she points out that "'triangulation points' like Tuskegee . . . deftly evoke nineteenth- and twentieth-century debates on black identity, southern history and politics, modernism and myth, and the role of the artist, all the while paying homage to what is 'very old'—classic in the truest meaning of that word."

Among other interesting details, in his 1996 *Bookmark* interview, "A Conversation with Albert Murray," Don Noble inspires Murray to talk about a rarely discussed juncture in his education, his pursuit of a master's degree at New York University. Murray explains to Noble that writing his master's thesis brought him to his conceptualization of futility and how that functions within the blues. Murray says that in writing his thesis he discovered that "Hemingway's confrontation was more like the blues [than was T. S. Eliot's]. Life is a low-down dirty shame that shouldn't happen to anyone—futility. All is futile. I appropriated that in my interpretation of the blues."

In "Albert Murray's House of Blues," Roy Hoffman captures another telling facet of Albert Murray by relating the details of a day in the late 1980s spent traveling with Murray in New York City. With Hoffman, the reader accompanies Murray inside the Strand Bookstore, for instance, where customers and clerks fawn over him, give him chocolate, and ask him for an autograph.

In "An Interview with Michele Murray," we see him through the eyes of his daughter, who recalls a childhood filled with famous visitors like Duke Ellington, exciting adventures to places like the Savoy, and a steadfast paternal encouragement that led her to a professional dancing career with the Alvin Ailey Company.

When I sat down with Mr. Murray in 2003, discussed his life, and recorded the interview published here as "Conjugations and Reiterations," Murray had just published his only book of poems, *Conjugations and Reiterations.* In the interview he explained to me how the poems, written over many years in longhand in a leather binder that he had bought when he sold the first installment of *Train Whistle Guitar,* captured in a highly crystallized poetic form thoughts he had pondered for decades as well as the highlights of his life adventure. The interview was recorded with the intention of serving as a teaching tool, and so I pressed Mr. Murray to discuss his time teaching at Tuskegee. Hundreds of Tuskegee students in my classes viewed this interview and were moved, inspired, and proud of their Tuskegee forebear, Albert Murray.

One such student is Maurice Pogue, who has since graduated from Tuskegee and gone on to graduate study in literature. In "Murray's Mulatto America," Pogue takes up the groundbreaking theme of Murray's *The Omni-Americans,* arguing that in it Murray "boldly subverts polemics of racial authenticity through the recuperation of the trope of the mulatto in an American idiomatic identity."

And finally, in the last two essays of the first part of *Albert Murray and the Aesthetic Imagination of a Nation,* Bert Hitchcock and Jay Lamar bring our reflections on the life and works of Albert Murray back home to the South, especially to his native Alabama. "Chinaberry Tree, Chinaberry Tree" illustrates Murray's powerful use of the tree to symbolize a unification of the diverse cultures and classes populating the South and southern literature. Hitchcock shows that in Murray's hands the chinaberry tree is a special agent of horizon-extending inspiration.

We conclude the first part of this book with "Scooter Comes Home," in which Jay Lamar contextualizes Murray's writing within the broader frame of Alabama writers and argues that for writers of Murray's circumstances, the context is most significant. As she says, "[i]f you had cast the fortune of a Negro child born in the early part of the twentieth century in a tiny south Alabama town, not even the most audacious prognosticator might have had the vision to see through that thick hedge of time and place." But it turns out that prickly hedge exactly suits our hero, Albert Murray, who "has bounded again and again into the places where more fearful folk hesitate to tread, urged on in his quest by a sense of destiny."

In the second part of this book, "Reminiscences and Appreciations," we wanted to give others whose lives have been forever touched by having known Albert Murray an opportunity to speak about what the experience has meant to them. The reminiscences begin with the well-known jazz trumpeter Wynton Marsalis (as told to Roberta S. Maguire) and internationally acclaimed literary scholar Henry Louis Gates Jr., and then move to writer and publisher Sidney Offit, who reflects on the later life of Albert Murray in Manhattan. Louis A. "Mike" Rabb, mentioned throughout the Ellison and Murray correspondence, knew Murray as a young man teaching at Tuskegee, and then throughout the years as Murray returned often to Alabama to visit with his lifelong Tuskegee friends.

Writers Sanford Pinsker, who wrote "The Bluesteel, Rawhide, Patent-Leather Implications of Fairy Tales"; Lena Horne's daughter, Gail Buckley; and Eugene Holley Jr. reflect on their own writing careers and how Murray shaped their thinking and personally inspired them. Radio host Greg Thomas and Paul Devlin flesh out for us the long, deep friendship between Murray and Michael James, nephew of Duke Ellington. And contemporary New York City artists Elizabeth Mayer Fiedorek and Carol Friedman, the latter the talented portrait artist who shot our cover photo, share with us glimpses of the man and the teacher who has always been willing to debate and deliberate any time and any place with those who want to know the secrets of the century that Albert Murray has collected through a lifetime of deep reading, engaged thought, and thoughtful discussion with the greatest thinkers of the twentieth century.

Albert Murray and the Aesthetic Imagination of a Nation is a tribute as well as a critical examination, and it is Team Murray's hope that it will serve as a starting point for years of intellectual discussion about the fiction, poetry, and cultural theories of an intense thinker and unique observer of American art and culture who has always been well ahead of his time.

Observations, Interpretations, and Conversations ■

1

In Response to Being Awarded a Citation for Distinguished Literary Achievement by an Alabamian (2003)

ALBERT MURRAY

It didn't take me very long to realize that fairy tales, fables, nursery rhymes, and fire circle and fireside and barbershop lies, store porch and cracker barrel tall tales and yarns, no less than the great national sagas, epics, and classical masterpieces regardless of geographical origin and cultural, which is to say environmental variations, applied to everybody.

Because they all are a form of art. And, according to Susanne K. Langer, the author of *Feeling and Form* and other philosophical studies in aesthetic theory, what all art represents or expresses is human feeling, how human beings feel about what they are aware of.

For me, this means that local circumstances and predicaments and the idiomatic procedures evolved to cope with them may have worldwide implication and application. Indeed, such is the function of fiction, which is also to say poetry, which is to say metaphor. Social science surveys are really about one place at a time. But the local metaphor is about all mankind.

I want readers to identify with the protagonist in my fiction, not in terms of social science survey–derived political ideology—but in terms of the universal implications of the hero's humanity as I hope I've been able to render it.

Scooter, the main character of *Train Whistle Guitar, The Spyglass Tree, The Seven League Boots,* and my current work in progress, is an Alabama boy who is by way of becoming an omni-American, which is to say the personification of the definitive ideals of the nation as a whole, as promulgated by the Declaration of Independence, the Constitution, the Emancipation Proclamation, the Gettysburg Address, and the Thirteenth, Fourteenth and Fifteenth amendments.

In other words, in Scooter I have tried to create and project what I hoped would be a captivating image of an Alabamian as an efficient protagonist whose briarpatch upbringing enables him not only to cope with but also to transcend the inevitable obstacles in the contemporary world at large.

Originally delivered as an acceptance speech, May 2, 2003, for the Distinguished Artist Award given by the Alabama State Council on the Arts.

2

King of Cats (1996)

HENRY LOUIS GATES JR.

What does it mean to be black? In part, it means rejecting all exclusionary answers to the question, as Albert Murray, the great contrarian of American cultural criticism, has inspired generations of thinkers to do.

In the late seventies, I used to take the train from New Haven to New York on Saturdays, to spend afternoons with Albert Murray at Books & Company on Madison Avenue. We would roam—often joined by the artist Romare Bearden—through fiction, criticism, philosophy, music. Murray always seemed to wind up fingering densely printed paperbacks by Joyce, Mann, Proust, or Faulkner; Bearden, typically, would pick up a copy of something daunting like Rilke's *Letters on Cézanne* and then insist that I read it on the train home that night.

In those days, Murray was writing Count Basie's autobiography—a project that he didn't finish until 1985. ("For years," he has remarked more than once, "when I wrote the word 'I,' it meant Basie.") But he had already published most of the books that would secure his reputation as a cultural critic—perhaps most notably, his début collection, *The Omni-Americans* (1970), which brought together his ferocious attacks on black separatists, on protest literature, and on what he called "the social science-fiction monster." Commanding as he could be on the page, Murray was an equally impressive figure in the flesh: a lithe and dapper man with an astonishing gift of verbal fluency, by turns grandiloquent and earthy. I loved to listen to his voice—grave but insinuating, with more than a hint of a jazz singer's rasp. Murray had been a schoolmate of the novelist Ralph Ellison at the Tuskegee Institute, and the friendship of the two men over the years seemed a focal point of black literary culture in the ensuing decades. Ellison's one novel, *Invisible Man,* was among the few unequivocal masterpieces of American literature in the postwar era, satirizing with equal aplomb Garveyites, Communists, and white racists in both their southern-agrarian and their northern-liberal guises. Murray's works of critique and cultural exploration seemed wholly in the same spirit. Both men were militant integrationists, and they shared an almost messianic view of the importance of art. In their ardent belief that Negro culture was a constitutive part of American culture, they had defied an entrenched literary mainstream, which preferred to regard black culture as so much exotica— amusing, perhaps, but eminently dispensable. Now they were also defying a new black vanguard, which regarded authentic black culture as separate from the rest of American culture—something that was created, and could be appreciated, in splendid isolation. While many of their peers liked to speak of wrath and resistance, Murray and Ellison liked to speak of complexity and craft, and for that reason they championed the art of Romare Bearden.

In terms of both critical regard and artistic fecundity, these were good days for Bearden, a large, light-skinned man with a basketball roundness to his head. (I could never get over how much he looked like Nikita Khrushchev.) He, like Murray, was working at the height of his powers—he was completing his famous "Jazz" series of collages—and his stature and influence were greater than those which any other African American artist had so far enjoyed. The collages combined the visual conventions of black American folk culture with the techniques of modernism—fulfilling what Murray called "the vernacular imperative" to transmute tradition into art.

After a couple of hours at the bookstore, we'd go next door to the Madison Café, where Romie, as Murray called him, always ordered the same item: the largest fruit salad that I had ever seen in public. He claimed that he chose the fruit salad because he was watching his weight, but I was convinced that he chose it in order to devour the colors, like an artist dipping his brush into his palette. He'd start laying the ground with the off-white of the apples and the bananas, and follow them with the pinkish orange of the grapefruit, the red of the strawberries, the speckled green of the kiwifruit; the blueberries and purple grapes he'd save for last. While Romie was consuming his colors, Murray would talk almost nonstop, his marvelous ternary sentences punctuated only by the occasional bite of a BLT or a tuna fish on rye. Murray was then, as now, a man with definite preoccupations, and among the touchstones of his conversation were terms like *discipline, craft, tradition, the aesthetic,* and *the Negro idiom.* And names like Thomas Mann, André Malraux, Kenneth Burke, and Lord Raglan. There was also another name—a name that never weighed more heavily than when it was unspoken—which sometimes took longer to come up.

"Heard from Ralph lately?" Bearden would almost whisper as the waitress brought the check.

"Still grieving, I guess," Murray would rasp back, shaking his head slowly. He was referring to the fire, about a decade earlier, that had destroyed Ellison's Massachusetts farmhouse and, with it, many months of revisions on his long-awaited second novel. "That fire was a terrible thing." Then Murray, who was so rarely at a loss for words, would fall silent.

Later, when Bearden and I were alone in his Canal Street loft, he'd return to the subject in hushed tones: "Ralph is mad at Al. No one seems to know why. And it's killing Al. He's not sure what he did."

The rift, or whatever it amounted to, used to vex and puzzle me. It was a great mistake to regard Murray simply as Ellison's sidekick, the way many people did, but he was without question the most fervent and articulate champion of Ellison's art. The two were, in a sense, part of a single project: few figures on the scene shared as many presuppositions and preoccupations as they did. Theirs was a sect far too small for schismatics. At the very least, the rift made things awkward for would-be postulants like me.

When *The Omni-Americans* came out in 1970, I was in college, majoring in history but pursuing extracurricular studies in how to be black. Those were the days when the Black Power movement was the mode and rage de rigueur. Just two years before, the poets Larry Neal and Amiri Baraka had edited *Black Fire,* the book that launched the so-called Black Arts movement—in effect, the cultural wing of the Black Power movement. Maybe it was hard to hold a pen with a clenched fist, but you did what you could: the revolution wasn't about niceties of style anyway. On the occasions when Ralph Ellison, an avatar of elegance, was invited to college campuses, blacks invariably denounced him for his failure to involve himself in the civil rights struggle, for his evident disdain of the posturings of Black Power. For me, though, the era was epitomized by a reading that the poet Nikki Giovanni gave in a university lecture hall to a standing-room-only crowd—a sea of colorful dashikis and planetary Afros. Her words seemed incandescent with racial rage, and each poem was greeted with a Black Power salute. "Right on! Right on!" we shouted, in the deepest voices we could manage, each time Giovanni made another grand claim about the blackness of blackness. Those were days when violence (or, anyway, talk of violence) had acquired a Fanonist glamour; when the black bourgeoisie—kulaks of color, nothing more—was reviled as an obstacle on the road to revolution; when the arts were seen as merely an instrumentality for a larger cause.

Such was the milieu in which Murray published *The Omni-Americans,* and you couldn't imagine a more foolhardy act. This was a book in which the very language of the black nationalists was subjected to a strip search. Ever since Malcolm X, for instance, the epithet "house Negro" had been a staple of militant invective; yet here was Murray arguing that if only we got our history straight we'd realize that those house Negroes were practically race patriots. ("The house slave seems to have brought infinitely more tactical information from the big house to the cabins than any information about subversive plans he ever took back.") And while radicals mocked their bourgeois brethren as "black Anglo-Saxons," Murray defiantly declared, "Not only is it the so-called middle class Negro who challenges the status quo in schools, housing, voting practices, and so on, he is also the one who is most likely to challenge total social structures and value systems." Celebrated chroniclers of black America, including Claude Brown, Gordon Parks, and James Baldwin, were shown by Murray to be tainted by the ethnographic fallacy, the pretense that one writer's peculiar experience can represent a social genus. "This whole thing about somebody revealing what it is really like to be black has long since gotten out of hand anyway," he wrote. "Does anybody actually believe that, say, Mary McCarthy reveals what it is really like to be a U.S. white woman, or even a Vassar girl?" But he reserved his heaviest artillery for the whole social science approach to black life, whether in the hands of the psychologist Kenneth Clark (of *Brown v. Board of Education* fame) or in those of the novelist Richard Wright, who had spent too much time reading his sociologist friends. What was needed wasn't more sociological inquiry, Murray declared; what was needed was cultural creativity, nourished by the folkways and traditions of black America but transcending them. And the work of literature that best met that challenge, he said, was Ellison's *Invisible Man.*

The contrarian held his own simply by matching outrage with outrage—by writing a book that was so pissed off, jaw-jutting, and unapologetic that it demanded to be taken seriously. Nobody had to tell this veteran about black fire: in Murray the bullies of blackness had met their most formidable opponent. And a great many blacks—who, suborned by "solidarity," had trained themselves to suppress any heretical thoughts—found Murray's book oddly thrilling: it had the transgressive frisson of samizdat under Stalinism. You'd read it greedily, though you just might want to switch dust jackets with *The Wretched of the Earth* before wandering around with it in public. "Very early on, he was saying stuff that could get him killed," the African American novelist David Bradley says. "And he did not seem to care." The power of his example lingers. "One February, I had just delivered the usual black-history line, and I was beginning to feel that I was selling snake oil," Bradley recalls. "And right here was this man who has said this stuff. And I'm thinking, Well, *he* ain't dead yet."

As if to remove any doubts, Murray has just published two books simultaneously, both with Pantheon. One, *The Seven League Boots,* is his third novel and completes a trilogy about a bright young fellow named Scooter, his fictional alter ego; the other, *The Blue Devils of Nada,* is a collection of critical essays analyzing some favorite artists (Ellington, Hemingway, Bearden) and expatiating upon some favorite tenets (the "blues idiom" as an aesthetic sub-strate, the essentially fluid nature of American culture). Both are books that will be discussed and debated for years to come; both are vintage Murray.

The most outrageous theorist of American culture lives, as he has lived for three decades, in a modest apartment in Lenox Terrace in Harlem. When I visit him there, everything is pretty much as I remembered it. The public rooms look like yet another Harlem branch of the New York Public Library. Legal pads and magnifying glasses perch beside his two or three favorite chairs, along with numerous ballpoint pens, his weapons of choice. His shelves record a lifetime of enthusiasms; James, Tolstoy, Hemingway, Proust, and Faulkner are among the authors most heavily represented. Close at hand are volumes by favored explicants such as Joseph Campbell, Kenneth Burke, Carl Jung, Rudolph Arnheim, Bruno Bettelheim, Constance Rourke. On his writing desk sits a more intimate canon. There's Thomas Mann's four-volume *Joseph and His Brothers*—the saga, after all, of a slave who gains the power to decide the fate of a people. There's André Malraux's *Man's Fate,* which represented for Ellison and Murray a more rarefied mode of engagé writing than anything their compeers had to offer. There's Joel Chandler Harris's *The Complete Tales of Uncle Remus,* a mother lode of African American folklore. One wall is filled with his famously compendious collection of jazz recordings; a matte black CD player was a gift from his protégé Wynton Marsalis. You will not, however, see the sort of framed awards that festooned Ellison's apartment. "I have received few of those honors," he says, pulling on his arthritic right leg. "No American Academy, few honorary degrees."

A quarter of a century has passed since Murray's literary début, and time has mellowed him not at all. His arthritis may have worsened over the past few years, and there is always an aluminum walker close by, but as he talks he sprouts wings. Murray likes to elaborate his points and elaborate on his elaborations, until you find that you have circumnavigated the globe and raced through the whole of post-Homeric literary history—and this is what he calls "vamping till ready." In his conversations, outrages alternate with insights, and often the insights are the outrages. Every literary culture has its superego and its id; Albert Murray has the odd distinction of being both. The contradictions of human nature are, fittingly, a favorite topic of Murray's. He talks about how Thomas Jefferson was a slaveholder but how he also helped to establish a country whose founding creed was liberty. "Every time I think about it," he says, "I want to wake him up and give him ten more slaves." He's less indulgent of the conflicting impulses of Malcolm X. Dr. King's strategy of nonviolence was "one of the most magnificent things that anybody ever invented in the civil rights movement," he maintains. "And this guy came up and started thumbing his nose at it, and, to my utter amazement, he's treated as if he were a civil rights leader. He didn't lead anything. He was in Selma laughing at these guys. God *damn*, nigger!"

Albert Murray is a teacher by temperament, and as he explains a point he'll often say that he wants to be sure to "work it into your consciousness." The twentieth century has worked a great deal into Murray's consciousness. He was fifteen when the Scottsboro trial began, twenty-two when Marian Anderson sang at the Lincoln Memorial. He joined the air force when it was segregated and rejoined shortly after it had been desegregated. He was in his late thirties when *Brown v. Board of Education* was decided, when the conflict in Korea was concluded, when Rosa Parks was arrested. He was in his forties when the Civil Rights Act was passed, when SNCC (Student Nonviolent Coordinating Committee) was founded, when John F. Kennedy was killed. And he was in his fifties when the Black Panther Party was formed, when King was shot, when Black Power was proclaimed. Such are the lineaments of public history—the sort of grainy national drama that newsreels used to record. For him, though, the figures of history are as vivid as drinking companions, and, on the whole, no more sacrosanct.

He is equally unabashed about taking on contemporary figures of veneration, even in the presence of a venerator. Thus, about the novelist Toni Morrison, we agree to disagree. "I do think it's tainted with do-goodism," he says of her Nobel Prize, rejecting what he considers the special pleading of contemporary feminism. "I think it's redressing wrongs. You don't have to condescend to no goddam Jane Austen. Or the Brontës, or George Eliot and George Sand. These chicks are tough. You think you'll get your fastball by Jane Austen? So we don't need special pleading for anything. And the same goes for blackness." He bridles at the phenomenon of Terry McMillan, the best-selling author of *Waiting to Exhale*—or, more precisely, at the nature of the attention she has received. "I think it's a mistake to try to read some profound political significance into everything, like as soon as a Negro writes it's got to be some civil rights thing," he says. "It's just Jackie Collins stuff."

At times, his pans somehow edge into panegyrics, the result being what might be called a backhanded insult. About Maya Angelou's much-discussed Inaugural poem he says, "It's like the reaction to *Porgy and Bess.* Man, you put a bunch of brown-skinned people onstage, with footlights and curtains, and they make *anything* work. White people have no resistance to Negro performers: they charm the pants off anything. Black people make you listen up. They're singing 'Old Man River'—'Tote that barge, lift that bale'? What the fuck is that? Everybody responded like 'This is great.' That type of fantastic charm means that black performers can redeem almost any type of pop fare."

Since discipline and craft are his bywords, however, he distrusts staged spontaneity. "He plays the same note that he perfected twenty-five years ago, and he acts like he's got to sweat to get the note out of his goddam guitar," Murray says of the contemporary blues musician B. B. King. "He's got to shake his head and frown, and it's just going to be the same goddam note he already played twenty-five years ago." Murray himself doesn't mind returning to notes he played twenty-five years ago—his nonfiction books explore the same set of issues and can be read as chapters of a single ongoing opus. Indeed, from all accounts, the fashioning of this particular cultural hero began long before the start of his writing career.

In Murray's case, heroism was a matter both of circumstance and of will. Certainly he has long been an avid student of the subject. Lord Raglan's classic *The Hero: A Study in Tradition, Myth, and Drama* (1936) is among the books most frequently cited in his writing, and it remains a part of his personal canon. Moreover, the mythic patterns that Lord Raglan parsed turn out to have had resonances for Murray beyond the strictly literary. According to Raglan's exhaustively researched generalizations, the hero is highborn, but "the circumstances of his conception are unusual," and he is "spirited away" to be "reared by foster-parents in a far country." Then, "on reaching manhood," he "returns or goes to his future kingdom," confronts and defeats the king or a dragon or some such, and starts being heroic in earnest. So it was, more or less, with Oedipus, Theseus, Romulus, Joseph, Moses, Siegfried, Arthur, Robin Hood, and—oh, yes—Albert Murray.

Murray was born in 1916 and grew up in Magazine Point, a hamlet not far from Mobile, Alabama. His mother was a housewife, and his father, Murray says, was a "common laborer," who sometimes helped lay railroad tracks as a cross-tie cutter and at times harvested timber in the turpentine woods. "As far as the Murrays were concerned, it was a fantastic thing that I finished the ninth grade," he recalls, "or that I could read the newspaper." But he had already decided that he was bound for college. Everyone in the village knew that there was something special about him. And he knew it, too.

He had known it ever since an all-night wake—he was around eleven at the time—when he had fallen asleep in the living room, his head cradled in his mother's lap. At one point, he surfaced to hear himself being discussed, but, with a child's cunning, he pretended he was still asleep.

"Tell me something," a relative was saying. "Is it true that Miss Graham is really his mama?"

"She's the one brought him into the world," Mrs. Murray replied. "But I'm his mama. She gave him to me when he was no bigger than a minute, and he was so little I had to put him on a pillow to take him home. I didn't think he was going to make it. I laid him out for God to take him two or three times. And I said, 'Lord, this child is here for something, so I'm going to feed this child and he's going to make it.'"

It was a moment that Al Murray likens to finding out the truth about Santa Claus.

Murray's birth parents were, as he slowly learned, well educated and securely middle class—people who belonged to an entirely different social stratum from that of his adoptive parents. His natural father, John Young, came from a well-established family in town. His natural mother had been attending Tuskegee as a boarding student and working part-time for John Young's aunt and uncle, who were in the real estate business. When she learned that a close encounter with John Young had left her pregnant, she had to leave town—"because of the disgrace," Murray explains. As luck would have it, a cousin of hers knew a married woman who, unable to bear a child of her own, was interested in adopting one. Murray doesn't have to be prodded to make the fairy tale connection. "It's just like the prince left among paupers," he says cheerfully. (In *The Omni-Americans* he wrote, apropos of the 1965 Moynihan report on the breakdown of the black family structure, "How many epic heroes issue from conventional families?")

As a freshman at the Tuskegee Institute—the ancestral kingdom he was fated to enter—Murray became aware of a junior whose reading habits were alarmingly similar to his. He was a music major from Oklahoma named Ralph Waldo Ellison, and what first impressed Murray about him was his wardrobe. "Joe College, right out of *Esquire*—he had fine contrasting slacks, gray tweed jacket. He would be wearing bow ties and two-tone shoes," Murray recalls. "In those days, when you checked out a book from the library you had a little slip in the back where you would write your name, and then they would stamp the due date." Consequently, when Murray took out a book by, say, T. S. Eliot or Robinson Jeffers, he could see who had previously borrowed the book. Time and again, it was that music major with the two-tone shoes.

Ellison left Tuskegee for New York before completing his senior year: his absence was meant to be temporary, a means of saving some money, but he never went back. Murray earned his BA at Tuskegee in 1939, and stayed on to teach. In 1941, he married Mozelle Menefee, who was a student there. He spent the last two years of the Second World War on active duty in the air force. "I was just hoping I'd live long enough for Thomas Mann to finish the last volume of *Joseph and His Brothers*," he says. Two years after his discharge, he moved to New York, where, on the GI Bill, he got a master's degree in literature from New York University. It was also in New York that the friendship between him and Ellison took off. Ellison read passages to Murray from a manuscript that would turn into *Invisible Man.* The two men explored the streets and the sounds of Harlem together; over meals and over drinks, they hashed out ideas about improvisation, the blues, and literary modernism. Even then, Murray had a reputation as a "great explainer."

The prominent black religious and literary scholar Nathan A. Scott, who was a graduate student in New York in the forties and had become a friend of Ellison's, tells about being in the Gotham Book Mart one day and noticing another black man there. "I was somewhat surprised to find this slight, dark man there, because I'd never bumped into a Negro there," Scott recounts. "And some young white chap came in, and they knew each other and immediately plunged into a spirited conversation, and at a certain point I overheard this chap say to the black man, 'Well, what are you working on these days?' To which the black chap replied, 'Oh, I am doing an essay in self-definition.'" (And Scott laughs loudly.) Later, at a dinner at Ellison's apartment, Ellison introduced Scott to his friend Albert Murray: "Immediately, I thought, By God, here is the chap who was doing that essay in self-definition! Inwardly, I laughed all over again."

If it was clear that the young man was interested in trying to write, it wasn't so clear what the results were. In the early fifties, Saul Bellow and Ralph Ellison shared a house in Dutchess County, and Bellow recalls seeing Murray from time to time down in the city. "I think he agreed with Ralph, in simply assuming that they were deeply installed in the whole American picture," Bellow says. He adds that Ellison talked about Murray's writing in those days, but that he himself never saw any of it. In 1952, Ellison published *Invisible Man.* The book was a best seller for several months, and garnered some of the most enthusiastic critical responses anyone could remember. It was soon a classroom staple, the subject of books and dissertations. It was read and re-read. Ellison, in short, had become an immortal. And Murray? With a wife and a daughter to support, he was pursuing a more conventional career—in the air force, which he rejoined in 1951.

As a military officer, Murray taught courses in geopolitics in the air force ROTC program at Tuskegee, where he was based for much of the fifties, and he oversaw the administration of large-scale technical operations both in North Africa and in the United States. While his military career has remained oddly isolated from his creative work—a matter of regret, in the opinion of some of his friends—the experience would leave him impatient with the pretensions of the by-any-means-necessary brigade. He says, in that distinctively Murrayesque tone of zestful exasperation, "Let's talk about 'the fire next time.' You know damn well they can put out the fire by Wednesday."

When Murray retired from the military in 1962, he moved to New York, and soon his articles began to appear in periodicals (*Life,* the *New Leader*). In 1964, Ellison wrote a letter about his old friend to one Jacob Cohen, who was planning to start a magazine. "Actually, I find it very difficult to write about him," the letter began. "I suppose because I have known him since our days at Tuskegee, and because our contacts since that time have been so constant and our assumptions about so many matters in such close agreement that I really don't have the proper sense of perspective." Ellison went on to say of Murray, "He has the imagination which allows him to project himself into the centers of power, and he uses his imagination to deal with serious problems seriously and as though he were a responsible participant in the affairs of our nation and our time." The following year, a panel of book critics, authors, and editors found *Invisible Man* to be the most widely admired novel published since the Second World War. Meanwhile, Albert Murray, then two years out of the air force, was scarcely known outside the circle of his acquaintances.

However asymmetric the public stature of the pair, people who spent time with Murray and Ellison in those days were impressed by the ease and intimacy of their friendship. In the late sixties, Willie Morris, then the editor of *Harper's,* eagerly sought their company: they provided him with a refreshing contrast to what he found a suffocating literary climate. He recalls, "In every way, they were like brothers—you know, soul brothers and fellow writers— but Ellison's star was so bright, and Al was just really getting started." Soul brothers they may have been; they were also brothers-in-arms. When Murray rose to do battle with the rising ranks of black nationalism, he knew he shared a foxhole with Ralph Ellison, and there must have been comfort in that.

It may seem ironic that the person who first urged *The Omni-Americans* on me was Larry Neal, one of the Black Arts founders. But Neal was a man of far greater subtlety than the movement he spawned, and he understood Albert Murray's larger enterprise—the one that he shared with Ellison—better than most. People who may not read Murray but like the *idea* of him reflexively label him an "integrationist"; seldom do they take in the term's full complexity. In Murray's hands, integration wasn't an act of accommodation but an act of introjection. Indeed, at the heart of Murray and Ellison's joint enterprise was perhaps the most breathtaking act of cultural chutzpah this land had witnessed since Columbus blithely claimed it all for Isabella.

In its bluntest form, their assertion was that the truest Americans were black Americans. For much of what was truly distinctive about America's "national character" was rooted in the improvisatory prehistory of the blues. The very sound of American English "is derived from the timbre of the African voice and the listening habits of the African ear," Ellison maintained. "If there is such a thing as a Yale accent, there is a Negro wail in it." This is the lesson that the protagonist of Ellison's novel learns while working at a paint factory: the whitest white is made by adding a drop of black. For generations, the word "American" had tacitly connoted "white." Murray inverted the cultural assumption and the verbal conventions: in his discourse, "American," roughly speaking, means "black." So, even as the clenched-fist crowd was scrambling for cultural crumbs, Murray was declaring the entire harvest board of American civilization to be his birthright. In a sense, Murray was the ultimate black nationalist. And the fact that people so easily mistook his vision for its opposite proved how radical it was.

But why stop with matters American? What did the European savants of existentialism understand about *la condition humaine* that Ma Rainey did not? In later works, most notably *Stomping the Blues* (1976), Murray took the blues to places undreamed-of by its originators. It has long been a commonplace that the achievements of black music have far outstripped those of black literature—that no black writer has produced work of an aesthetic complexity comparable to Duke Ellington's, Count Basie's, or Charlie Parker's. This much, for Murray, was a point of departure: he sought to process the blues into a self-conscious aesthetic, to translate the deep structure of the black vernacular into prose. Arguably, LeRoi Jones attempted something similar in his celebrated *Blues People* (1963), but there sociology gained the upper hand over art. (Ellison, writing in the *New York Review of Books,* complained that Jones's approach was enough to "give even the blues the blues.") To Murray, the blues stood in opposition to all such reductionism. "What it all represents is an attitude toward the nature of human experience (and the alternatives of human adjustment) that is both elemental and comprehensive," he wrote in

Stomping the Blues, and he continued: "It is a statement about confronting the complexities inherent in the human situation and about improvising or experimenting or riffing or otherwise playing with (or even gambling with) such possibilities as are also inherent in the obstacles, the disjunctures, and the jeopardy. It is also a statement about perseverance and about resilience and thus also about the maintenance of equilibrium despite precarious circumstances and about achieving elegance in the very process of coping with the rudiments of subsistence."

Though Murray's salvific conception of the blues may seem fantastical, it represented precisely the alternative that Larry Neal and others were searching for. In truth, you could no more capture the sublimity of music in earthbound prose than you could trap the moon's silvery reflection in a barrel of rainwater, but there was heroism, surely, in the effort.

Nor was it only literature that could be revivified by jazz and the blues. That was where Bearden came in, and that was why his friendship with Murray had to be understood as an artistic alliance. Bearden's mixed-media works could serve as a cultural paradigm for the kind of bricolage and hybridity that Murray favored.

In recent stanzas entitled "Omni–Albert Murray" the young African American poet Elizabeth Alexander writes, "In my mind and in his I think a painting is a poem / A tambourine's a hip shake and train whistle a guitar." Certainly Murray proved an authoritative exponent of Bearden's works, the titles of which were frequently of his devising. The literary scholar Robert O'Meally remembers being with Bearden and Murray in Books & Company when the two were trying to decide on a name for whatever picture Bearden had brought along that day. O'Meally recalls, "It might be that Al Murray's eye was caught by the figure of a woman in one corner of the image. And he'd say, 'Who's that?' And Bearden would be looking embarrassed, because the woman in question had been an old girlfriend of his. Maybe Bearden would say, 'Oh, she's just a woman I once knew from North Carolina.' And then Murray would say, 'I've got it. Let's call it *Red-Headed Woman from North Carolina.*' Or, 'I know, call it *Red-Headed Woman from North Carolina with Rooster.*' And Bearden would go and write that on the back of his painting."

Murray stood ready to assist in other ways, too. When, in 1978, I asked

Bearden if he would conduct a seminar on Afro-American art at Yale, where I was teaching, his immediate response was, "Why don't you ask Al?" But this particular appointment called for an artist, and Bearden finally did accept, though with genuine reluctance and vehement protestations of pedagogic incompetence. So reluctant was he that I was astonished by the remarkably well-organized and cogent weekly lectures he had prepared—always neatly double-spaced and fifty minutes in duration, the precise length of the academic lecture's hour. Comprehension soon dawned. Bearden, taking matters into his own hands, had found a way to bring Murray along to New Haven; the critic had ghostwritten Professor Bearden's erudite lectures.

But did Murray have debts of his own to acknowledge—in particular, to his Tuskegee schoolmate? The very similarity of their preoccupations proved a source of friction. Now it was Murray—here, there, and everywhere— spreading the glad word about the literary theorist Kenneth Burke, about Lord Raglan, about the luminous blending of craft and metaphysics represented by André Malraux and by Thomas Mann. Ellison's claim, at least to Kenneth Burke and Lord Raglan, seems clear: they were part of the swirl of ideas at Bennington College in the early fifties, when Ellison was living nearby and socializing with the faculty. One writer who had been friendly with both Murray and Ellison since the forties assures me that he has no doubt as to who was the exegete and who the originator: "This is not to say that Al was simply some sort of epigone. But *all* the fundamental ideas that are part of *The Omni-Americans* came from Ellison. Al made his own music out of those ideas, but *I* know where they came from. The course of thought that Murray began to follow in the sixties was a result of Ralph's influence, I think there is no doubt about this at all."

That has become something of a consensus view. In recent appreciation of Murray, the jazz critic Gene Seymour writes that on such subjects as improvisation, discipline, and tradition, Murray (and, by extension, disciples of his like Stanley Crouch and Wynton Marsalis) sounds "like an echo." He maintains that the recently published volume of Ellison's collected essays "makes clear [that] Ellison was the wellspring for the ideals advanced by Murray, Crouch, and Marsalis."

It's a thorny subject. At one point, Murray tells me about V. S. Naipaul's visit with him in the late eighties—a visit that was recorded in Naipaul's *A Turn in the South.* Naipaul wrote, "He was a man of enthusiasms, easy to be with, easy to listen to. His life seemed to have been a series of happy discoveries." At the same time, Naipaul identified Murray as a writer who "was, or had been, a protégé of Ralph Ellison's." Murray makes it clear that this gloss does not sit well with him. He counters by quoting something that Robert Bone, a pioneering scholar of African American literature, told him: "I've been trying to figure out *who* is the protégé of *whom.*"

Bone, an acquaintance of both principals, suggests beginning with a different set of premises. "On Murray's part, it must have been a terribly difficult thing for him to have been overshadowed by Ralph in terms of the timing of their two careers," he says. "In a way, they started out together at Tuskegee, and then they cemented that friendship in New York, but Murray got such a later start in his career as a writer. So when he came on the scene Ralph was, of course, a celebrity." What escapes us, Bone says, is that many of the positions with which Ellison was associated were ones the two had mulled over together and corresponded about—especially "the link between Afro-American writing and Afro-American music." Reverse all your assumptions, though, and one thing remains constant: "Murray, I think, naturally must have felt a good deal of envy and resentment." Where others see Darwin and Huxley, Bone sees Watson and Crick. Of Ellison and Murray he says, "There was a time when they were both young aspiring writers, and they shared these ideas and they worked on them together, but Ralph got into print with them first, by a kind of accident." Speaking like a true literary historian, he adds, "I think these matters will be resolved when Murray leaves his papers—he has a box full of correspondence with Ellison. I think that that correspondence is going to bring out the mutuality of these explorations and discoveries."

It's clear that, beneath Ellison's unfailingly courtly demeanor, his own internal struggles may have taken their toll. The fire, in the fall of 1967, is often mentioned as a watershed moment for him, one whose symbolic freight would only increase over the years. He had been busy that summer in his Massachusetts farmhouse, making extensive revisions on his novel in progress—Murray recalls seeing a manuscript thick with interlinear emendations during a visit there. At times, Ellison had called Murray to read him some of his new material. The fire occurred on the very evening that the Ellisons had decided to return to New York. Murray says, "He packed up all his stuff and got everything together, put it in the hallway leading out, with some cameras and some of his shooting equipment. Then they went out to dinner with Richard Wilbur. On the way home, when they got to a certain point, they saw this fire reflection on the skyline, and the nearer they got, the more it seemed like it was their place. And as they turned in, they saw their house going up in flames." Ellison had a copy of the manuscript in New York, but the rewriting and rethinking that had occupied him for months were lost. "So he went into shock, really. He just closed off from everybody." Murray didn't hear from him until Christmas. In the months that followed, Ellison would sometimes call Murray up and read him passages—trying to jog Murray's memory so that he would jog Ellison's. "It took him years to recover," Murray says. Meanwhile, Murray's career was following an opposite trajectory. As if making up for lost time, he spent the first half of the seventies averaging a book a year; during the same period, Ellison's block as a novelist had grown to mythic proportions. Bellow says, "Ralph was suffering very deeply from his hang-up, and it was very hard to have any connection with him. He got into a very strange state, I think."

Did Ellison feel betrayed? It seems clear that he did. ("Romie used to call it 'Oklahoma paranoia,'" Murray says, musing on the *froideur* that settled between them.) Did Ellison have reason to? That's harder to answer. The African American poet Michael S. Harper, an Ellison stalwart, says, "The most important word I ever heard Ralph say was the word 'honor.' I happen to know some of the difficulties they went through when Albert was in a phase of making appearances in white literary salons, and reports came back from various people." Theories of the estrangement abound. One writer acquainted with the two men says that Ellison had learned that Murray was bad-mouthing him; another suggests that Ellison simply felt crowded, that Murray was presenting himself as Ellison's confidant—"as the man to see if you want to know"—in a way that Ellison found unseemly. The chill could make things awkward for acquaintances. One of them says, "I remember on one occasion Ralph and I were lunching at the Century Club, when Al saw me in the downstairs lobby. He came up immediately and we chatted briefly, and as we were talking to each other Ralph walked away and would have nothing to do with Al." Theirs had become a difficult relationship.

Murray, for his part, is inclined to see the matter in almost anthropological terms, as falling into the behavior patterns of out-group representatives amid an in-group: "Here's a guy who figures that he's got *his* white folks over here, and he got them all hoodwinked, so he don't want anybody coming in messing things up." In anthropological terms, the native informant never relishes competition. "Hell, it was probably inevitable," Willie Morris says of the estrangement.

For all their similarities in background, education, sensibility, even dress (they shared a tailor, Charlie Davidson, himself something of a legend in sartorial circles), the two men inclined toward rather contrasting styles of public presentation. A private man who in later years grew intensely aware of being a public figure, Ellison had contrived a persona designed to defeat white expectations of black brutishness. Hence the same words come up again and again when people try to write about him—words like *patrician, formal, aristocratic, mandarin, civilized, dignified.* James Baldwin once observed, shrewdly, that Ellison was "as angry as anybody can be and still *live.*" It was this banked anger that kept his back so straight in public settings, his manners so impeccable; even his spoken sentences wore spats and suspenders. Murray, who enjoyed verbal sparring as much as anybody, lacked that gift of anger, and as a conversationalist he had always taken delight in the saltier idioms of the street. (Imagine Redd Foxx with a graduate degree in literature.) The writer Reynolds Price, a friend of both Ellison and Murray, says, "Ralph had a kind of saturnine, slightly bemused quality. I thought Al always seemed the more buoyant person."

Writing is at once a solitary and a sociable act, and literary relationships are similarly compounded of opposites. So it was with Ellison and Murray, two country cousins. Many people speak of Ellison's eightieth-birthday party—to which Murray had been invited and at which he delivered a moving tribute to his old schoolmate—a significant moment of reconciliation. "I think it was Ellison's way of reaching out to Murray," a friend of Ellison's says.

Then, too, for all his companionability, Murray's literary inclinations ran strongly toward the paternal. He takes deep satisfaction in that role, and there are many who can attest to his capacity for nurturance. James Alan McPherson, one of the fiction writers who have most often been likened to Ellison, recalls a time in the late seventies when he was in Rhode Island with Michael Harper, the poet, and Ernest J. Gaines, whose novels include *The Autobiography of Miss Jane Pittman.* In a moment of mad enthusiasm, they hit on the idea of going to New York and letting Ellison know how much they admired him. When they phoned him, he told them, to their unbounded joy, that they should come right down. And so, after an almost mythic trek, these young black writers arrived at Riverside Drive to pay a visit to their hero.

"Mr. Ellison can't see you," they were told at the door. "He's busy working."

They were crushed. They were also adrift: with the destination of their pilgrimage closed to them, they had no place to go. "So we called Al Murray, and he picked up the slack," McPherson recounts. "He brought us to his apartment, where he had some apples and some bourbon and some fancy French cheese. And he said, 'Have you ever met Duke Ellington's sister?' We said no, so he took us over to meet Duke Ellington's sister. And he said, 'Do you want to see the Bearden retrospective?'" He took them to the Brooklyn Museum and on to the Cordier and Ekstrom gallery, where Bearden was then showing his work. "And I'll always remember Al for that," McPherson says. (Murray tells me, "Most guys forget that I'm just two years younger than Ralph, but they feel closer to me because I'm more accessible. They kid with me all the time.") Perhaps, in the end, Ellison was the better student of Lord Raglan; he knew that patricide, or some variant of it, was a staple of heroic literature. McPherson says, quietly, "Ellison didn't want sons."

For McPherson, what crystallized things was a ceremony that City College held in 1984 to honor Ellison. McPherson and Harper were both there to give tributes. At the luncheon, Harper tapped on his glass and handed Ellison a wrapped box, saying, "Ralph, here's a gift from your sons."

"Then you'd better open it yourself," Ellison replied dryly. "I'm afraid it might explode."

Albert Murray has now reached the age where his progeny have progeny, two of the most prominent in his line being, of course, Stanley Crouch and Wynton Marsalis. Both are frequent guests at Lenox Terrace, and Marsalis tells me of dinner table conversations that roam from Homer to Galileo, from the commedia dell'arte to Faulkner and Neruda. "Murray has given me a first-class education," he says. And he speaks eloquently about the impact that *Stomping the Blues,* and Murray's very notion of jazz as an art form, had on him; he speaks about tradition, blues idioms, a poetics of inclusion. As he puts it, "I'm a Murrayite." Crouch, whose writing brilliantly championed Murray's difficult aesthetic and emulated his pugnacious style of critique, says, "I think he's one of the foremost thinkers to appear in America letters over the last twenty-five years." (He also suggests that Murray would have been a far worthier candidate for a Nobel Prize than Toni Morrison.) "The last of the giants," McPherson calls him.

There is much to be said for having descendants. They spread the insights you have given them. They worry about why you are not better known. (Crouch has a simple explanation for Murray's relative obscurity: "It's because he spent all that time on the Basie book—there was that very long silence. I think what happened was that his career lost momentum.") They remind you, fetchingly, of your own callow youth. And they take inspiration from your fearless style of analysis and critique and apply it to your own work—though this can be a mixed blessing.

No doubt it's the ultimate tribute to Murray's legacy of combative candor that his most fervid admirers are quite free in expressing their critical reservations—notably with regard to the new novel. *The Seven League Boots* has the distinction of being the least autobiographical of Murray's three novels: its protagonist leaves Alabama with his bass and joins up with a legendary jazz band—one not unlike Ellington's. The band is blissfully free of quarrels and petty jealousies, and Murray's alter ego, Scooter, inspires only affection in those he encounters. Indeed, this is, in no small part, a novel about friendships, about literary and intellectual conversations and correspondences, including those between Scooter and his old college roommate. On a trip across the Mississippi River Bridge, Scooter finds himself thinking about my old roommate again. But this time the writer he brought to mind was not Rilke but Walt Whitman, about whom he had said in response to my letter about joining the band for a while. . . . *According to my old roommate, old Walt Whitman, barnstorming troubadour par excellence that he was, could only have been completely delighted with the interplay of aesthetic and pragmatic considerations evidenced in the maps and mileage charts and always tentative itineraries.* . . . It was Ralph Waldo Emerson who spoke of "melodies that ascend and leap and pierce into the deeps of infinite time," my roommate also wrote, which, by the way, would make a very fine blurb for a Louis Armstrong solo such as the one on "Potato Head Blues."

In the next few pages, there are allusions to, among others, Melville, James Joyce, Van Wyck Brooks, Lewis Mumford, Constance Rourke, Frederick Douglass, Paul Laurence Dunbar, and Antonin Dvořák. Perhaps the critic's library overstocks his novelistic imagination. In the *Times Book Review,* the novelist and critic Charles Johnson—who must be counted among Murray's heirs, and is certainly among his most heartfelt admirers—described it as "a novel without tension." It may well be that the pleasures this novel affords are more discursive than dramatic, more essayistic than narrative. Murray tells me, "I wrote hoping that the most sophisticated readers of my time will think that I'm worth reading." They do, and he is.

The poet Elizabeth Alexander writes:

Albert Murray do they call you Al
or Bert or "Tuskegee Boy"?
Who are the Omni-Ones who help me feel?
I'm born after so much. Nostalgia hurts.

You could say of him what he said of Gordon Parks: "Sometimes it is as if he himself doesn't quite know what to make of what he has in fact *already* made of himself." Sometimes I don't quite, either. On the one hand, I cherish the vernacular; on the other, I've always distrusted the notion of "myth" as something deliberately added to literature, like the prize in a box of Cracker

Jack. And though my first two books can be read as footnotes to *The Omni-Americans*, I, like most in the demoralized profession of literary studies, have less faith in the cultural power of criticism than he has. All the same, I find his company immensely cheering.

We live in an age of irony—an age when passionate intensity is hard to find outside a freshman dining hall, and when even the mediocre lack all conviction. But Murray was produced by another age, in which intelligence expressed itself in ardor. He has spent a career *believing* in things, like the gospel according to Ma Rainey and Jimmy Rushing and Duke Ellington. More broadly, he believes in the sublimity of art, and he has never been afraid of risking bathos to get to it. (I think the reason he took so long to write Basie's life story is that he wanted to step *inside* a great black artist, to see for himself how improvisation and formal complexity could produce high art.)

The last time I visited him at his apartment, I sat in the chair next to his writing desk as he talked me through the years of his life and his formation, and made clear much that had been unclear to me about cultural modernity. "Let me begin by saying that Romie frequently got me into trouble," Ralph Ellison told mourners at a 1988 memorial service for Bearden. "Nothing physical, mind you, but difficulties arising out of our attempts to make some practical sense of the relationship between art and living, between ideas and the complex details of consciousness and experience." In this sense, Murray, too, has always spelled trouble—for critics and artists of every description, for icon-breakers and icon-makers, for friends and foes. You learn a great many things when you sit with him in his apartment, but, summed up, they amount to a larger vision: this is Albert Murray's century; we just live in it.

Reprinted from the *New Yorker* Apr. 8, 1996: 70–81.

3

Trading Twelves

The Omni-American Literary Identity of Albert Murray and Ralph Ellison

JOHN F. CALLAHAN

"I'm fired up and ready to go."

Forgive me for borrowing Senator Obama's campaign chant. I do so because Albert Murray foretold the call Barack Obama is making to the American people as far back as 1970 in the case he made for multifaceted American identity in *The Omni-Americans.* During the presidential campaign I heard that same omni-American accent in the voice of my four-year-old African American, Irish American granddaughter. When I asked her on the telephone what her mother, my daughter, was doing in Nevada, she replied, "Mama's helping *the* Barack Obama." Her use of the definite article turned her words into an incantation. "*The* Barack Obama," she repeated, "he's a very serious man." *This little girl gets it,* I thought, and so as Senator Obama became the focus of former president Bill Clinton's scorn in South Carolina, I was tempted to suggest that the campaign enter my granddaughter in the lists against Clinton as Barack Obama's chief surrogate—I know I'm biased, but I don't think there's much doubt about who the American people would have chosen.

In any case I am fired up by the marvelous connections made in the symposium that resulted in this book between Albert Murray and classical, American, and European literary traditions, and between Al Murray and vernacular American and African American forms, especially the blues. Indeed, the multitoned, multifaceted quality of Albert Murray's writing and presence celebrated in the essays in this volume recalls a hilarious and magical passage from Ralph Waldo Ellison's *Juneteenth* in which the Reverend Hickman calls the roll of the most memorable black preachers who performed at a climactic long-ago Juneteenth night celebration, describing "that little Negro Murray, who had been to a seminary up north and could preach the pure Greek and the original Hebrew and could still make all our uneducated folks swing along with him." Hickman, backed by Ellison, assures congregants and readers alike that the Reverend Murray was "not showing off, just needing all those languages to give him room to move around in" (134).

In the Albert Murray symposium we heard calls for a biography of Albert Murray. One will surely come. And when it does, I hope the biographer will rely upon *Trading Twelves: The Selected Letters of Ralph Ellison and Albert Murray* just as future Ellison biographers should make use of his correspondence with Murray as a barometer of his "cold [vernacular] Oklahoma Negro eye." As I'll show presently, the Ellison of *Trading Twelves* wrote in a rollicking, riffing, take-no-prisoners idiom that revealed the man behind the masks thrown up by biographers; by others, who thought they had Ellison figured out; and, at times, by Ralph's own somewhat misleading magisterial persona. In ways more personal and perhaps even more revealing than either man's literary works, the Ellison-Murray correspondence from 1950 to 1960 shows each man coming into maturity, and remaining, at least to the other, the same person before, during, and after Ellison's great success with *Invisible Man,* and long before Murray's first book was published. In this connection biographers of Albert Murray should take care to avoid Arnold Rampersad's tendency to rely on *Trading Twelves* as merely discrete letters rather than probe it as a correspondence, which accelerates into a succession of rolling call-and-response jazz riffs. Taken together, their letters are the steel-cut grist for an intense, evolving friendship. The two men were implicit and explicit collaborators in what Murray characterized as their common project as "heirs and continuators of the most indigenous mythic pre-figuration of the most fundamental existential assumption underlying the human proposition as stated in the Declaration of Independence, which led to the social contract known as the Constitution and as specified by the Emancipation Proclamation and encapsulated in the Gettysburg Address and further particularized in the Thirteenth, Fourteenth, and Fifteenth Amendments" (*Trading Twelves* xiii).

Certainly the Murray-Ellison correspondence in *Trading Twelves* yields particular *and* comprehensive insight about the themes discussed in this volume on Albert Murray's work and life. Murray's letters to Ellison and Ellison's responses constitute a profound, unguarded exploration of what it means to be an American, black, and omni; what it means to be an artist in an experimental nation whose culture and politics are works in progress; and, finally, what it means to embrace the rights and responsibilities of friendship on both the higher and "the lower frequencies" of democratic equality.

The Ellison-Murray correspondence, which in sweep and intensity hearkens back to letters exchanged by Melville and Hawthorne, is one of the most instructive and fascinating American literary correspondences of the twentieth century. Imagine if Ernest Hemingway had been more of a resilient blues man in his own interior life, capable of the vulnerable, compassionate honesty displayed by F. Scott Fitzgerald in their correspondence. For although the Fitzgerald-Hemingway letters are rich and suggestive, despite the fits of combat and the emotional lacunae on Hemingway's part, one wishes that in their respective skins Hemingway and Fitzgerald had imagined themselves as members of the same jazz combo, bringing their best to each other after the fashion of Ralph Ellison and Albert Murray. Of course the Ellison-Murray correspondence lasted for only one of the more than five decades of their acquaintance; although they saw each other when they could from time to time, theirs is primarily a long-distance friendship. For that very reason, and because their occasional meetings reinforced affinities and confidences they shared with no one else during these ten years, their letters illuminate nooks and crannies of American culture, literature, politics, and personality often kept in the shadows.

The keynote is friendship. Yet if the letters of *Trading Twelves* were inspired by the spirit of fraternity shared by Murray and Ellison, they came into print through the good offices of John Jameson's twelve-year-old Irish whiskey. The full story goes back as far as 1979, the beginning of my own friendship with Ralph Ellison, when Mr. Jameson also figured as the catalyst he became twenty years later for Albert Murray and me. But first, a word about my meeting with Ellison. In response to "The Historical Frequencies of Ralph Waldo Ellison," a piece I'd written arguing that his essays suggested a way to read the classics of American literature as well as *Invisible Man,* he invited me to 730 Riverside Drive. There, I glanced at my watch after a late-afternoon chat during which we sat across from each other in front of windows that looked out on the Hudson and, in the distance, the Palisades on the Jersey side, and spoke in language reminiscent of set pieces from the late novels of Henry James. It was five minutes to 5 o'clock. Without warning, Ellison slapped his hand on the glass coffee table and broke the stiff formality of the academic—or was it the therapeutic?—hour.

"Well, John, would you like a drink?"

Frozen by the modulation, I replied as if I were kin to Invisible Man. "Why, yes, Mr. . . ."

"What?" he growled, his disappointment palpable.

"Sure, Ralph," I recovered.

"That's bettah," he said, lapsing into his Oklahoma drawl. He disappeared into the kitchen, soon returning with a bottle of Jack Daniels, which he put on his side of the table, and a bottle of Jameson for me.

There's a revealing, bittersweet coda to this story. About ten years into our friendship, visiting at the Ellison summer home in the Berkshires, I yielded to an urge to call him out about the bottle of Jameson's.

"Ralph," I began, "do you mind if I ask you something?"

"Why, no," he said.

I blundered on. "Since we met, I've always wondered what the hell you would have done with that Irish whiskey if you hadn't liked me."

Thinking that my line easily met the threshold of jacks or better required to open a hand in a mean game of five-card stud poker, I forgot that Ralph Ellison didn't live, even for an instant, on such narrow categorical frequencies. He looked at me—just looked at me—for a while, then shook his head in exasperation.

"For God's sake, John, I like Irish whiskey, too."

Even in kidding you could not tempt Ralph Ellison to traffic in stereotypes of race devised and practiced by his countrymen. As for me, I learned a lesson. Five years later, after Ralph passed away, *Juneteenth* came out, and Albert Murray graciously agreed to read a passage at the Barnes and Noble flagship store in New York. I say "graciously" because, months before, after Albert had read the galleys of *Juneteenth,* word came from an acolyte that he wanted to talk to me. I hardly knew Al Murray, and with some trepidation I called him. Those of you who know him won't be surprised to hear that he launched into a half-hour-long account of a section of the novel in progress I had not included in *Juneteenth.* Narrated by the white, Kentucky-born-and-bred reporter, Welborn McIntyre, book 1, Murray felt, expressed, in black *and* white, the restless American expansiveness necessary to complement what he considered the *Negro*-centric world of book 2.

I listened but let *Juneteenth* stand without book 1. After the public launch of the book, I paid a visit to tell Al how personally grateful I was for his reading and his earlier advice. Before taking my leave, I presented him with a bottle of Jameson's twelve-year-old whiskey, whereupon he went into the alcove of his study and emerged with a black binder full of letters whose provenance he explained in that gravelly tenor voice of his. "Ralph wrote me these from 1950 to 1960. I think they'd make a sharp little volume."

I took them to read overnight. Twice since Ralph's passing, I'd heard Albert read in public a hilarious letter about Ralph going all over Rome in search of the proper ingredients for pigs' feet. Now, reading them together, consecutively, I realized the letters summoned Ralph's defiant mind and spirit in all its brilliant improvisation, mimicry, and occasional bawdiness. But something was missing, and I resolved to tell Albert what it was when we met again the next afternoon.

"Lots of people would read them, if they had a chance," he said as soon as I was seated.

"Yes," I said, "but what about your end of the correspondence?"

"Not many people would care about mine."

I resisted the impulse to argue the point. "Albert," I said instead. "Let me read them, and give you an honest opinion."

Murray hesitated. He is a man of proud humility and humble pride. I quickly saw that he was loath to poach on what he considered his friend's greater achievement and reputation. But we talked some more, and finally he said, "All right, read mine. No promises, understand." He insisted we seal the terms of the deal with a stiff drink of the Jameson's, still standing unopened in his liquor cabinet. No question about it; that was the true beginning of *Trading Twelves.* A month later Albert ran his preferred title by me, and I've always felt that after I pushed it with the Modern Library as perfectly expressive of the letters' verbal approximation of the in-chorus and out-chorus signatures of so many of the swing tunes he and Ralph loved, my vote of confidence nudged our relationship from collaboration to friendship.

Let me foreground the Murray-Ellison correspondence in the very different lives the two men led from 1950 to 1960. Murray was an officer in the air force and an English instructor at Tuskegee, making side trips to France in 1950 and to Casablanca in a military capacity from 1955 to 1958. Except for a stint at the Salzburg Seminar in American Studies during the fall of 1954 and two years at the American Academy in Rome from 1955 to 1957, Ellison was rooted in New York. (These two intervals, by the way, turned out to be the only time of any duration Ellison passed outside the United States, and perhaps his letters from Rome are more American by virtue of being somewhat provincial.) From the fall of 1957 until the correspondence halts in 1960, Murray rises in the air force ranks to become an officer at the Reserve Flying Center in Long Beach while Ellison divides his time between New York City and Saul Bellow's house in the woods of Tivoli a hundred miles up the Hudson.

More than anything else, on every page the letters in *Trading Twelves* reveal two individuals increasingly comfortable and at ease with one another. Theirs is the symbiosis of friendship—a mutually beneficial connection between two men unmarred by competitiveness, perhaps because they are thoroughly formed in style and personality when they commence their literary journey. Alternately hare and tortoise, tortoise and hare, they stimulate and challenge each other in the manner of a collaborative competition between jazz brothers who like each other and jam at cutting sessions for love of music, not from any corrosive rivalry. Maybe this is because each man plays a different instrument. Ellison's voice is that of a horn man improvising long, meditative solos on trumpet broken by fierce irreverent runs of cacophony, while Murray swings along on piano in an offhand syncopation that he accelerates with sudden earthy velocity.

As they become regular correspondents, each chooses a playful comradely informality only rarely broken by tenderness. For example, perhaps because of his military habits, Albert signs his letters "Murray," even when he writes Ralph from Algeria in 1956 that he's suffered a *mild* heart attack. In response to this letter, Ellison's customary salutation of "Dear Albert" becomes "Dear Ole Albert"; touchingly, he ends with "Love to lovable Mokable and Miqueable [Mozelle and Michele Murray] from Ralphable" (*Trading Twelves* 169, 172). Perhaps in silent acknowledgement of his friend's intimacy and his own mortality, for the first time Murray signs his reply, "Albert" (174).

In any case, consulting these letters (biographers take heed), one sees each man summon qualities in the other that he did not often have on display otherwise. Writing to Murray, Ellison let down his hair, the thinning of which was a running joke between them. As he sat down to write, the very thought of Murray seemed to let loose a wild, uproarious streak in Ralph that few people knew, especially in his later years. During the final edit of *Invisible Man*, Ellison writes of an apparent crevasse of sensibility between him and his distinguished editor and friend, Albert Erskine. "Erskine's having a time deciding what kind of a novel it is, and I can't help him," he confides. "For me, it's just a big fat ole Negro lie, meant to be told during cotton picking time over a water bucket full of corn, with a dipper passing back and forth at a good fast clip so that no one, not even the narrator himself, will realize how utterly preposterous the lie actually is. I just hope someone points out that aspect of it. As you see I'm more obsessed with this thing now than I was all those five years" (*Trading Twelves* 21). Some twenty years later Murray was to riff in response that "[i]t was as if Ellison had taken an everyday twelve bar blues tune (by a man from down South sitting in a manhole up North in New York singing and signifying about how he got there) and scored it for full orchestra" (*Omni-Americans* 167).

In his letters to Murray Ellison also expresses a sometimes unflinching, unforgiving frankness, especially about old unhealed hurts experienced at Tuskegee, where Murray had seen Ellison from afar and imagined him as a sheerly Olympian upperclassman. And generosity, a trait of Ellison's given maddeningly short shrift in the Rampersad biography, is abundantly part of his comradeship with Murray. Months before *Invisible Man*'s publication, Ellison is as intensely interested in and arrested by Murray's work in progress as Murray is about *Invisible Man*. When Murray sends him the manuscript, Ellison writes back with palpable excitement and pleasure: "Yes, maybe we'll have books published during the same year" (*Trading Twelves* 25).

Ralph Ellison's response to a draft of what would not become Murray's finished, published *Train Whistle Guitar* until much later reflects both the praise and truth telling of a writer writing as a friend to both the author and his book. After he and Fannie [Ellison's wife] have both read the manuscript, Ralph writes, "[W]ithout further delay let me say that we both think that you've written yourself a book. I found it beautifully evocative and poetic (indeed, I'm not sure if it's a novel or a narrative poem)" (*Trading Twelves* 27). Murray scholars will know that Ellison identified the very issue of form that kept Murray's manuscript on the boil for more than twenty years. Notice, though, the deft and generous way Ralph elaborates on his point: "For while I disagree with hardly any of his [your narrator's] formulations on the nature of fiction nor with his theories of jazz, etc., I think the reader is deprived of his, the reader's, adventure because here you turn from presenting process to presenting statements" (28). As Ralph's literary executor and posthumous editor, I would note my view, more than fifty years later, that Ralph's subsequent revisions composed on his PC from the 1980s and early 1990s have less narrative crackle, less narrative tension, and more essayistic statement and inadvertent slow motion than the earlier typescripts from the late fifties, sixties, and early seventies.

At any rate, about his own novel in progress Al Murray was not shy, responding to Ralph's 1952 letter with a confident burst of learned African American vernacular.

> [T]here are some other bop riffs that I did hope would operate. Miss Eunice was rendered in bop and was supposed to operate *crucially*. I felt that that was the only way to render her this time (since she's going to be used again!) EUNICE means HAPPY VICTORY, man, and I can't say a hell of a lot about that yet. In my mind it also suggests union, oneness, equilibrium. Notice that the full name is Eunice Purifoy. I was hep to eunuch implications too, but in the sense of un-readiness, unfitness. Remember, this guy must fear abortions in the sense that he is unready, he *is* a eunuch and I described her to look as much like that Egyptian princess that Mzle [Mozelle] looks like as I could—but in another sense he is NOT a eunuch at all but a prince in disguise preparing to—well, he's running around with Falstaff and them. (*Trading Twelves* 32)

Likewise, when Ralph delivers his "Brave Words for a Startling Occasion" address upon receiving the National Book Award, Murray declares himself a fellow recruit in the same literary battalion: "Proteus is the right kick, boy; and it is my kick, too. Both the writer and the hero have got to learn to riff on it. You got to be nimble or nothing, I keep trying to tell them (& myself too)" (*Trading Twelves* 37). Nor in Ellison's view was Murray engaging in bravado. Later in 1953 Ellison declares allegiance to his friend's vernacular learning and his originality as a thinker and writer whose style, substance, and point of view all have that *swing:* "I hope you'll get work done on your book and that you'll start turning out essays on jazz which can later be part of a book. You have the stuff and I think it'll do you good to have part of your identity anchored outside Tuskegee. Thus far you've stayed there and transcended its limitations. You've evolved the stuff, so now put it on the line. You're the only one I know who makes sense of all the ramifications and since it looks like no one is going to do anything with this material we might as well get started" (80). I love Ellison's shift from the somewhat avuncular *you* of the younger, unpublished man to the *we* of full partner and collaborator. Certainly Ellison and Murray each were of the mind that neither would realize his objective—

what Murray called creating "stories to provide American literature with representative anecdotes, definitive episodes, and mythic profiles that would add up to a truly comprehensive and universally appealing American epic" (xiii)—unless both of them made a distinctive and connected contribution to the common project.

Reading a very early draft of an episode from Ellison's second novel sent from Rome in 1956, Murray responds with a riff calling Ralph to keep on keeping on. "You writin' good, boy, real good, blowin' good, cuttin' good, keen and deep. If you getting any of this stuff working in there with old Cleofus & em you still swinging that switchblade and you aint got nothing to worry about. For my money you're *in* there with that shit, man." And he closes with his own report. "Me, I've finally begun to get a few notes down for that jazz novel I've got to take a crack at" (*Trading Twelves* 118–19).

Still in Rome a year later and frustrated by what others are writing (and failing to write) about the black heroes of African American folklore and culture, Ellison urges Murray to get cracking on the blues.

> Hell, [Stanley Edgar] Hyman don't know that Ulysses is both Jack the rabbit (when that Cyclops gets after his ass) and Jack the Bear, Big Smith the Chef, John Henry and everybody else when he starts pumping arrows into those cats who've been after his old lady. Or if he does recognize this, it's only with his mind, not his heart . . . : Mose can't rise vertically so he's restless; he can't get a good job here so he goes there—missing the fact that there is a metaphysical restless built into the American and Mose is just another form of it, expressed basically, with a near tragic debunking of the self which is our own particular American style. I really thought I'd raised that boy [Hyman] better than that. *But hell, I keep telling you [Albert] that you're the one who has to write about those blues.* (*Trading Twelves* 166; my emphasis)

Again, their styles are so attuned to one another that at times you wonder who is speaking, Ellison or Murray?

Here and elsewhere in his letters Ellison continues to use his influence to push Murray's literary fortunes. Then and now Murray has been the first person to tell the world about the help that he got from Ralph Ellison. In his testimony Albert gives chapter and verse that Ralph did not just talk the talk; he walked the walk. "When I was settled in New York," he remembers in one of his notes to *Trading Twelves*, "my first published item was a long review of several books that *Life* asked me to do because Ralph had suggested that one of the literary editors get in touch with me. It was also upon Ralph's generous recommendation that editor Myron Kolatch asked me to do reviews for *The New Leader*. My collegial relationship with Ralph was also to lead to my personal and professional relationship with Willie Morris, who as editor-in-chief of *Harper's* not only published an episode from my novel *Train Whistle Guitar* but also gave me the assignment that turned into *South to a Very Old Place*" (*Trading Twelves* 188). Murray's series of acknowledgements suggests an ease in his own skin and the conviction that the quality of his work has repaid a great writer and friend's unreserved confidence in his talent.

Toward the end of the correspondence Murray writes Ellison trenchant and prophetic comments on the artificial landscape of Southern California and its mesmerizing influence on the coming suburbanization of America. "So far what I've seen of this part of southern California has been mostly boomtown stuff. A big shiny supermarket, even the homes & gardens seem to have been bought in a supermarket" (*Trading Twelves* 191). Pithy, trenchant, and on the case, Albert Murray's been in California for only a month, and he nails the meretricious seductiveness of the place. In the meantime, on his end, Ralph riffs on his students at Bard College and his larger conviction that this privileged cohort coming of age in the late fifties has embraced an inheritance of excess:

> They all expect to be entertained but I played the dozens *at* them and signified about them in so many different ways that I don't think they found many places to hide from confronting the connection between their identities, social and personal, and the major concerns of the American novel. I wasn't nice at all. I hit them with their ignorance . . . and their easy smugness towards the South, then tried to shake some of the shit out their vague and inflated notions concerning the superiority of European fiction. . . . I know Bard is something of a special case but the picture I get of what the American whites who matured during the thirties are doing to their children is frightening. (205)

Ellison's letters from Bard were not just jeremiads against the undiscipline of others; he sometimes took council with Albert about his (Ralph's) tendency to accept invitations to write essays about American literature and American culture, and in so doing, neglect the novel that mattered so much and was such a struggle for him. In response to Murray's gentle listening, Ralph comes clean about his need to have it both ways, despite breaks in focus and concentration that threatened his fiction: "Nevertheless I'm still planning to put together a book of essays. Right now I'm working up a piece on Negroes in Southern fiction titled *The Seer and the Seen* for an anthology edited by some southern boys and scheduled by Anchor. If this goes well I'll use it along with the other stuff. I've been finding interesting things in Hemingway and Fitzgerald which might well work into a broader piece on the same subject" (*Trading Twelves* 206).

In the same 1959 letter Ellison finds his way back to what was behind his novel in progress and essays alike: "When you start lifting up that enormous stone, the Civil War, that's kept so much of the meaning of life in the North hidden, you begin to see that Mose is in the center of a junk pile as well as in the center of the cotton boll. All the boys who try to escape this are simply running from the problem of value—Which is why those old Negroes whom I'm trying to make Hickman represent are so confounding, they never left the old original briar patch. You can't understand Lincoln and Jefferson without confronting them" (*Trading Twelves* 206).

So it went. In 1960 Ralph, exhilarated from revising and editing a fifty-page excerpt from book 2 of his novel to run as the lead piece in the first issue of Saul Bellow's new, short-lived magazine, writes Murray on *Noble Savage* letterhead. Then, months later, he responds to Murray's news of finishing a new chapter of *his* novel by taking pains to recruit his friend to be a fellow contributor, as if Albert's presence would confirm the worth of the much-ballyhooed magazine. "Dear Albert," he writes,

> I had Fanny get off a copy of the *Noble Savage* to you a couple of weeks ago, but have been so busy that only now am I getting around to the follow up letter. I hope it gives you some idea of what we're up to—although I'm not a very active editor at the moment—and I hope you'll let us see something of what

you're writing. . . . At any rate, we're out to provide a magazine which will make it unnecessary for a good writer to even think about *P.R.* [*Partisan Review*] or *Hudson,* or any of the other academic house organs, and any criticism we publish will be by writers, not critics. Best of all, we have a top word rate of 5 cents per—which ain't bad at all." (*Trading Twelves* 221)

Ellison's playful fraternal spirit of democratic equality typifies the generosity that went back and forth between him and Murray—a watermark in their correspondence, and the gold coin of their friendship.

Throughout this discussion I have used the Ellison-Murray friendship and correspondence as a lens through which to view Albert Murray as an American man of letters. Earlier, I teased you by quoting the beginning of what may be at once the wittiest, most serious, and most playful appraisal of Murray's genius in a passage from Ellison's second novel. What is also remarkable about this unlikely tour de force is that Ralph names the character in question Murray—not Albert or Al or, more likely, a completely different first name to throw readers off the scent, but simply *Murray.* Even more uncanny is how righteously Ellison nails his friend. Aptly, in the passage the Reverend Hickman—whom, Ellison had written in his last letter to Murray, was "moving more and more into the role of hero and the old guy is so large that I've just about given in to him" (*Trading Twelves* 222)—does the heavy lifting.

   Bliss, the little boy Hickman raised who runs off and becomes a racist senator from a New England state, is assassinated by the omni-American son he has long denied. Dying, he calls Hickman to him, and Hickman remembers the ministers, their sermons, the black church, the sacred calling, and the rigors and trials of doing the Lord's work. Right behind Hickman, in the kind of out-chorus Al Murray loved, Ralph signifies on his debt to his friend. "But as I was saying," Hickman riffs,

   what's more important, Revern' Murray's education didn't get him separated from the folks. Yeah, and he used to sit there in his chair bent forward like a boxer waiting for the bell, with his fists doubled up and his arms on his knees. Then when it came his turn to preach, he'd shoot forward like he was going to leap right out there into the congregation and start giving the Devil some uppercuts. Lord, what a little rough mister! One night he grabbed a disbelieving bully who had come out to break up the meeting, and threw him bodily out into the darkness; tossed him fifteen feet or more into the mule-pissed mud. Then he came on back to the pulpit and preached like Peter. . . .

"Yes," the Senator said, "I remember him." (*Juneteenth* 137–38)

"Little rough mister," indeed! Ellison's Murray is a man of the world doing the Lord's work in a rough-and-tumble way, using his fists when necessary. And of course the cream of the joke is that both Ellison and Murray considered art the Lord's work for the writer, just as moving the nation closer to its ideals is the citizen's work. As citizen-writers, both men challenged the conventional grain. They neither sought nor shirked combat. They wrote as omni-Americans on behalf of a republic of letters committed to the continuing quest for a more perfect union.

Originally given as the keynote address to the symposium "Albert Murray and the Aesthetic Imagination of a Nation."

his mood from shock and anxiety, to an enthusiastic
anticipation that was always there whenever we were
doing whatever we were doing in California.

② So what can I tell you, my man, he said before I
could even say hello, you already know that Hollywood is
75 per cent if not 90 per cent pop song romance. Sunset
Boulevard and blue horizons indeed. So what can I tell you
fellow. Old Dice go it bad and gotta try to make it good.
So I got over that attack of cornballitis.

③ man, he went on, I realize what had hit me right after
we came outside and you headed across the street to
the arcade to 43rd street. Suddenly there was this
irrepressible need to hear her voice again as soon as
possible so that I could be sure that I hadn't made
the whole goddamn thing up. So I decided to call her
up and ask if I could pop by the boutique.

④ Which he had done from a phone in the lobby of the
bank at the corner of Fifth Avenue, and she had said yes
and as he hung up he suddenly realized that the
relationship that he was trying to develop with her was
only incidentally and at most only temporarily connected
with a film production that neither of them had ever

I said Hey, man next time around. after all I
plan to be here for at least two years, he said Hey but
that's not what I really mean. fellow. This is something

a part of the nucleus of the world famous Count BASIE band.
④ Those guys. That music, he said as we finished
Miss Defense Hightower you told me about had you

Handwritten Murray manuscripts. Photograph by Carol Friedman.

4

Cosmos Murray and the Aesthetic Imagination of a Nation

Barbara A. Baker

What impresses me most about Albert Murray is his drive. As a young man studying on the campus of Tuskegee Institute (University), he seemed already to understand that the classes he was taking and the books he was reading should come together in some grand scheme; race and region and culture and life, and most importantly art, are not only connected to each other but create a synergy that speaks beyond America to the greatest stories ever told. He wouldn't rest until he had found a way to articulate what he knew, until he found a metaphor that aptly captured the interconnectedness of the greatest artists of all times with the life of a gifted young Alabamian.

In his first books, he named the blues idiom statement his primary metaphor for this understanding, and just as artists of every stripe have riffed on the basic blues statement over the course of its development in American aesthetics, Murray has defined, redefined, conjugated, reiterated, elaborated, and extended his use of the metaphor over the course of his long and productive writing career. Not just the music but the ethos of its creators and the circumstances of its creation play into blues as the main metaphor in Cosmos Murray, the name he has given his grand scheme, which is culled from Murray's extensive reading across myriad topics, decades of discussion with some of the most original thinkers of the twentieth century (including Ralph Ellison), and an inventive, musically oriented commitment to the idea that American art can be situated in the pantheon of world-class aesthetic achievement.

The musicality of Cosmos Murray is most closely associated with the hero of the blues who exemplifies a pragmatic utility for its listeners that explains the endurance of that specifically American art form. Within his framework, Murray seeks to assign this pragmatic usefulness to American art through key concepts: "the representative anecdote," a story that serves as an example of heroic engagement with the obstacles ever present in human experience; "antagonistic cooperation," the constant threats and aggravations that generate the necessity for heroic action; and "the vernacular imperative," the artist's obligation both to establish functional relevance within the vernacular communication of the people and to stylize experience within artistic traditions. Cosmos Murray—laid down in *The Omni-Americans* and *The Hero and the Blues* and riffed on throughout all of his other works—holds that the blues idiom statement, informed by our mulatto culture, best illustrates a uniquely American aesthetic that equals fine art at its finest because within it are representative anecdotes forged in antagonistic cooperation that fulfill the vernacular imperative.

In orchestrating a comprehensive vision of American aesthetics that emphasizes the centrality of African American contribution to American identity and art, Murray has elevated his Alabama-bred perspectives to elegant statements of universal relevance in twenty-first-century aesthetic discourse. One could say that Murray has selected pragmatic functions associated with classic art and playfully imagined how they apply to the life and art that he has observed; and then, through something akin to incantation, he has spoken the relevant facets forward into a new aesthetics. In Murray's case, talking is as essential as writing. A vernacular virtuoso of both the spoken and written word, in his theories, Murray prioritizes expressions associated with black vernacular, particularly blues, but he usually insists on referring to "the blues idiom" rather than simply the music, perhaps to emphasize the rhythmic nature of blues phrasings that are characteristic of American speech patterns. In any case, for most who have really listened to him, his formulations about the American cultural landscape and the art that emanates from it seem surprisingly ahead of their time, like revelations about truths that one senses but does not know, or at least not well enough to articulate. Murray is rarely at a loss for words because he never shrinks from calling things out the way they are. Equally impressive as his drive is Murray's breathtaking cultural chutzpah, as Henry Louis Gates Jr. has called it (chapter 2).

His breathtaking chutzpah was evident from his first book, *The Omni-Americans: New Perspectives on Black Experience and American Culture* (1970), in which he articulated a perspective on American race that was not widely held or easily accepted at the time on either side of the mythical color line. Deeply influenced by Constance Rourke's study of American humor, Murray absorbed her contention that the American character is made up of equal parts Yankee, backwoodsman, American Indian, and Negro, and that any person who hoped to identify with an American character necessarily would be embracing all of these facets of it. Immigrants, for instance, according to Murray, by *"the very act of arrival . . .* emerge from the bottomless depths and enter the same stream of American tradition as those who landed at Plymouth. In the very act of making their way through customs, they begin the process of becoming, as . . . Rourke would put it, part Yankee, part backwoodsman and Indian—and part Negro!" (*Omni-Americans* 20–21). In his insistence that all Americans must identify with (among other things) their blackness, Murray's ideas are not unlike Ralph Ellison's in "The Art of Fiction," in which he says that African American experience is one that all Americans must identify with and recognize "as an important segment of the larger experience . . . not lying at the bottom of it, but intertwined, diffused in its very texture" (172). Ellison and Murray, of course, are the coconspirators behind the idea.

"Identity," Murray boldly announced in *The Omni-Americans,*

is best defined in terms of culture, and the culture of the nation over which the white Anglo-Saxon power elite exercises such exclusive political, economic, and social control is not all-white by any measurement ever devised. *American* culture, even in its most rigidly segregated precincts, is patently and irrevocably composite. It is, regardless of all the hysterical protestations of those who would have it otherwise, incontestably mulatto. Indeed, for all their traditional antagonisms and obvious differences, the so-called black and so-called white people of the United States resemble nobody else in the world so much as they resemble each other. And what is more, even their most extreme and violent polarities represent nothing so much as the natural history of pluralism in an open society. (22)

So in Cosmos Murray, American culture is mulatto, by which he means non-white and pluralistic, and the American aesthetic imagination is its product.

Murray is even more direct when the American mulatto imagination is applied to his own aesthetic formulations. Consider "Premier Cru U.S.A." from his only collection of poems, *Conjugations and Reiterations* (2001), for example, in which the speaker says, "[T]he anecdotes that most immigrants find most representative are those horatioalgerisms that relate and reiterate how the white human trash of europe interacting with other human trash of west africa and elsewhere in accomplishing what the redskin elite of the forest primeval had no aztec, inca, mayan or toltec plans for became the demographic cream of the crop" (43–44). For Murray there is only one kind of American, and that is the omni-American—the sum of the human trash deposited on this country's shores, a composite blended beyond recognition of its parts and transformed through interaction and antagonistic cooperation into the demographic cream of the crop. The transformed composite omni-Americans are "the progeny of all that mayflower, middle passage and steerage flotsam and jetsam" (44).

And this progeny creates uniquely American art that reflects its mulatto makeup. The mulatto aesthetic plays out in the art of William Faulkner, who for Murray is the "hamlet-hounded master of mulatto metaphors among Macbeths in county courthouse castles out-demographed by ever in-creeping miscegenated thickets" ("William Faulkner" 52). It plays out in the art of Hemingway, who referred to himself as an honorary Negro. Of the fiction of Ernest Hemingway Murray says, "[B]y the very nature of its emotional authenticity, its stylized precision, its flesh-and-blood concreteness, and the somehow relaxed intensity of its immediacy, [it] qualifies not only as the blues but as classic Kansas City blues" (*Blue Devils* 181). As Murray illustrates in *The Blue Devils of Nada,* the mulatto aesthetic applies to the art of Romare Bearden, of Count Basie, of Louis Armstrong, and of Duke Ellington. As Joe Wood puts it, "'[M]ulatto culture' has given as much to black people as blacks have given to it" (95). The mulatto American aesthetic that this culture generates plays out most authentically in the blues, which has a personal resonance for me, as well. What I have always loved about Murray's insistence that all Americans are incontestably mulatto is that, especially with my own blues orientation, he allows me to embrace the black part of my aesthetic imagination.

To be sure, African Americans created blues, which is fine art, which is stylized experience. But not until Albert Murray said so did most people acknowledge that blues is "a celebration of human existence in all its complexity" (*Blue Devils* 181) and that there is

> no other attitude towards experience more appropriate to the ever-shifting circumstances of all Americans or more consistent with the predicament of a man in the contemporary world at large. Indeed, the blues idiom represents a major American innovation of universal significance and potential because it fulfills, among other things, precisely that fundamental function that Constance Rourke ascribes to the comedy, the irreverent wisdom, the sudden and adroit adaptations she found in the folk genre of the Yankee-backwoodsman-Negro of the era of Andrew Jackson. It provides "emblems for a pioneer people who require resilience as a prime trait." (*Omni-Americans* 59)

Murray embraces, and then extends to the blues idiom, Rourke's suggestion that pioneer-era comedy captured the resilience of the American character. He claims the universal relevance of the American blues idiom by assigning to it the artistic capacity to express resilience against the limitations of life. As Murray explains in *The Hero and the Blues,* "the fundamental condition of human life . . . [is the] ceaseless struggle for form against chaos, of sense against nonsense" (16). And a people's art is its expression against inevitable entropy and chaos; it is the "expression of all human hope" (64). Echoing André Malraux, Murray elaborates by saying that "all art is a revolt against man's fate, against the limitations of human life itself" (62).

Rourke would have it that the terror of the wilderness that early Americans faced required special resilience. Murray further extends Rourke's paradigm to twentieth-century relevance by drawing together America's special quality of resilience with its uniquely mulatto blues aesthetic by saying "[I]n its orientation to continuity in the face of adversity and absurdity—the blues idiom lyric is entirely consistent with the folklore and wisdom underlying the rugged endurance of the black American. . . . blues-idiom dance music challenges and affirms his personal equilibrium, sustains his humanity, and enables him to maintain his higher aspirations in spite of the fact that human existence is so often mostly a low-down dirty shame" (*Hero* 36–37).

Murray's only published blues idiom lyric, "Aubades: Epic Exits and Other Twelve Bar Riffs," or simply "Epic Exits," from *Conjugations and Reiterations*, is probably his best artistic representation of how this principle works, and the poem also draws together the other pragmatic elements that Murray consistently attributes to universal fine art: the representative anecdote, antagonistic cooperation, and the achievement of the vernacular imperative. The poem's narrator may be an even more precise rendering of a resilient individual in heroic confrontation with the entropy and chaos inherent in the human condition than is Scooter, the protagonist in Murray's fictional trilogy-plus-one. Critics complain that in his fiction Murray often simply makes Scooter reiterate recapitulations of Cosmos Murray. One of Murray's very first readers, Ralph Ellison, for example, in 1952, gently criticized Murray's draft of *Train Whistle Guitar* because he could not distinguish whether the manuscript was "a novel or a narrative poem" (*Trading Twelves* 27). Ellison felt that "the reader is deprived of his, the reader's, adventure because here you turn from presenting process to presenting statements" (28). John Callahan speculates that Murray benefited from Ellison's criticism (while, ironically, the same lack of narrative tension may have confounded Ellison and contributed to his failure to complete the long-awaited follow-up to *Invisible Man*). In the meantime, the poem that Murray had been refining for years in a leather-bound notebook that he bought with the money he earned from publishing the first excerpt from *Train Whistle Guitar* became "Epic Exits" and was finally published forty-nine years after Ellison's initial criticism. The speaker of "Epic Exits," not unlike the narrator in *Invisible Man,* does not so much mouth formulations on the nature of fiction or theorize about blues and jazz as he embodies a blues attitude and illustrates a blues-oriented disposition toward the circumstances of life.

The narrator of "Epic Exits" swings in that uniquely American way that only the blues feel provides. When you read the poem, you sing the poem. If you are an American, you know the tune. "Early in the morning, I hear the rooster crow (twice). / Hear the freight train coming whistle moaning low" (3). Sounds occupy the center of the speaker's experience, and his thoughts are coaxed into his consciousness through what he hears. The sounds of the crowing rooster and the oncoming freight train inform his awakening sensibility as he prepares to embark on his life's journey, which is described throughout the rest of the poem. I would add that the crowing rooster might further suggest the mulatto orientation of American blues and the emulation of black style that many American blues musicians, especially nonblack musicians, so admire and strive to achieve in their own renditions. Put another way, every person on the bandstand wants to crow even if, or especially if, the implication of the word "crow" suggests blackness. Again, you see Murray calling out what most people know: when it comes to the blues, the aesthetics associated with black vernacular is the most positive and the most essential element in the aesthetic imagination that creates America's music.

Artistic renderings, musical and spoken, that manifest aesthetics associated with black vernacular are often associated with the African American Vernacular Tradition, which can be defined as the continuity of expression by black Americans in the United States from the first days of contact to the present. Examples include spirituals, black sermons, work songs, gospel, blues, jazz, soul, and hip-hop music. These forms of expression maintain their continuity through improvisation and extension of the vernacular forms from one performer to another, as illustrated clearly in Ken Burns's documentary film *Jazz,* in which Albert Murray appears. But in Cosmos Murray, the tradition is an omni-American tradition (nonblacks having provided antagonistic cooperation if nothing more) that speaks to and for all Americans. Murray primarily emphasizes the most sophisticated manifestations of the tradition, such as the jazz performances of Louis Armstrong and Duke Ellington, which Murray calls fully orchestrated blues statements because they share artistic qualities with world-class literature.

In his poem, Murray extends the well-known American blues tune to an American story—or, as he would say, a representative anecdote—but in Cosmos Murray, even though there is no one-to-one relationship between music and literature, there is an omni-American conflation of artistic purpose. As Murray says in *The Hero and the Blues,*

> The implications for contemporary American writers, whether black or white, should be easy enough to grasp: Precisely as white musicians who work in the blues idiom have been simulating the tribulations of U.S. Negroes for years in order to emulate such musical heroes as Louis Armstrong, Lester Young, and Duke Ellington, and such heroines as Bessie Smith and Billie Holiday, so in fiction must readers, through their desire to imitate and emulate black storybook heroes, come to identify themselves with the disjunctures as well as the continuities of black experience as if to the idiom born. Moreover, the basis for such omni-American fiction is already in existence. (50)

Blues as fiction is an example of the primary function of art. From the moment they stood upright, humans began creating narratives to capture experience, to entertain, delight, testify, and teach. Although every human is a storyteller, stories that contain "a symbolic representation of survival and achievement" become great literature, the epic, and the blues because they serve the pragmatic function of the "representative anecdote," a term Murray borrows from Kenneth Burke's *Attitudes toward History* (*From the Briarpatch File* 13). The representative anecdote teaches us the best way to struggle against inevitable and universal entropy (Wood 96), and Murray's omni-American representative anecdote provides examples of a specifically American confrontation with chaos because they occur within the context of the American, down-home experience.

In Cosmos Murray, however, American stories are not unique; they are not meant to be, otherwise they would not be representative, just as Richard Wright's Bigger Thomas is not emblematic of any human we know. Murray says Bigger "is not even a reliable reflection of the norms of *abnormal* U.S. Negro behavior" (*Hero* 94–95). Murray seeks to create the opposite of Bigger Thomas, the storybook, epic hero of the blues who is "the object of admiration or emulation. Even when he fails, there is something in his deportment that inspires others to keep trying. Even his difficulties are considered desirable" (49–50).

The speaker of "Epic Exits" exhibits this desirable deportment by dealing with "the experience of oppression," for example, "in terms of the dynamics of antagonistic cooperation" (*Hero* 49). As Murray told Don Noble in an interview (see chapter 9), he borrowed the term "antagonistic cooperation" from his late friend Joseph Campbell, who probably borrowed it from Heinrich Zimmer. Antagonistic cooperation is an aesthetic strategy that allows one to view a menace as an opportunity for creativity and respond within what Kenneth Burke, in *Attitudes toward History,* has called the "frame of acceptance" (*From the Briarpatch File* 5). Rather than adopting a "frame of rejection" and complaining or lamenting about an unfortunate circumstance, one accepts the necessity for struggle as an opportunity and "riffs on it," as old grandpa and the speaker of "Epic Exits" do in the poem.

When the speaker becomes conscious of the world around him through the moaning of a faraway train, he thinks of "old grandpa" who

> snagged the underground freedom train
> booked his passage through the grapevine
> stashed his pack
> and prayed for rain, I mean heavy rain. (4)

Murray, the speaker of the poem, and old grandpa all view racism "as an American-born dragon which should be destroyed, but . . . also regard it as something which, no matter how devastatingly sinister, can and will be destroyed because its very existence generates both the necessity and the possibility of heroic deliverance" (*Hero* 49). Just as slavery is the dragon that inspires old grandpa to snag the northbound freedom train, the image of the train supplies continuity in the ongoing heroic confrontation with harsh actualities.

In *Stomping the Blues* and *The Blue Devils of Nada* Murray elaborates on the train's significance to the northbound and upwardly mobile movement of black people during the great migration. The train was an awesome beacon, impossible to ignore as it snaked through every southern burg, tantalizing would-be heroes into forward movement and hope. Not only did its metaphorical weight hearken back to the underground railroad, but its driving, moaning sound, which is onomatopoetically re-created in folk blues, informed the aesthetic imagination fueling American music from the turn of the century through the heyday of Duke Ellington and, I would add, on through the birth and persistence of rock and roll. In American music, one can hear the onomatopoeia of the train reverberating back to the puffing steam engines and forward through the sounds of the A train barreling through New York City. Murray writes,

> once was the north star
> then it was the L and N
> not talking about cincinnati
> not telling nobody where or when

and

> going down to the railroad
> down to the railroad track
> grab me an arm full of freight train
> ain't never ever coming back. ("Epic Exits" 5–6)

The speaker of "Epic Exits" rides the wave of possibility provided by the blues-drenched American soundtrack.

The narrator's story is a "horatioalgerism" much like that told by Booker T. Washington in *Up from Slavery*. It is also Albert Murray's story. It is a bildungsroman following the development of a young man who is well aware of America's dark past; so he enters into a heroic and aesthetic confrontation with it. For example, the speaker hears the sawmill whistles calling him and the other members of his community to their menial jobs, but he rejects them and listens instead to the school bell ringing:

> early in the morning
> hear the sawmill whistles blow
> then when the school bells ring
> it's my time to be ready to go

and

> When folks called me schoolboy
> I never would deny my name
> I said you've got to be a schoolboy
> if preparation is your aim. (7–8)

Then, as Murray told me, he refers specifically to Tuskegee in the poem, saying

> early in the morning
> listening to the radio
> first week on the campus
> four chime time years to go. (9)

and then specifically to his wife, Mozelle, another Tuskegee graduate,

> I said what I said
> and her smile said we shall see
> ain't no line of jive gonna ever make a
> fool of me. (11)

Murray has said, "You write about what you know about. Try to get how you really feel about it. If your sensibility is comprehensive enough and your craft is good enough, then what you come out with is probably a representative anecdote. . . . the problem of the artist is to take . . . idiomatic particulars and process them in a way that gives them universal impact" (qtd. in Wood 101–2), and in so doing, fulfill the vernacular imperative. He uses the word "imperative" very much like the word "obligation" because in Cosmos Murray the artist has a social commitment "to human well-being and self-realization" (*Hero* 26). In this regard, Murray's sense of obligation is akin to a spiritual commitment with both existential and religious overtones. As John Callahan puts it, Murray and Ellison were doing "the Lord's work," and for them, "the Lord's work" is to create art that, like the blues, functions as an "existential device or vehicle for coping with the ever-changing fortunes of human existence" (Murray, *From the Briarpatch File* 5).

In *The Blue Devils of Nada,* Murray refers to the pantheon of great American art (into which he inducts the works of Duke Ellington) as a metaphorical temple: "it refers to all of the gods, heroes, outstanding champions and achievers of a particular people or nation" (76) into which artists must earn their way "as gods and heroes have always had to do" (77). Artists fulfill their obligations and earn their way into the pantheon by tapping into human experience and realizing the universal implications of specific situations, knowing and engaging all of the formal artistic traditions through which experience has been stylized into enduring art forms, and devising tactics that extend these traditions by contextualizing them within vernacular communication that encompasses the essential nature of experience. To process the idiomatic particulars of the raw experiences of life into universal statements of relevance and appeal is to accomplish the vernacular imperative as Ellington did in music, Hemingway did in fiction, and as Murray does in poetry.

For Murray, "Ellington's place in music is equivalent to that of Hemingway and Faulkner in literature" because he concerned himself "with the actualities of life in an American landscape" and "was able to process it into such fine art and to such international effect" (*Blue Devils* 79). Hemingway, too, "wrote as accurately as possible about how he really felt about the things he really knew." His heroes are blues heroes, and his conflicts are blues conflicts because like those in blues problems, they "are always based on confrontation and acknowledgment of the fundamental facts of life without illusion, facts that are sometimes as incomprehensibly absurd as they are ugly" (216).

Through the autobiographical horatioalgerism as told by the speaker of "Epic Exists," Murray also includes the ugliness of the fact that life is a "low-down dirty shame," and he presents himself as someone who confronts and slays the dragons, but can never really defeat chaos and entropy; he can only keep the blues at bay by swinging in the blues tradition. Like Hemingway and Ellington, he accomplishes the vernacular imperative both by writing what he knows and by referring to the masters and extending the aesthetic traditions that he inherits. Murray says that "creative effort means entering" a colloquy "with the form" (qtd. in Wood 97). In this sense he resembles the high modernists because he knows, refers to, and responds to the masters of the tradition, but in Murray's case they are the masters of both the literary and the blues tradition.

It is Murray's conflation of the art of both the literary masters and the blues/jazz masters that delights and confounds, resonating logically for the musically oriented at the same time it presents some challenges for his less musically inclined readers. Since there is no one-to-one relationship between music and literature, describing the blues idiom often relies on evoking the principles of continuity and improvisation that are central to its evolution within our vernacular traditions and applying those concepts to the ongoing development of literary art. The vernacular thread that runs from the spirituals to gospel music, from soul music to blues and jazz, resembles the vernacular traditions at work within literary art. As Murray learned from Malraux, "the artist derives not from nature itself but from other artists," and "the sense of life which any given artist expresses always involves an interaction with other works of art" (*Hero* 65).

In Murray's treatment, the blues idiom equals classic literary art because it attracts other artists who continue to develop it beyond itself, just as, for example, *The Odyssey* attracted Joyce, and Dostoyevsky's *Notes from the Underground* attracted Ellison, and the continuity between these works is created as one author expands (or improvises) on the creation of the other. According to Cosmos Murray, vernacularly contextualized continuity and improvisation refer to tradition at the same time they create artistic tradition. As he says in *The Hero and the Blues,*

To refer to the blues idiom is to refer to an established mode, an existing context or frame of reference. But then not only is tradition that which continues; it is also the medium by which and through which continuation occurs. It is . . . precisely that in terms of which the objectives of experimentation are defined, and against which experimental achievements are evaluated. . . . It is for the writer, as for the musician in a jam session, that informal trial and error process by means of which tradition adapts itself to change, or renews itself through change. It is, that is to say, the means by which the true and tested in the traditional regenerates itself in the vernacular. (72)

Cosmos Murray is succinctly aesthetically captured in the blues form of "Epic Exits" largely because the poem is a regeneration of the vernacular into the tradition Murray knows best. As he told Tony Scherman, "We all learn from Mann, Joyce, Hemingway, Eliot and the rest, but I'm also trying to learn to write in terms of the tradition I grew up in, the Negro tradition of blues, stomps, ragtime, jumps and swing. After all, very few writers have done as much with American experience as Jelly Roll Morton, Count Basie and Duke Ellington" (132). His blues jam "Epic Exits" functions successfully as an artistic rendering of stylized experience because he houses his grand scheme within the tradition that both Murray and America grew up with, the blues tradition.

Murray, however, is clear on the point that the blues idiom is not some primitive inheritance he was born with. It is a matter of mastery and stylization:

Though few students of American culture seem aware of it, but as those who are truly interested in promoting "black consciousness" in literature should note, what makes a blues idiom musician is not the ability to express *raw* emotion with primitive directness, as is so often implied, but rather mastery of elements of esthetics peculiar to U.S. Negro music. Blues musicians do not derive directly from the personal, social, and political circumstances of their lives as black people in the United States. They derive most directly from styles of other musicians who play the blues and who were infinitely more interested in evok-

ing or simulating raw emotion than in releasing it—and whose "*primitiveness*"
is to be found not so much in the *directness* of their expression as in their pro-
nounced emphasis on stylization. In art both agony and ecstasy are matters of
stylization. (*Hero* 83)

Ultimately, Albert Murray's best art, rendered in the blues tradition, lays
bare both the agony and ecstasy of his own personal conception of life in all
its striving and chafing against the chaos and entropy of the human condition. He takes seriously the responsibility that comes with mastering form
and demonstrating that, in blues, American artists have rendered the fundamental facts of life that inform all fine art. As he says, "[N]o social or political
responsibility is greater than that which comes with the realization that there
is more earthly chaos and human confusion than there is form and that he
who creates forms and images creates the very basis of human values, defines accurately or not what is good and what is not, and in doing so exercises immeasurable influence on the direction of human aspiration and effort" (*Blue Devils* 220–21).

Nothing is more fundamental to establishing order than one's own conception of life, and Murray's is both sobering and invigorating. Cosmos Murray embraces the agony and the ecstasy, the tragedy and the comedy, and
even melodrama and farce through the blues idiom statement, which accepts
"the fact that whole shebang could come apart at any time—your universe,
everything you know. . . . ultimately it doesn't matter whether you succeed
or fail. You're gonna die" (Murray qtd. in Scherman 133). This is the farce of
life, but it is not evil. "It's as impersonal as nature" (135). If you view the infinite antagonism of entropy and chaos as cooperative, then the struggle of
the human condition becomes opportunity (134). It becomes the quest for
the castle as seen in the great epics of literature. The speaker of "Epic Exits,"
for instance,

> finds no enchanted castles
> there were no magic keys
> nor was there anyplace on this planet
> that was a realm of total ease. (14)

Murray as the autobiographical speaker of the poem calls out the truth as it is. His blues advice has always been: it's not about winning or losing; "it's about how many bars can you swing?" (Murray qtd. in Scherman 136). The speaker of "Epic Exits," learns, too, that

> the world ain't promised me nothing
> it don't owe nobody nothing at all
> makes no difference to the universe whether you walk, swim, fly or crawl. (15)

In Cosmos Murray, one must confront this reality and keep on crawling, or walking, or—if at all possible—swinging with as much poise as one can muster, just as Albert Murray has always done. Whether his artistic achievement fulfills the lofty goals of Cosmos Murray or not will, of course, finally be left to the discretion of the ages. But for those of us who find ourselves in confrontation with the human confusion and chaos of our time, Murray's efforts serve as a heroic example of immeasurable influence on the direction of our aspirations.

5

Albert Murray and Visual Art

PAUL DEVLIN

Paul Devlin: I find it interesting that you and Romie were both pitchers in baseball. Could it have been partially in retrospect because a pitcher is like a ritual dancer?
Albert Murray: Yeah, well, you know, pitchers are interested in line.
—2007 interview

You can't have haute cuisine without folk cuisine and nothing respects folk cuisine more than haute cuisine. You hear what I'm saying?
—Albert Murray, interview with Janis Herbert, 1993

Do you like the Tamayos? That was what she was already saying as I looked around. And when I said, Very much, she said, Well good for you and good for Rufino. The next time I see him I must tell him that I found a bass player in a library looking at two of his pieces while a big Beverly Hills party was going on downstairs.
—Albert Murray, *Seven League Boots*

As you know, I pay just as much attention to painters as I do to writers because, except technically, their problems are the same. They seem to move in the same direction at the same time. (Wallace Stevens to Jose Rodriguez Feo, May 4, 1948).
—Beverly Coyle and Alan Filreis, *Secretaries of the Moon*

Albert Murray has a profound knowledge of and interest in visual art. Unlike writers such as John Updike or John Ashbery, who have impressive side careers as art critics (and artists), Murray is not just a critic and explicator of art (or dabbler in art), but was intimately involved in the production of some of the most important visual statements in American art in the second half of the twentieth century, especially with the great critical and financial successes of his friend and collaborator Romare Bearden.

Any discussion of Albert Murray and visual art must focus on his friendship and collaboration with Bearden. As Henry Louis Gates Jr. wrote in "King of Cats," "[Bearden's] friendship with Murray had to be understood as an artistic alliance. Bearden's mixed-media works could serve as a cultural paradigm for the kind of bricolage and hybridity that Murray favored" (see chapter 2 in this volume). The Murray-Bearden friendship-collaboration-alliance has been the subject of much critical commentary in the voluminous scholarship on Bearden, which has been proliferating now for four decades. Indeed, the vast majority of the work done on the Murray-Bearden collaboration (aside from "King of Cats") has been done in the context of larger projects involving Bearden. This discussion, however, may well be one of the first instances of Bearden being brought into a larger project involving Murray. It is well known and well documented that Murray gave titles to many of Bearden's pieces, ghostwrote technical articles and other pieces for Bearden,[1] wrote catalog essays for Bearden's shows, and at times contributed (or edited) literary text that appeared alongside Bearden's work at exhibitions.[2] Bearden paintings have appeared on at least four of Murray's book covers, and Murray has been a lecturer on Bearden's work at the nation's most prestigious art museums.[3]

This essay will explore Murray in relation to Bearden and present what I hope is an original take on their remarkable relationship. Before heading in that essential and inevitable direction, it will be necessary to take a brief, Bearden-free excursion into the wider world of Albert Murray's engagement with visual art so we can more fully appreciate the extent of it. Ultimately, this may shed light on his literary aesthetics in his fiction and nonfiction.

Albert Murray's relationship with visual art is rich and complicated. A few quick anecdotes might be of interest here. When Murray lived in Paris in 1950, studying at the Sorbonne courtesy of Tuskegee and the GI Bill, he lived in the same building as Henri Matisse.[4] The modernist master lived on the third floor; Murray lived on the eighth. Matisse often worked with his door open, and Murray would see him through the old-fashioned open elevator, sitting in bed cutting up paper dolls or working on the sketches for the stained glass windows of the chapel he designed at Vence, which was under construction from 1948 to 1951. Impressed by the sketches he would see through the door, Murray did what any hip student of art would do: took a trip down to Vence to see Matisse's then uncompleted Notre Dame du Rosaire chapel. Later that summer, Murray was dining in a crowded and undoubtedly chic restaurant when the frail Matisse walked in. Shouting "Maestro! Maestro!" the crowd gave him a standing ovation.[5] This presented Murray with an example of what he considers the context about which he writes: that of the heroic artist, the culture hero, not unlike Bearden or Duke Ellington or Louis Armstrong.

During that spring, summer, and early fall of 1950, Murray moved in a circle that included art patron Peggy Guggenheim's daughter and at times Peggy herself. Murray appreciated collectors like the Guggenheims because they made the greatest works of all the ages available to the American public. Murray voiced his appreciation of the great collectors through his tribute to Isabella Stewart Gardner (the founder of Boston's Gardner Museum) in his 1997 talk/essay "Riffing at Mrs. Jack's Place." One study of Gilded Age art collectors that Murray considers indispensable is *The Proud Possessors* by Aline Saarinen. The proud possessors, who flooded America with Europe's (and the world's) art in the generation or two before Murray was born, made a more complete artistic education not only a possibility but something of a mandate for a student, and later, a writer like Murray.

Murray has been friends with many artists over the years. He conducted long interviews with the painters of the generation before him, such as

Charles Alston and Hale Woodruff.[6] Murray (through Bearden) was also close to younger painters in the Spiral Group (the civil rights–era association of black painters), such as Norman Lewis and Richard Mayhew.[7] In 2002, I accompanied the Murrays to an opening for Mayhew at the ACA Gallery in Chelsea.[8] Professor emeritus at Penn State, Mayhew is a master of abstract landscapes in startling colors. His mastery of color reminded Murray of Titian (1485–1576). That day Mayhew said to Murray, "You are my inspiration," and shortly thereafter sent him a painting.

It is interesting that a painter, Paul Resika, was responsible for Murray's entrance into that most Olympian of cultural organizations, the American Academy of Arts and Letters. Resika was instrumental, along with the biographer and critic R. W. B. Lewis, in nominating Murray for membership.[9] Murray joined in 1997 and became a very active participant in the academy's affairs from 1997 to 2005. Beginning in the 1970s, Murray and Resika (who has certain similarities with Mayhew as a painter) belonged to the same midtown social club. Resika is a big, burly, and down-to-earth guy, a serious jazz listener, and a serious reader. He is kind of a quintessential New York character: *gruff,* with a big white beard, a nice sports jacket, and a no-nonsense demeanor. Murray and Resika became good buddies and frequent lunch companions throughout the 1980s and 1990s. Murray made it a point to try to attend Resika's frequent shows at the Salander O'Reilly Gallery, which was on Seventy-ninth Street, a short walk east of the bank branch Murray preferred to use on Madison Avenue. Resika also attended many of Murray's events, such as his book parties.

I have often thought that Resika's work, with its bright tones and representational (though spare and narrative-resistant) images, reminded me (certainly) of Matisse but also of the poetry of Wallace Stevens. The aesthetic appeal of Resika's work, for Murray, may have been his alignment in a sort of serene, minimalist aesthetic space that includes not only Stevens (whom Murray has read more than he's discussed), but also Bach, Count Basie, Hokusai, Tolstoy, Matisse, and Hemingway—the group that Murray discusses in his essay "Comping for Count Basie." In this piece Murray wrote about the style that all these artists seem to have in common, "the style of old age" (citing Hermann Broch's essay "The Style of the Mythical Age"), in which, among other things, vocabulary loses importance to syntax (*Blue Devils* 43–44). Resika (and Mayhew) clearly fall into Broch's aesthetic category. This is perhaps why Mayhew reminded Murray of Titian. Broch cites Titian as a prime example of this style.

I am aware of two pieces by Resika that Murray owns. The most important is a busy, vibrant charcoal portrait of a trumpet player blowing the blues away titled *Wynton,* which hangs perpendicular to and hugging the large window in Murray's apartment that faces out onto 132nd Street. Directly across the room is a Bearden sketch of Duke Ellington, in which Duke's arm is raised, as if conducting a band. In Murray's arrangement, it is as if Bearden's Duke is conducting Resika's Wynton from across the room. Murray also owns an abstract sketch of himself (yet a very good likeness) by Resika, done on a cocktail napkin at a black-tie dinner.

Murray also dabbled in visual art himself. Not only did he move in a circle of accomplished visual artists, but his friends in other arts were also visual artists. Murray once said, "My three most sophisticated friends were Ellison, Bearden, and Duke" (qtd. in Gelburd 58). Ellison was an accomplished sculptor and semiprofessional photographer. Duke Ellington originally planned to be a painter and to study painting on a scholarship to the Pratt Institute, until he decided to focus on music. (Murray also dabbled in music, playing the bass for a time.)

In addition to some sketching,[10] Murray tried his hand at making sculptures. His sculptures, however, are more like standing collages of metal than traditional sculptures. For a few months in 1961, Major Murray was in charge of an air force scrap depot at Hanscom Air Force Base in Bedford, Massachusetts. He used his time in this position, which must have involved all sorts of supremely mundane matters, to collect bits of scrap metal—screws, fittings, little parts of various kinds—that he pieced together into sculptures of standing figures, using rectangular magnets as torsos. The sculptures he created, some of which were to decorate his New York apartment for the next five decades, are primeval looking, austere, like gods or relics from another epoch, but clearly composed of materials from our century, whose technological innovations Murray never feared or had a problem with. Indeed, Murray in this case was "swinging the machine."[11]

Furthermore, some of his sculptures look not unlike Bearden's famous *Conjur Woman* figures. They were both interested in the "primitive," but more to the point, in *Picasso's* interest in the primitive, and how the modern and primitive intersect in modern art. The word *primitive,* though, holds a positive connotation for Murray (as well as for other students of André Malraux's aesthetics). As Murray told Gail Gelburd, "Primitive art is fine art in that it is the product of the ultimate extension, elaboration, and refinement. Folk art is crude by comparison. Now this jumps forward to the great 'Bearden achievement': his very special awareness of the ritualistic dimension of stylization saved him from genre, from being just provincial" (57).

Murray and Bearden shared an aesthetic sensibility that I will call " down-home pragmatic romanticism." (Note the lowercase *p* and lowercase *r*.) It is what helped their careers take off after they renewed their friendship in New York in 1962 and ultimately may make them difficult for scholars of both literature and art to approach. From one point of view, Murray and Bearden were—like, say, T. S. Eliot and Ezra Pound—"Late Romantic High Modernists" in both their tastes and creations. This aesthetic position has been studied extensively as one that often goes hand in hand with a highly conservative and sometimes fascist political slant (while Bearden and Murray were devotees of American liberalism).[12] Richard Powell ("Changing") has noted that Bearden, for instance, was a fan of the "romantic" (Powell's term) scholar of mythology and religion Mircea Eliade. Mircea Eliade is also a favorite of Murray's. Murray owns quite a few of Eliade's books and thinks very highly of them. Before coming to teach at the University of Chicago, Eliade had, in Romania (like Paul de Man in Belgium), questionable associations with his country's fascist government.

Similarly, but in a nonpolitical sense, Myron Schwartzman (who wrote the first major book on Bearden) has described the strong influence of Nietzsche on Murray, partially through Thomas Mann (and thus on Bearden). Nietzsche's problems, of course, are well known. In 1981, Murray recruited his longtime friend Joseph Campbell, the prolific scholar of mythology (who often cites the work of Eliade), to appear in a documentary, *Bearden Plays Bearden,* to comment on the mythological implications in his work. After Campbell's 1987 death, he was dealt many charges of anti-Semitism by the writer Brendan Gill and others (though these charges are disputed by at least one of Campbell's Jewish friends).

Murray and Bearden, through other sets of influences, were able to side-step the pitfalls that may have arisen from absorbing these potentially dangerous influences. In the 1930s, young Murray and Bearden were both shaped by several figures who fled from Nazi persecution. At Tuskegee in the 1930s, Murray was heavily influenced by the work of Nobel Laureate Sigrid Undset. At the same time, Bearden studied under George Grosz at the Art Students League. Murray and Bearden were influenced by the refugee scholar of Indian religions Heinrich Zimmer.[13]

What redeemed Murray and Bearden, who held Romantic beliefs in Genius and Spirit (as well as modernist fascination with ritual), from the more negative conclusions of such an ideological bent (that is, fetishizing the folk and their "spirit," which helped create the Third Reich in Germany; the fetishism of the solitary genius cum Nietzschean superman) was their pragmatism, born of the pragmatic strain of the African American experience and cultural memory. Neither artist fell into the Romantic trap (and later mark of worldwide fascism) of believing in a "golden age." Murray demolishes any space for discussing an American golden age in his essay "Situation Normal: All Fouled Up" at the end of *The Omni-Americans.* And both knew that white anthropologists were a little square. Since both came from "the folk," they would not romanticize them into a "volk," a people more pure and noble than the people next door. They also knew, along with Constance Rourke, that America's "folk" (actually all Americans) were culturally "part Negro, part Indian, part backwoodsman, part Yankee." Murray encapsulated his thoughts on racial or ethnic or cultural purity in comments he made at Harvard's 1973 Alain Locke Symposium: "I, for one, am always running in the opposite direction of anything that looks like it's about to be pure—or has any presumptions of purity. I just don't think human life can be that way" (qtd. in Cruse 16).

Bearden, for his part, spent three decades as a special, part-time New York City social worker assigned to the city's gypsy population. Murray and Bearden were both informed by certain authors and ideas that had questionable associations, but neither was tripped up by them, which is perhaps one of the reasons both men clicked so nicely. It is by no means a given that resistance to "purity" springs from African American experience. As Mark Christian Thompson shows in his recent study *Black Fascisms,* the twentieth century saw many black fascist movements that could have seduced a less hip Bearden or Murray.

Thus, Murray's and Bearden's appropriation of European modernist attitudes and styles (which more often than not grew out of or were extensions of Romanticism) did not end with any kind of rote imitation of European modes (such as the work of African American painters traveling through France in the 1920s, for example, the early work of Hale Woodruff) or with the simple depiction of black life in America through a European-derived form (such as the naturalism of Richard Wright). Instead there was a pragmatic appropriation by both men of what they found useful in a European tradition, which they respected and admired, but never fetishized or idealized to the exclusion of their own experience. In terms of structural and formalistic devices, both learned a great deal from Europe.

But in their finished products, *jazz* plays a central role in terms of both subject matter and formalistic creative processes. Murray, for instance, credits Thomas Mann with giving him the idea that a novel could be structured like a piece of music. But where Mann had Wagner or Beethoven in mind, Murray's novels are structured like Duke Ellington compositions (Edwards 87). In his catalog introduction to Bearden's "Of the Blues" exhibition, Murray notes that Bearden follows a similarly jazzy procedure. Furthermore, in *The Omni-Americans,* Murray uses Mann's ideas about time in the prologue to *Joseph and His Brothers* in order to sidestep discussion of African cultural patrimony over African American culture (13–14). Bearden learned much from, say, the collages of Juan Gris and George Braque, yet in many of Bearden's collages, there is a much different spatial relationship, an out-of-proportionness not found in Gris or Braque. Murray sees this as "analogous to the leap-frog sequences in jazz" (qtd. in Patton 8).

The ultimate European modernist common denominator between Bearden and Murray is André Malraux, most specifically, his landmark revisionist history of art, *The Voices of Silence,* which greatly influenced them. *The Voices of*

Silence is discussed at length by Murray in his study of fiction, *The Hero and the Blues*. What Murray took most from Malraux is his theory of stylization—that all art is human experience "stylized" (65). Murray also completely appropriated Malraux's "Museum without Walls": "Now," says Murray, "we live in terms of *all* art" (*From the Briarpatch File* 158).

This is also precisely what Bearden took from Malraux. It's as if they saw Malraux's multiculturalism (something truly new at the time) as an antidote to rigid and unacceptable attitudes about race in America. Sarah Kennel, in her essay on Bearden's dialogue with European art, writes, "[F]or Malraux, the photographic reproduction functions as a democratizing and universalizing force" (141). This "universalizing force" must have seemed like a magic potion to two men who were surrounded, on the one hand, by racist white people and, on the other, by patronizing white people. Kennel goes on to write, "While Malraux's book contributed to Bearden's understanding of the history of art as a repository of forms and objects available to and awaiting transformation by the modern viewer/artist, Bearden's grasp of both the pedagogical and democratizing possibilities of a photographic history of art preceded the publication of *The Voices of Silence*" (142). It may have, but the fact remains that not long after the American publication of *The Voices of Silence* (1960), Bearden began seriously to work with photographs—a process that showed its first fruits during his tremendously successful 1964 photomontage show. It also must be kept in mind that much of *The Voices of Silence* was published in periodicals, such as the *Hudson Review,* before it came out as a book. Murray owns many of these original articles. I believe *The Voices of Silence* is one of the factors responsible for Bearden's rejection of oil paints and abstract expressionism (which he practiced throughout the 1950s). The point to take note of for our purposes is that this may have been the result of his having read Malraux—through Murray. Indeed, Gail Gelburd has hypothesized that Malraux is responsible for making Murray *and* Bearden see that their southern, black experience had universal character (53).

In his photomontage, Bearden uses what he learned from abstraction and gives it what I'm calling a "mimetic nod"—a "headfake" at representation. This enabled him not only to address the civil rights movement from a stance still abstract enough to satisfy his own aesthetic requirements (which social realism did not) but also brought him into what Murray calls "the ritual dimension [that] takes [Bearden] beyond his province" (qtd. in Gelburd 57).

Moreover, Murray and Bearden also took from Malraux the idea of "art *through* art"; however, they did not rigidly adhere to the idea. There seems to be an uneasy coexistence in Bearden and Murray of art both as a closed, self-referential system and as one permeated by experience. Of course, in real life, as most people would agree, art is a little bit of both. Experience, the black experience in particular, was not something they were willing to dismiss in the mysteries of the creative process. While close to their own idiom, its depiction is reflected through a larger lens, that of the world's art. As Murray puts it: "Not that Bearden's work is ever idiomatic in any ethnic, folk, or provincial sense. Being a visual artist, his definitive influences . . . have always been other visual artists, not musicians. Thus his fundamental objectives and procedures are best understood in the context of his apprenticeship to the works of George Grosz, Peter de Hooch, Vermeer, classical Chinese and Japanese flat painting, the Byzantine designers, African sculptors, such pre-Renaissance Siennese as Duccio and Lorenzetti, plus the Cubism of Picasso, Braque, and Leger, and Mondrian (whom Bearden sees as a direct extension of de Hooch and Vermeer)" ("Of the Blues" 2). This is pure Malraux. Yet at the same time, in terms of Bearden's subject matter, there is strong experiential, idiomatic content.

Addressing the ubiquitous presence of jazz (blues) musicians in Bearden's work, Murray writes: "Blues musicians, it so happens, were not only far more prevalent in the Harlem of his formative years than were, say, ballet dancers in the Paris of Edgar Degas, but the music itself, perhaps because its typical use was as an element of mere entertainment, was infinitely more obvious in comprehensive reflection of the actual textures of every day life in America than classical ballet has ever been of life in Europe" ("Of the Blues" 2).

Thus, their allegiances to modernism and to the traditions of Europe in general were always pragmatic, never dogmatic. Put less diplomatically, their procedures (Bearden's specifically) consisted of an "aesthetic ransacking of high art and culture" (Patton 14). But, in cases where Bearden's own idiom offered what another culture's offered, he chose his own culture's model: "I listened for hours to the recordings of Earl Hines at the piano. Finally, I was able to block out the melody and concentrate on the silences between the notes. I found that this was very helpful to me . . . in my placement of objects in my paintings and collages. I could have studied this integration and spacing in Greek vase painting, among many examples, but with Hines I ingested it within my own background" (qtd. in Patton 10). Hines, the jazz pianist and bandleader, was first, before influencing Bearden, perhaps the primary non-painterly influence on the (white) American painter Stuart Davis (1892–1964), a friend of and influence upon Bearden. Davis himself was overwhelmingly influenced by the "numerical precisions of the Negro piano players" (Kelder 2). Above all "Negro piano players," Davis was influenced by Hines. As Murray put it, "Davis was forever regaling [Bearden] about Earl Hines, whose fantastic sense of interval Davis claimed had been of crucial significance to his own development" ("Of the Blues" 2).

This poses a dilemma. Although Davis genuinely adored Earl Hines, even naming his own son Earl, was he guilty, or at least a bit unethical, in his own "aesthetic ransacking" of jazz? Bearden clearly did not think so; he was "deeply moved" by Davis's study of jazz (Patton 12). However, when one does not show due respect to a work from a culture that is not one's own, or if the work is condescended to by a member of an oppressor's culture, it can become sad and awkward, leading to outrage and disgust. W. H. Auden's travesties of blues lyrics, while well meant, are an example of the sad and awkward. At the same time, this did not prevent Murray from saying "[Auden] couldn't write the blues but he could write everything else" (*From the Briarpatch File* 153).

In the foreword to *Mitchell and Ruff: An American Profile in Jazz,* a book in which William Zinsser, the white journalist, tells the story of two black jazz musicians, Murray writes, "[O]rdinarily when people enter an unfamiliar situation there are two common reactions. One is insecurity, which results in xenophobia: fear, hostility, or condescension. The other is to see the situation as exotic, or weird, or dangerous and to find it fascinating—as all those people did who used to go slumming in Harlem" (x–xi). What Murray and Bearden strove for, and I believe achieved, for their part, was this same fine line between xenophobia and exoticism. It is this line that is still so much of a problem today in academia and elsewhere. It seems to me that Auden was "slumming" in the blues, whereas Theodor Adorno, for instance, approached jazz by way of the xenophobic rant. Beyond the two "common reactions" that Murray defines, Zinsser navigates a third course, a realm of true, honest identification. Here is the conundrum as Bearden similarly saw it: "In the twenties, Benny Goodman used to come up to Harlem a lot. He was teaching himself about jazz the only way he could, and he had to become a little black to learn it. By the same token, when I started copying and learning from those pictures by Vermeer and Delacroix and the rest, in a sense I was joining the white world. It's all a little more complicated than some people try to make out" (qtd. in Tompkins 237).

In the 1968 essay "Rectangular Structure in My Montage Painting," ostensibly by Bearden, but acknowledged by Bearden scholars to have been ghostwritten by Murray, Murray-and-Bearden wrote, "The drawings of Grosz on the theme of the human situation in post World War I Germany made me realize the artistic possibilities of American Negro subject matter" (11). If Bearden's teacher and mentor, Grosz, could make him see certain possibilities in his own experience, it stands to reason that a Bearden painting could make a young German (or anyone) see new possibilities in his or her own experience. As Mikhail Bakhtin once said, "In the realm of culture, outsideness is a most powerful factor in understanding. It is only in the eyes of another culture that foreign culture reveals itself fully and profoundly (but not maximally fully, because there will be cultures that see and understand even more)" (7).

This "outsideness" may be a key to understanding why Bearden and Murray saw so much in European modernism, and perhaps they arrived at a conclusion similar to Bakhtin's and hoped that they could make white people see hitherto unseen things in black culture. As Murray once said (in response to being asked what distinguished his work from Ralph Ellison's), "[In Ellison there is] a certain amount of explanation of black folks stuff for white folks, which I refuse to do. He would say certain things which I wouldn't say" (Edwards 85).

There is an analogy in this regard between Murray and Ellison and Bearden and the painter Jacob Lawrence. In addressing the differences between the two painters, Murray said, "Do you know what I mean by [genre painting]? If you look at a painter like Jacob Lawrence, his painting is genre—what Negroes look like, how they live, the way their neighborhood looks. These are the peasants represented as art, like the wonderful peasant life of France" (qtd. in Edwards 92).

Murray's off-the-cuff comparison of himself and Bearden to Ellison and Lawrence is a critique of what anthropologists would call "the informant"— the cultural explainer to the outsider. Murray is enforcing obscurity for the outsider, and assuming that the thoughtful insider will "get it." Taken in its full complexity and expressed through the most sophisticated formalistic techniques as they saw them, African American culture would be seen on its own terms.

Richard Powell suggests that Bearden's use of jazz overwhelmed his modern European influences, such as Picasso and Mondrian. Powell writes, "One finds especially in Albert Murray's essay ["The Visual Equivalent of the Blues"] a plausible and pliant equation in his discussion of Bearden's style and the aesthetic pull of black music" ("Art History" 184). Powell sees this, paradoxically, as a reason why Bearden is sometimes ignored by the art-critical establishment and precisely why he should not be (183).[14] There is a parallel here with the case of Murray. Who has been better reviewed in more high-end publications than Murray? Yet he still seems unable to get traction among critics. Bearden is so conversant with modernism and Western tradition generally and equally conversant with jazz that perhaps no, or very few, critics are equally conversant and thus willing to try to figure out what is going on. Murray claims that "[Bearden's] blues idiom orientation to vamping and riffing and otherwise improvising . . . leads him to dominate his subject matter . . . as the jazz musician does" (*Blue Devils* 139).

It is in this real engagement with jazz and blues rhythms and creative procedure that Bearden reinvents collage; he approaches it with no plan. One piece of paper is put down in response to another piece, in much the same way that a jazz jam session operates. Yet his engagement with jazz and his own African American heritage of improvisation is not meant to esotericize the noninitiated out of critical discourse with his paintings. When asked by

Callaloo editor Charles Rowell what exactly Bearden meant by improvisation in regards to painting, Bearden turns around and explains what he means not in terms of Duke Ellington, which he surely could do, but in terms of von Clausewitz, of all people. Bearden replied to Rowell's question of what is improvisation by saying, "There is a very well known book titled *Vom Kriege*. The author, Karl von Clausewitz, says that the solution to a battle is very simple. The difficulty, he said, is that you have so many choices as to which one to pick as the right one. The answer to your question is the same" (qtd. in Rowell, "Inscription" 435).

Pick and choose, old pardners, choice of tools, weapons, ancestors, to paraphrase Murray. At any rate, Bearden and Murray are inextricably intertwined, and it is ultimately, though not entirely, through Bearden that Murray will have forever left his complex mark on the visual art of the United States and the world. Few writers who know so much about visual art can say the same. Murray was lucky to have had such a friend, and so was Bearden.[15]

Notes

1. Gates writes in "King of Cats," "When, in 1978, I asked Bearden if he would conduct a seminar on Afro-American art at Yale, where I was teaching, his immediate response was, 'Why don't you ask Al?' . . . Bearden, taking matters into his own hands, had found a way to bring Murray along to New Haven; the critic had ghostwritten Professor Bearden's erudite lectures" (see chapter 2 in this volume). Although this has been disputed by the art dealer June Kelly (see Price and Price), who said she saw drafts in Bearden's handwriting, I would suggest that Bearden may have rewritten the lectures in his own hand, perhaps for purposes of legibility, as most people find it easier to read their own handwriting than someone else's. Murray is also thought to have ghostwritten Bearden's Carnegie-Mellon commencement address, which appeared in the *New York Times* under the title "Humility" on June 21, 1975.

2. See, for instance, the catalog to Bearden's *Collages,* May 6–June 6, 1981, Cordier and Eckstrom, "Profiles/Part II: The Thirties." The title page says, "Picture titles and text reviewed and edited by Albert Murray."

3. Bearden's work has appeared on the cover of Murray's *Train Whistle Guitar* (first edition), *Stomping the Blues* (Vintage paperback edition, 1982), and on the first editions of *The Blue Devils of Nada* and *The Magic Keys.* Murray has lectured on Bearden

at the Mint Museum (1980), the Brooklyn Museum of Art (1981), the Whitney Museum of American Art (2004), and the Metropolitan Museum of Art (2005), among other places.

4. The summer of 1950 in Paris is also when and where he met and became friends with Bearden.

5. Murray has recounted this story about Matisse many times over the years, including on a panel at the Whitney Museum in 2004. The section about the visit to Matisse's chapel was recounted to me in a taped interview in November 2007.

6. Murray interviewed Alston (1907–77) and Woodruff (1900–1980) in the late 1960s. His interview with Alston (who was Bearden's cousin) was done for the Smithsonian. His fascinating interview with Woodruff was published in the catalog to the 1979 exhibit *Hale Woodruff: Fifty Years of His Art,* at the Studio Museum in Harlem.

7. Murray owns a large, colorful abstract painting by Norman Lewis, which hung for many years above his CD collection, overlooking the Murrays' dinner table. Murray often said, mysteriously, that the painting "makes me think of Mongolia." Perhaps this is why he has always kept the novels of Frederick Prokosch below the painting, instead of on a bookshelf.

8. ACA also has a long affiliation with Bearden and published a book on him in 1989. I documented Mayhew's quote in an e-mail to Philip Clark on May 21, 2002. A little more than a year later, a picture of Murray and Mayhew together at the National Gallery's opening gala for the Bearden exhibit appeared on the cover of the *Washington Post*'s style section.

9. Albert Murray told me on several occasions that Resika had proposed him for the American Academy of Arts and Letters. Resika confirmed this in February 2009, adding only that after having the idea, he "brought it up with one of Al's writer-friends," who must have been R. W. B. Lewis. The academy had confirmed Resika's involvement for me, but not the depth of it, by phone. R. W. B. Lewis wrote Murray's citation (essentially the list of reasons why he believed Murray belonged) upon his entry into the academy (letter from Virginia Dajani to Paul Devlin, November 20, 2007).

10. Murray was included, along with about a hundred other prominent writers (and a few other cultural figures, including Bearden) in the 1976 book *Self-Portrait: Book People Picture Themselves,* which was put together by Strand Bookstore clerk Burt Britton with the encouragement of Murray's friend the writer Anaïs Nin. Some of the authors take their sketch-assignment more seriously than others, and Murray is among the most serious, producing a fine likeness, one that I imagine could not be created by someone who did not practice.

11. To borrow the title of Joel Dinerstein's admirable book.

12. Until he turned to Dada-inspired collage in the 1960s (right around the time he rekindled his acquaintance with Murray, which began in 1950), Bearden was an outstanding abstract expressionist, working in a tradition that was associated with Jungian psychology and not exactly associated with progressive politics.

13. To further complicate matters, Murray was introduced to Zimmer's work (*The King and the Corpse,* in particular) by Campbell, who was Zimmer's literary executor.

14. For a more in-depth discussion of this phenomenon, namely, the one that leaves Bearden out of so many anthologies, see the discussion by Richard and Sally Price in *Romare Bearden: The Caribbean Dimension.*

15. I strongly believe that they were essential to each other's careers. Their careers took off when they renewed their friendship in New York in 1962.

6

Murray and Mann

Variations on a Theme

Lauren Walsh

> Nor is there any such thing in literature as a simple story about one individual in one time, place and circumstance. All stories are examples of some essential aspect of human experience in general, and each is recounted precisely because what it implies has general implications.
> —Murray, *The Hero and the Blues*

As you enter Albert Murray's Harlem apartment, you find yourself facing, at the far end of the room, a wall of windows that blaze with a dazzling white light on a sunny springtime afternoon. And as you involuntarily shift your glance away from the flood of sunlight that is too bright until your eyes have had a chance to adjust, you take in the immense bookshelves that line the left wall of the room. The bookshelves, in fact, snake throughout Murray's apartment, and he knows every book on those shelves, not only where each individual title finds its home, but particular literary passages from them as well; that is, he can, very likely, quote you lines from most of those books—and there are hundreds of them.

In one particularly vast section of the shelves that is devoted to American and European modernism, you find a number of authors that Murray has cited as his personal literary influences: Faulkner, Malraux, Eliot, and, of course, Hemingway, of whom he has said, "[H]e was the master of epoch-making style" (Seymour 54). But it is Thomas Mann, whom Murray has repeatedly referenced, if not always elaborated on, who holds a special role in the development of this singular American writer. Indeed, says Murray, Mann "is my number one 20th century" author (qtd. in Lamb). Mann is also the writer who taught Murray that the various disciplines he had studied at Tuskegee Institute (Tuskegee University since 1985)—all the seemingly disparate knowledge he had gained—in fact could be synthesized into an understanding of human motivation and activity. In other words, Albert Murray recognized in Mann's literature a nascent philosophy that Murray himself was to bring to the fore in his own essays and fiction, giving that philosophy new depth and meaning pertinent to American letters, the era of blues and jazz, and the politics of the twentieth-century United States. Murray's writings, from *The Omni-Americans* to *The Hero and the Blues* to *Train Whistle Guitar* and beyond, work together as variations on specific themes: the concept of a universal aesthetic statement and the function of myth in the portrayal of human endeavor, both of which tie to the third theme, the depiction and purpose of an epic hero. Thomas Mann's multivolume *Joseph and His Brothers* was integral to the development, elaboration, and refinement of these themes.

It was not until 1939, in the week after he graduated from Tuskegee, that an acquaintance told Murray about Thomas Mann: "If you like Hemingway and Faulkner then you have to read Mann. He is the greatest living author" (Murray qtd. in Walsh). Murray recounted that this otherwise ordinary conversation was, in fact, to become a turning point in his development as an artist. The two men made a trade that day. Murray, at this point, does not even recall what book he gave away in the trade, but only that he got the better end of the deal. He received Mann's *Joseph in Egypt*. As the story goes, he sat down on a stoop, began reading immediately, and within a few pages knew that this writing held great resonance for him. But then he stopped reading.

Joseph in Egypt is not first in the *Joseph* novel series, and Murray had to read this author right. He went to a local bookstore where he purchased *Joseph and His Brothers,* the first volume of the series.[1] The *Joseph* texts, and especially the character of Joseph himself, were to have a great impact on Murray's subsequent thinking and writing.

Thomas Mann's *Joseph and His Brothers* is a novel that took sixteen years to write. Published over four volumes, the novel was not only periodically put on hold while Mann worked on other publications, but was composed at a time of great historical adversity. While Mann was writing, the Weimar Republic crumbled, National Socialism took hold, and ultimately World War II devastated the European continent. All the while, Mann continued his project, which is a political and social commentary of his times set in the framework of a biblical narrative: the Old Testament stories of Jacob and Esau, and Jacob's son Joseph, who was sold into slavery by his jealous brothers, but who prevailed and eventually became a beneficent and socially proactive Egyptian leader. In response to the troubling state of contemporaneous affairs and of his protracted work on *Joseph,* Mann wrote that the novel was "my staff and my stay on a path that often led through dark valleys. It was my refuge, my comfort, my home, my symbol of steadfastness, the guarantee in the tempestuous change of things" ("Foreword" v). In effect, the writing of this novel was a way of navigating desperate times. In this, Murray sees in his literary forebear a relation to the blues.

Murray has written time and again on the role of the blues as an aesthetic statement that conditions us to a realistic recognition of the sufferings in life and to productive resilience in the face of privation. What he finds in Mann is a perspective that is quite similar, although Mann, in 1930s Germany, responds to the hardships of a time and place Murray did not know personally. And yet Murray, through the lens of Mann, takes up an idea of the universal human condition, the common experiences of human endeavor that transcend specific locales. The blues hero, Murray has noted, doesn't deny the limitations of his setting, but acknowledges them in order to rise above them. And where Mann embodied elements of this, his protagonist Joseph, as we shall see, was even more of a true blues hero, a riff-style improviser and literary antecedent to Murray's celebrated character, Scooter. In essence, in seeing a connection to the blues in Joseph, Murray makes a profound literary realization that informs his future writing: he grasps from Mann's biblical retelling and simultaneous critique of 1930s Germany that enduring notions of adversity and resilience—universal attributes of human existence—are powerfully communicated through the blues persona. Joseph inspires the creation of a variant on that persona: Murray's epic blues hero. But to see how this plays out in his protagonist Scooter, we first need to understand Mann's influence on the role of universality and the place of the mythic in Murray's nonfiction writings and his general philosophy of storytelling.

In order to be an effective storyteller, Murray explains, the writer must invoke the universal through the language of the local. In other words, he must speak in the vernacular of his characters' setting, but the implications should be broad enough to reach and hold meaning to a far more universal readership. Murray says, "That's the only objective for an ambitious writer: to take those idiomatic particulars and make something universal out of it that is true for mankind at large" (qtd. in Lamb). To this end, Murray invokes what I think of as the "once upon a time" test, which appears in *The Hero and the Blues* and elsewhere. He offers the brilliant insight that contrary to one's initial assumption, the "once upon a time" trope doesn't at all refer to one place or one time. Rather, it gestures toward the idea that "'time after time in place after place such and such came to pass.' . . . Human existence, [the storyteller] postulates, is thus and so." Furthermore, in providing a general yet fundamental essence of human existence, the storyteller also offers us a view toward the ethically or morally "tried and true." Such stories present lessons: "This is good. That is bad. Do this. Avoid that" (*Hero* 93). The "once upon a time" tale presents a framework for seeing, evaluating, and learning from and about the human condition.

And sure enough, one locates this idea of the "once upon a time" in Mann's own *Joseph and His Brothers*. "What concerns us here is not calculable time," Mann writes in the "Prelude," which is to say that his focus is not on any one specific historical moment but on the universals that carry throughout time. "The phrase 'once upon a time,'" he continues, embodies a "double sense of past and future and therewith its burden of potential present" (29–30). Mann, we can see, is playing with ideas that Murray will, half a generation later, develop into a full aesthetic philosophy on the role of universality, and hence, the "once upon a time" idiom is a signifier of that universality.[2]

Moreover, the universal—for both Mann and Murray—is inextricably linked to the narrative function of mythologies, broadly interpreted. In fact, Murray addresses this very connection in *The Omni-Americans,* where he privileges Mann's influence on his thinking, opening that text with a discussion of none other than *Joseph and His Brothers.* Murray describes a Mannian depiction of "the essential nature of the space-time continuum of human experience" (in other words, the "once upon a time") and goes on to explore Mann's idea that "the whole of history itself is largely mythological" (13). Legends, myths, folktales, and, in Mann's case, the stories of religion are narratives to teach us about ourselves—that is, about human nature. The mythologies are the framing devices for imparting an essential knowledge about who we are. "Mann uses scripture, 'the wisdom of the ages,' to get at truths, at contemporary wisdom of humanity," Murray told me during one of our conversations. Mann isn't so much working through the biblical story on any religious level, but working out what it shows us about people and how they respond to their conditions; be it ancient Egypt or 1930s Germany, underlying truths exist for any time and place. And as Murray recognized, the lessons of Mann are transportable to American history too. "Mann can sneak contemporary knowledge into any setting!" Murray enthused admiringly. "He goes back to a fable, to religion, to find the meaning in the contemporary, to investigate the complexity of human behavior" (Walsh).

Indeed, critical discussions of Thomas Mann's *Joseph* novel frequently invoke the concepts of the mythic and the universal. Hannelore Mundt, for example, has written, "The narrator, who exists in a specific yet unidentified time and place, invites his readers to travel back with him in time, into the 'well of the past' [Mann, *Joseph and His Brothers* 3] to explore the universal nature of man in the realm of myths and legends that provide insights into archetypal human nature" (138). This is precisely the idea that Murray will put into play in an American setting in his own novels. And while Mann's fiction uses the frame tales of Jacob and Joseph, what it teaches ultimately are fundamentals of human activity through assessments of interpersonal relations and power dynamics of sociopolitical structures and of personal attributes, both the flawed and the estimable, such as narcissism and integrity. More-over, Mann examines creativity and the role of the artist as well as issues of passivity versus assertiveness in terms of a greater social good.

Such things are, in Murray's words, "the complexities," "the raw material," of life. He is referring, in other words, to the fundamental "common ground" experiences, anxieties, and attributes shared by all humanity. It is the task of the artist to stylize those complexities, those source materials, into a univer-sal aesthetic statement. And where does one first find that idea of "raw mate-rial?" We need look no further than the translation of *Joseph and His Brothers* that Murray read as a recent college graduate, where the terms "raw mate-rial" and "chaos"—now signature Albert Murray terms—appear together on a page that makes plain Mann's notion of a timeless universal.[3] Indeed, Mann's narrator traces the idea of universality throughout time immemorial, that is, back to the beginnings of Time; he refers to the creation of "the earthly uni-verse out of confusion and chaos" and describes how this story of origin (an-other mythic tale) provides "raw material" for understanding life. Discussing Joseph, the novel's hero, the narrator continues, "He was a human being *like ourselves,* thus he must appear to us, and despite his earliness in time just as remote as we, mathematically speaking, from the beginnings of humanity" (*Joseph and His Brothers* 14; emphasis added). In employing the first person plural, which invokes the reader's personal identification with this premodern protagonist and does so with the sense of a collective appreciation, Mann puts forth an idea that Murray will expand: it is the recognition of a com-mon human condition, of shared experiences, and it should cast our minds to Murray's words on time after time and place after place.

Beyond the ideas about universality and mythic frameworks, Mann's ability to integrate information—historical, religious, mathematical, or political—also hugely impressed a young Albert Murray. Mann synthesized knowledge in a way that made it wisdom, and that was eye opening to Murray. He told me once that everything he'd learned in school—"the science, the psy-chology, Freud, relativity, everything"—all made sense after Mann. They aren't just pieces of knowledge; they tie together and the implications matter. It's all necessary, Murray asserted, in order to try to understand the complexity of human endeavor. This, he said with grave appreciation, is the scope that literature can have (Walsh). And then he told me to go to the tremendous bookshelves and pull down his copy of Mann's *The Magic Mountain.* In fact, he owns two copies, one much older than the other, and he asked for the older version—the one he had read as a young man. As I lifted the novel from its place on the shelf, Murray began quoting to me, from memory, a line that I found on the back of the book jacket: "The first great novel toward the making of which have gone the full intellectual resources of the twentieth century."[4] It is quite an impressive claim. One might even say grandiose, and yet Murray would counter any arguments that this accolade oversteps actuality. For Murray, Mann is not just a writer but also a thinker and philosopher, one who combines literary genius with historical, political, and scientific intellect. And while Mann may exhibit the epitome of this kind of cognizant writing, Murray expects similar from any serious writer.

Murray recognized and valued that Mann's exploration of universality and human endeavor elevated his writing from entertainment to socially and politically engaged fiction. After reading Mann, he asked: What does it mean to have access to vast historical, scientific, social, and anthropological understanding, and how should the informed and concerned artist use that knowledge toward greater ends? In answer he says that first, writers must be knowledgeable in contemporary developments and debates and, by extension, passionately interested in those disciplines of innovation; and second, they must synthesize that knowledge and present it eloquently to their readers. The ramifications, Murray tells us in *The Omni-Americans,* are immense: "Perhaps every serious writer proceeds on the assumption that a sufficiently vernacular and revolutionary image can be created to initiate a millennium during his generation" (226).

These ideas are echoed in Murray's *Train Whistle Guitar,* when the mentor figure, Luzana Cholly, tells the young protagonist and his friend that "the young generation was supposed to take what they were already born with and learn how to put it with everything the civil engineers and inventors and doctors and lawyers and bookkeepers had found out about the world and be the one to bring about the day the old folks had always been prophesying and praying for" (30). Here, Murray seems to shift the burden away from the artist onto a child protagonist, and yet that character is, in fact, semiautobiographical. In giving advice to the young character, Cholly dramatizes Murray's own values and instills them in Murray's alter ego. He is told how to be a serious thinker—one who, in the tradition of Mann, makes use of contemporary knowledge and also recognizes the principles of "once upon a time." *Train Whistle Guitar* attempts both to capture a time and place and also to speak more broadly to a universal readership through and about the complexities of modern life.

Murray's first novel, which serves as my model for exploration of the universal, the mythic, and the epic hero within his fiction, has been hailed as "perhaps the most phenomenal African American Bildungsroman written to date" (Carson 291). It charts the growth of Scooter, a young African American boy in a small southern town in the 1920s. *Train Whistle Guitar* brings its readers into that time and place, introducing us to the people Scooter knows, and the social, political, and racial experiences that he and those around him live. At the same time, it brings us out of that time and place because the lessons that Scooter learns, we realize upon reflection, are lessons that apply broadly: the function of history; the value of family; principles such as conviction, determination, and respect. "Superbly evocative and a poetic epic, the novel shows its hero discovering through the story of his forebears that he is obligated to make the high end of its aspirations come true through his own accomplishments," writes Stanley Crouch. He continues: "In ways that bring together the archetype and the plausible character, Murray invents figures who represent certain backgrounds and are composites of Negro American history in the flesh—ex-slaves, folk blues players and sophisticated jazzmen, World War I veterans, schoolteachers, and so on. This allows the boy to look history in the face and listen to what it has to say through the people who know what they know" (168–69). The lesson is that there is a timelessness to life's experiences; history functions as a mirror onto the present (as Mann put it, the past carries "a presentness"). Early on in the novel, Scooter alludes to a basic, if not yet fleshed-out, understanding of this: "Because I knew even while [something] was happening that it wasn't just happening then. I didn't know very much about historical cause and effect then, but I knew enough to realize that when something happened it was a part of something that had been going on before" (66). There we have one half of the "once upon a time" that Murray picks up from Mann. Scooter, though unaware of just how significant his statement is, implies that history looks more like "time after time" than an isolated moment in time.

And what of the "place after place" that Murray explains as the other half of the meaning behind "once upon a time"? *Train Whistle Guitar* tells the careful reader that although the story's setting is textually Gasoline Point, Alabama, it is metaphorically Anyplace, USA. In *From the Briarpatch File*, Murray writes, "All of my books are about the basis and possibilities of heroic action that are endemic to life in the United States in our time" (10), and in an interview with Brian Lamb, he explains that he strives "to deal with experience that is idiomatically American, but deal with it with a technique that would give it universal appeal and affect." Thus, Murray revises the idea of rootedness in his efforts to create "representative anecdotes, definitive episodes," that add up to a "comprehensive and universally appealing American epic" (*Trading Twelves* xxiii).

Gasoline Point implies a place of origin from which one metaphorically fills up the gas tank and then has the capacity to go anywhere. Such is the significance of passages like this one: "You couldn't see the L & N Bridge from the skiff boat landing where we were standing then, but we knew where it was because it was also the gateway through which the Chickasabogue, which was really a tributary, flowed out into the Mobile River which led down into Mobile Bay which spread out into the Gulf of Mexico which was part of the old Spanish Main which was the beginning of the Seven Seas" (40). The local, we are shown explicitly, connects outward to the universal. While there is a stress on one's point of origin, there is as much an emphasis on outward extension and encompassing experience. The twofold pronunciation of the word *mobile* (mo-beel as the city; mo-bil as the adjective) only fuels this sense of expansion; the Mobile River and Bay may be fixed points on a map, but ironically their very place-names convey an embodied *mobility*. Indeed, Scooter experiences a perceived mobility precisely in response to "seeing places on a map": "I had just shut my eyes and opened them and found myself in another place on another day" (41).[5] If the first passage illustrates a universality attained through plotted terrain, the second demonstrates that a global per-spective can occur on the imaginative level as well.

And lest we miss those references to "time after time in place after place," the phrase "once upon a time" itself makes a few appearances in the novel, most significantly in the very beginning, when Murray ties it into one of the mythic narratives that he employs in this novel.[6] Where Mann used religious account as the mythic framework for *his* text, Murray gives us the American folktale of Brer Rabbit—one of the narrative tools that underscores the role of the universal throughout *Train Whistle Guitar*. And while Brer Rabbit speaks to an "insider" status—stories of subversion from the inside out—Murray will show us that through an internal or vernacular language one can neverthe-less get at the universal. Indeed, in a letter to Murray, Ralph Ellison describes how Murray's fictional character "turns himself inside out—and we see the whirling world that made him" (*Trading Twelves* 28). The individual's experi-ence comprises a "world" of collective social and historical factors, and in this case, those conditions are depicted through the lens of a folktale. Thus, like Mann's choice of a biblical setting in order to convey broader wisdom, the mythlike tale of Brer Rabbit originates with a specific culture and in a particu-lar time and place, but widens to a greater audience through Murray's appro-priation and use of it.

The mythic, we'll recall, is a story of tradition that offers insight into the human condition. It therefore allows the storyteller to talk *beyond* the scope of the specific, instead taking up essential issues of human activity and en-deavor. In speaking about Gasoline Point at the start of the novel, the narra-tor imparts, "[O]nce upon a time it was also the briarpatch, which is why my nickname was Scooter, and is also why the chinaberry tree (that was ever as tall as any fairy tale beanstalk) was, among other things, my spyglass tree" (3). Invoking the "once upon a time" and the Brer Rabbit story (as well as the fairy tale of Jack and the Beanstalk), Murray establishes from the out-set that Scooter's story of an African American boy growing up in the South will embody a fabled quality. In Murray's version, however, the sense of fable as "make-believe" is undone by the reality of Scooter's surroundings, which include brawls and murder, characters gone insane, and a stunning realization about his parentage. *Train Whistle Guitar* makes myth of Scooter's real-world experiences—through the very language of the myth of Brer Rabbit—and thus it both acknowledges Scooter's trials as experiences faced by others and also renders Scooter's life and encounters accessible to others.

One of the ways that the Brer Rabbit references achieve the universal is through the use of a trickster hero—an archetypal character of many cultural, religious, and historical traditions. That Scooter is overtly linked to Brer Rabbit on numerous occasions ("My name is also Jack the Rabbit because my home is in the briarpatch" [4]) signals his status as such a hero.[7] Scooter, like the rabbit, embodies a wit and agility. And while Brer Rabbit stands as one iteration of the archetypal trickster, in Joseph we find another. In fact, Murray would have known of Brer Rabbit long before reading Mann, but encountering an adapted version of the trickster in Joseph likely confirmed for him the universality of the trickster figure. Ultimately, it is the trickster Joseph whose trajectory more similarly parallels Scooter's. And so while Murray was familiar with the Brer Rabbit lore from an early age, it was through the lens of Mann that the import of the Brer Rabbit myth as a universalizing device could be more fully realized—thus, the use of the Brer Rabbit allusions as well as their conceptual connection to Thomas Mann. Where Brer Rabbit functions as an example of Murray's utilization of a vernacular mythic tradition, it is back to Joseph that one can look to find a basis for Murray's figure of the hero.

For Murray, a trickster is playful, devilish, rascally, and, notably, resilient; he may get into trouble, but he also always learns from or remedies his mistakes. A trickster might, for example, skip school to spend a day as an explorer with Little Buddy Marshall. He could also, knowing full well what the adults would say, lose his virginity under a kitchen table to Deljean McCray. And he may, just as well, pretend to lie sleeping while actually eavesdropping in order to learn that his birth mother is not the woman who raised him. Scooter, like the literary tricksters who precede him, is nimble and quick ("I also used to call myself Jack the Nimble and Jack the Quick"); he leans upon his "trickster stick" (31). He is, according to the character Deljean McCray, a "mannish rascal"—or perhaps, in literary homage, one could read that as a "Mann-ish rascal." Murray's protagonist rarely employs flat-out trickery;

instead, he navigates tricky situations and in so doing he, rather like the blues hero, prevails. And while Scooter is never tested with life-and-death challenges, in placing him in and around some serious (even dangerous) circumstances, Murray portrays a protagonist, familiar with a breadth of experiences, who acknowledges the limitations of his setting while also maintaining equanimity and perspective. Thus, Scooter is a mixture of trickster hero and blues hero, the combination or culmination of which can be thought of as Murray's epic hero—and again, this idea will trace back to a Mannian influence.

In Joseph we see a trickster character who, in his youth, is immature and self-concerned, even wily and self-serving. Murray puts it a little more bluntly: "Joseph is a cocky, conceited S.O.B.," he joked one day as we looked together at the opening pages of *Joseph in Egypt,* where sure enough the text begins with an enslaved Joseph needling one of his captors. Provoked to respond, the captor states mockingly, "Thou'rt a good one!" and continues, "Thou art and remainest a funny fellow," finally jabbing with, "[T]hy tongue runs on like a lizard's tongue" (3–4). Indeed, Mann crafts his Joseph with a tongue of wit, not to mention a face of beauty. Joseph, the cunning hero, takes advantage of those good looks when it works well for him, and in similar fashion, he takes advantage of his brothers at times, setting them up for censure from their father. He is, again and again, referred to as "charming," a trait that reads two ways: it implies, on the one hand, his manipulative personality (as a *charmer* whose powers of persuasion are potent) and also refers, on the other, to a nascent goodness within (a *charming* fellow who is amiable). While Joseph's roguish traits are often immature and sometimes even cruel, Mann nevertheless presents a character that will grow beyond his youthful flaws.

Murray's protagonist, who shares Joseph's rascally and devilish attributes, is never as condemnable as Joseph is at times. Murray plays with the idea of the hero, inventing his own variant of the archetype. Moreover, Murray notes that the trickster element is not just in the Joseph character himself, but also in the way Mann writes his character; "Mann is singin' it to you, he's playin' with you," Murray said to me, in an effervescent voice that dramatized that very significance of his words. The mischievous tone and playful technique of Mann's writing let those pages resonate their stories. For Murray, Mann is "a poet, a singer and composer" (Walsh). And why exactly does Murray find this style so effective? Because, he told me, it's fun, it's playful, it gets the reader hooked, and that's how the writer imparts a lesson.

The lessons Joseph learns (and in turn delivers to his readers) are essentially lessons in progressive thinking and service for the good of others. "It is Joseph, the seer and provider, with his fabulous fusion of poetic imagination and political skill, who is best equipped of all Mann's protagonists to confront and come to realistic terms with the problems of contemporary existence," writes Murray in *The Hero and the Blues* (56–57). What Murray identifies in Joseph is rather like what Luzana Cholly asks of Scooter when he tells the boy to stay in school and to use his education in order to better the conditions of society.[8] Furthermore, Murray sees in Joseph's development a link to the blues tradition, noting that "Joseph goes beyond his failures in the very blues singing process of acknowledging them and admitting to himself how bad conditions are" (*Hero* 58). That is, Murray sees Joseph not only as a trickster figure but also as a blues hero—as that character capable of both conceding the blues and also stomping them away. He is severely challenged, for instance, when his brutal brothers first intend to leave him for dead in a well and then only slightly mitigate their conduct by instead selling him into bondage to migrant traders. Joseph, however, is not undone by these circumstances; rather, in acknowledging the gravity of his situation, he comes to terms with the behavior—his own arrogance—that resulted in his brothers' angry actions. And though his period of enslavement persists for hundreds of pages, the hero himself rises above contextual limitations in developing a keen belief in self-determination.[9]

In addition, Murray observes the blues not only in Joseph's character but also in the way Mann employs a stylistic rhetoric that is, interestingly, reminiscent of the idiom. Murray's own style, of course, is overtly blues-inflected and his character goes on, in fact, to become a blues musician in a later novel. Thomas Mann, meanwhile, has no such association with this music; he was not a jazz or blues writer. And yet Murray, with a careful eye—not to mention an attuned musical ear—recognized in Mann's prose something nascent that could be brought out fully in an American novel. Murray translates Mann's "music"—as Murray himself calls it—to its full blues potential in the modern American epic.

One finds an example of such nascent "music" in a scene early on in *Joseph and His Brothers,* where Mann portrays the young Joseph standing by a well, whispering "murmured singsong" of legends and ancestors. Mann then goes on to describe an "improvisation" where "all sorts of remote allusions and associations" mingle as Joseph sings a "variant and extension" on the original riff (64). Murray's writing better captures the swing, the movement of a jazz-style literature, and I prefer his use of "extension, elaboration, and refinement" to Mann's "variant and extension."[10] Nevertheless, one can see how Mann's ideas and words held special resonance for Murray. The import of "improvisation" to a jazz writer is clear. But those "allusions and associations" hold meaning as well, especially if one thinks of the technique of "signifying," adopted by some blues musicians, which creates a framework of shared discourse through references and insinuations of a specific vernacular. Murray put it best when he referred to "a little chicken butt signifying. . . . That is an indispensable part" of southern ritual (*Omni-Americans* 191). It could certainly be said that Murray playfully extended, elaborated, and refined what he originally found in Mann.

Joseph, it turns out, is the quick and nimble character who frees himself from his enslavement and returns—wiser, more humble, more honorable—to become a leader and provider. He matures to a critically reflective character, and he learns "about the rational perception of the world, science, and the world of progress" (Mundt 143); this knowledge readies him to act as a leader. In many ways, he is Scooter's literary ancestor. Scooter returns home at the end of *Train Whistle Guitar* after having been away at college, and he too, at this stage, takes on the aura of a more experienced, more purposeful, more learned persona. Of course, we know that one of the lessons emphasized to Scooter throughout the novel is the importance of education. Even during Scooter's period of youthful transgressions, Murray signals the personal and educational maturation that is to come: "I was to become a schoolboy above and beyond everything else, for all the absolutely indispensable times I was still to play hooky with Little Buddy Marshall" (54). But education doesn't come just in the form of books and exams. Scooter "realizes that his possibilities of survival, not to mention achievement, are predicated on his perpetual nimbleness," says Murray (*From the Briarpatch File* 10). This, in fact, is what the protagonist has been learning all along. Through the stories of elders, through personal mentors as well as figures of legend, and especially through mythic traditions (that perpetual nimbleness is attributable to Brer Rabbit), Scooter learns life lessons, and in discovering those fundamental lessons he also learns ways to navigate his personal time and place—the racially segregated South.

And yet, writes Stanley Crouch, "Murray became the first Negro writer since Ellison to so unflinchingly embrace an American identity that transcended race while working so well within the specifics of his own cultural background's variations on the elements that define and delineate national feeling of and for life" (150). Scooter may be fixed in a narrative time and space, but the novel and its lessons are not. *Train Whistle Guitar* depicts the challenging circumstances that breed confidence, ambition, and transcendent resistance. "The whole idea is resilience. . . . you got to have the resilience, the elegance in your movement, the hipness in your outlook that will get you through the briar patch, you see?" explains Murray (qtd. in Lamb). And how better to achieve that than through a universalized blues hero, an epic hero whose connection to a mythic narrative gives a broader scope to the interpretation of his setting's idiomatic particulars? This realization as it plays out in Murray's literature is indebted to Thomas Mann, who taught him that local particulars always have a universal resonance. Indeed, one would think the blues hero is an *American* archetype. And yet Murray finds a blues hero inspiration in a German author's rendering of a biblical tale.

The role that Mann played in shaping Murray's development was surely significant, and there are yet many other paths of Mannian influence that remain unexplored. Mann's *Joseph the Provider* (the fourth volume), for example, paints a picture of "blendedness," showing how seemingly opposite cultural and religious spheres can interlace and interact productively: "Through Joseph, Mann points out that a socially and morally responsible individual will be able to address both spheres. . . . [He proposes] a mutual recognition and interaction" (Mundt 151). We might notice that Murray himself offers a similarly astute position in *The Omni-Americans,* where he puts forth bold ideas on American mulatto culture. He said once, speaking extemporaneously during an interview:

> I try to establish a basis for a national image, for a national identity, and you know I've defined our culture as mulatto. You know, it's all interwoven, and it's most ironic that a nation which has achieved such magnificent innovations in communication and transportation could be stuck with [this] type of provincialism . . . because [this nation] should lead the world in terms of tolerance, if you want to use that word, in terms of sophistication—that is, the appreciation of things which are different, that there are always two different ways of approaching. You've got xenophobia or you have exotica. You could get a healthy mix of both. You could be a little worried because they're different, but you could also be fascinated because they're different. You make a synthesis, and it's yours and it's universal. (qtd. in Lamb)

That sounds a lot like mutual recognition and interaction and at the same time brings in Murray's concern with making the best use of contemporary knowledge. In Mann, he respected a writer who put his learning toward literature of a social good. In Scooter we see a character always taught to take his education to the next level—to make good on that education and to better his generation. Murray reasonably asks here: Why should a country so ahead in academic, technological, and commercial development still seem to lag so far behind when it comes to social tolerance and societal progression? And thus we see the import of the storyteller. He or she is, as we learn in *The Hero and the Blues,* also a mythmaker, and the mythmaker, we know, is a value maker. Murray writes to capture the essentiality of human existence and to offer perspectives on how to wade through the complexities, the predicaments, of life, "and in so doing [the writer] not only evokes the image of possibility, but also prefigures the contingencies of a happily balanced humanity and the Great Good Place" (*Hero* 11).

That Great Good Place might initially evoke the image of a Mannian biblical setting, yet Murray's tremendous bookshelves stand as towering proof of the wealth of literary raw materials he has drawn upon. When you're dealing with the likes of Albert Murray, a man who can recite lines from books he read six decades ago, never underestimate how much he has thought through the themes, philosophies, styles, and ramifications of the many authors whose works line his shelves. Yet at the end of the day, Murray will tell you that the key to understanding his books is actually quite simple: "[M]y stories are really about what it means to be human" ("Regional Particulars" 3).

Notes

1. Murray's copy (trans. H. T. Lowe-Porter, Knopf, 1934) titles the first volume *Joseph and His Brothers,* which is also the title of the entire four-volume novel. Other editions title the first volume *The Tales of Jacob.*

2. Incidentally, as one of the many ways that Murray marks his admiration for Mann, he entitles the third lecture in *The Hero and the Blues* "The Blues and the Fable in the Flesh," which is but a slight extension and variation on a chapter subheading in volume 1 of *Joseph and His Brothers:* "The Fable and the Flesh."

3. One can think of Murray's "chaos" as an extension of "the complexities" of life. On many occasions, Murray has talked to me about the role of chaos and entropy as factors that characterize our existence—the factors we're constantly struggling with or against, as we try to gain control over this or that aspect of life. In an interview with Brian Lamb in 1996, Murray explains the connection between menacing entropy and the blues that stomp it away. For more on Murray's use and description of "raw materials," see, for example, his essay "Regional Particulars and Universal Statement in Southern Writing" (1989).

4. The quote is from Ludwig Lewisohn (1945 Knopf edition, trans. H. T. Lowe-Porter).

5. Murray describes in the Lamb interview how he, as a young boy, was taken with geography lessons and with the study of maps, and thus one notes this as a point of autobiographic intersection between Murray and his character.

6. "Once upon a time" also appears on pages 15 and 67.

7. See also page 67: "And I said my name is Jack the Rabbit and my home is in the briarpatch."

8. Recall that Cholly advises Scooter both to develop his natural talents and to draw on up-to-date knowledge—"what the civil engineers and inventors and doctors and lawyers and bookkeepers had found out about the world" (30)—in order to cultivate practical and realistic responses to the problems of contemporary existence.

9. A discussion of the blues, of course, is a discussion of yet another mythic tra-

dition. Murray has written quite beautifully and extensively on this idea in *The Hero and the Blues, Stomping the Blues,* and *The Blue Devils of Nada,* and without rehashing those concepts here, it will suffice to say that the blues infuses *Train Whistle Guitar* as much as the popular folk tradition of Brer Rabbit. In so doing it adds to the essence of universality that Murray strives for in his writing.

10. See Murray's reference to a "*playful* extension, elaboration, and refinement" (emphasis in original) in, for example, "Regional Particulars."

7

Dewey's Pragmatism Extended

Education and Aesthetic Practice in *Train Whistle Guitar*

ROBERTA S. MAGUIRE

Albert Murray readily acknowledges a debt to Alabama's Tuskegee Institute, as it was there he began the process that led to his becoming a writer and, as he describes himself, "all-purpose literary intellectual" (Pinsker 207). He recalls not courses especially, but rather Tuskegee's marvelous library as the site of his real learning while at college. He has said that his major in education was something he "just did on the side" (qtd. in O'Meally 83). Taking their cue from Murray, scholars and interviewers have so far ignored the influence of Murray's coursework in education on his original approach to American culture and aesthetic theory. But because Murray did take this coursework seriously—which his decision to pursue graduate work in education for a term at the University of Michigan supports—I propose that we pause to consider how perhaps that major in education provided a foundation for Murray's startling originality.

The education curriculum at Tuskegee endorsed one theorist in particular: John Dewey, the leading proponent of "progressive" education, which de-emphasized transmitting knowledge to students as passive receptors in favor of structuring the learning environment so that students would be active participants. Murray was so intrigued by what he learned about Dewey in the classroom that, as he told Robert O'Meally, on his own he investigated Dewey's work further (118). What he discovered was that Dewey's progressive positions on education grew out of the larger philosophical framework of American pragmatism, which Dewey himself helped found. Deweyan pragmatism is based on the assumption that all philosophical questions are rooted in "ordinary, lived experience" (Boisvert 16). Following from that, something like "truth" is no longer immutable, divorced from lived experience, but rather shaped by time and circumstances; human existence can be recognized itself as a condition of contingency and plurality shaping and shaped by the natural and social environment; and rigid compartmentalization—separating human beings into body versus mind, education into teaching versus learning, art into fine versus useful—is the enemy of understanding and social progress. These positions made such an impression on Murray that among the first books he acquired for his own library were Dewey's 1934 treatise on aesthetics, *Art as Experience,* and *The Philosophy of John Dewey,* a 1939 scholarly overview. Both books remained on Murray's shelves throughout his writing career.

Murray's encounters with Dewey's ideas while he was an undergraduate had a lasting effect on his thinking. While these ideas are deeply embedded in his work, they can still be teased out, suggesting that Murray should himself be seen as a contributor to and shaper of the intellectual tradition of pragmatism, a distinctively American mode of thought and arguably our country's major addition to philosophy. Murray's contributions are evident in two great themes of his work—education, harkening back to that undergraduate major, and aesthetics, Murray's preoccupation out of the classroom while at Tuskegee—two themes that come together so well in his first novel, *Train Whistle Guitar,* as to allow readers to conclude themselves what Murray argues in all his work: contrary to the dominant mid-twentieth-century representation of the African American community as victimized and degraded—outside the mainstream of American culture—black U.S. culture is the quintessential American culture. Those who claim the culture and are shaped by it possess a heightened openness to change, which, as "adaptability," just happens to be the human trait on which Dewey's pragmatism is based. When extended and refined through experience, with education being a crucial dimension of experience, that African American openness to change becomes art, indispensable equipment for coping with contemporary life.

To see how *Train Whistle Guitar* accomplishes this requires setting out some of the major points Dewey makes about education, beginning with his "technical definition": education is "that reconstruction or reorganization of experience which adds to the meaning of experience, and which increases ability to direct the course of subsequent experience" (*Democracy and Education* 89–90). Such reconstructing or reorganizing occurs through "communication," which for Dewey is "a process of sharing experience till it becomes a common possession" (11). This educative process occurs formally and informally, in and out of school, and how to keep "a proper balance between the informal and formal" Dewey sees as "one of the weightiest problems with which [a] philosophy of education has to cope" (10), for while he recognizes that societies, in growing more complex, increasingly rely on formal schooling, he warns of the creation of an "undesirable" split "between the experience gained in more direct associations and what is acquired in school" (11). Their integration he sees as crucial for the ongoing renewal of a social group (12).

For a social group to renew itself, Dewey explains, does not mean it simply repeats its history. This is where formal schooling plays such an important role: in a democracy, "it is the office of the school environment . . . to see to it that each individual gets an opportunity to escape from the limitations of the social group in which he was born, and to come into living contact with a broader environment" (*Democracy and Education* 24). By developing a curriculum that integrates subject matter with social context, schools allow for students to develop "better habits" than those of the social group's current "adult society" (92). The pedagogy required for developing such habits requires that students be "fully enlisted in doing something," while the educator makes sure "that the doing requires observation, the acquisition of information, and the use of constructive imagination" (161). The subjects that lend themselves best to this mode, according to Dewey, are geography and history, which function "to enrich and liberate"; they are "the two great school resources for bringing about the enlargement of the significance of a direct personal experience" (255).

The premise of *Train Whistle Guitar* suggests Dewey's technical definition of education: the novel is Scooter's narration of significant events and people from his childhood spent in Gasoline Point, Alabama, a small, all-black community outside of Mobile. The reader understands Scooter-as-narrator to be an adult, removed from Gasoline Point in time and geography. His reflection on past events is a reconstructing or reorganizing through memory of experience, and it is in this reconstructing that his experiences gain meaning. For both Murray and Dewey, if education begins with the reconstructing of experience (which, by the way, Murray does say outright in *The Omni-Americans*, but without an attribution to Dewey), so too does art. According to Dewey, art is everyday experience intensified and refined (*Art as Experience* 74); Murray's related definition is that art is a "stylization" of experience through a process of "extension, elaboration, and refinement" (*Omni-Americans* 54; *Blue Devils* 94). According to both men, the goal of such aesthetic practice is to give meaning to past experience that in turn suggests possibilities for the future, indicating that they also see art as a subset of education—or, at times, education as a subset of art; as Murray says in *The Omni-Americans*, teaching "is an art, a fine art" (213). The overall structure of *Train Whistle Guitar* sets up an environment conducive for learning, with two different sets of teachers and learners. On one level, Scooter is both teacher and pupil, as his retelling of the past gives it a meaning for him that he uses to direct his future endeavors, which we see played out in Murray's other three novels that, together with *Train Whistle Guitar*, constitute the Scooter tetralogy. On another level, Murray the artist is teacher, and we the readers are the learners.

When we focus on Scooter as the teacher and learner, we see key elements of Dewey's educational philosophy concretized. The novel begins with Scooter recalling his beloved chinaberry tree, and the brief chapters that follow introduce Little Buddy, Scooter's best friend, and Luzana Cholly, the nomadic guitar-playing bluesman idolized by Scooter and Little Buddy. Those chapters are concerned with two adventures the young boys have. In one they hop a train leaving town in imitation of Luzana Cholly, and in another they set out on foot for the nearby shipyards. Formal schooling, while clearly in the background, is still woven through those early chapters. Scooter's first mention of school occurs during his recollection of how his and Little Buddy's train hopping meant that the boys were "not only . . . running away from home [but] were also playing hooky" (18); then Luzana Cholly brings school up after he discovers the two boys in an empty boxcar and returns them to Gasoline Point by way of a "slow-poking" local (28).

Scooter re-creates how Luzana Cholly, recognizing his responsibility to correct his young admirers' romantic view of his wandering life, told the boys to stay in school and add the knowledge they acquire to everything already known, so that they could "bring about the day the old folks had always been prophesying and praying for." His parting words to the boys: *Make old Luze proud of you. . . . You going further than old Luze ever dreamed of. Old Luze ain't been nowhere. Old Luze don't know from nothing"* (30). In that episode we have Dewey's ideal educative process, whereby experience is shared and reconstructed. The reconstruction is put into motion through Luzana Cholly's instruction, and through this instruction, the bluesman, who surely knows more than the "nothing" he claims, embraces another aspect of Dewey's educational philosophy: if the social group to which the boys belong—the southern black rural community—is to renew itself, it must not repeat his choices, as romantic as they might seem. He knows that school provides the boys with the opportunities they need, introducing them to the "broader environment" necessary to bring about the change the community needs.

In Scooter's recounting of the book's second adventure, a day he and Little Buddy played hooky to head out for the shipyards, he reveals how formal schooling was never far from his mind. As young boys would, Scooter and Little Buddy celebrate their freedom in a playful call-and-response that appears to dismiss the importance of school:

> Hey, that's all right about your goddamn school, Little Buddy said. Hey, call us the goddamn school this time.

We got your goddamn school, I said. I got your goddamn school right
here. (39)

Michael Borshuk reads that as a jazzlike critique of social convention—formal
schooling—which clearly, on its surface, it is (177–78). But underlying that
bravura performance is Scooter's guilty conscience, which alters the meaning
to be taken from it. Scooter recalls how, walking through the woods, the boys
could hear the morning's last school bell: "But schoolboy that I was even then,
as faint as the bell sound was, the minute I heard it I could also feel the way I
always felt and see them lining up at the flagpole; and I couldn't keep myself
from knowing exactly how long it would be before the Pledge of Allegiance
and the high society march would be over and Miss Lexine Metcalf would be
calling my name twice and looking up before marking me tardy" (38). The informal experience of sneaking out to the shipyards and the formal experience
of school, no matter Scooter's boyhood desire, remain intertwined. That they
must to achieve Dewey's "proper balance between the informal and formal"
the rest of the book develops.

This balance is especially apparent during Scooter's recollection of the
communal fireside gatherings at his home. With Scooter always in his "same
chair in my same place in the corner" (63), the adults tell stories about John
Henry, Stagolee and Billy Lyons, Railroad Bill. From these stories the conversation would turn more philosophical and broadly historical—to freedom
and the Civil War and on to Reconstruction, which Scooter tells us would in-
evitably lead to the topic of "Education" (68). And he recalls that as he grew
older, these fireside conversations would come to focus on him as "the hope
and glory" because of his progress at school. Scooter's school seems to have
had in place in the 1920s precisely the sort of curriculum that Dewey was calling for in 1916, when he published *Democracy and Education.* Central to the
curriculum at Scooter's all-black school, we learn, were geography and history, Dewey's "two great . . . resources for bringing about the enlargement
of the significance of a direct personal experience." When remembering how
he would be invited to share with his elders evidence of the education he was
getting, Scooter recalls, "[S]ometimes it was Geography and sometimes it
was History, and sometimes I had to tell it, and sometimes I had to get the

book and read it to them" (68). He would read or recite from the Constitution, the Declaration of Independence, Frederick Douglass's orations, even *Poor Richard's Almanac.* Once one of the townsfolk rewarded Scooter with a $5 bill, proclaiming that "we all going to be drawing down interest on him" (74). Not to be outdone, Scooter's Uncle Jerome that day stood to preach a sermon about his nephew, which led Scooter to look at the mantelpiece, which held an "old-fashioned pendulum clock." The clock, Scooter told us earlier, "was Papa's heirloom from that ancestral mansion of ante-bellum columns and gingham crisp kitchens in which his mulatto grandmother had herself been an inherited slave until Sherman's March to the Sea but which I still remember as the Mother Goose clock" (56). The day of his uncle's sermon, Scooter "heard the Mother Goose clock and outside there was the Valley Forge bitter wind in the turret-tall chinaberry tree" (75). Informal and formal schooling combine, allowing Scooter to expand his own history beyond his immediate experiences so that his context can include not only his parents' and their parents' pasts, but the entire nation's, going back to the Revolutionary War.

Another example of how vernacular experience and formal schooling combine: from town elder Unka JoJo the African, Scooter initially learns of the *Clotilde,* which had carried to the United States "one of the last if not the very last shipload of African captives" (79), Unka JoJo among them. His understanding grows from thinking it was a reference to the Old Testament story of Jonah and the Whale to it being a United Fruit Company boat to realizing it was a slave ship, once he "finally began to pay close enough attention during the New Year's Day ceremonies celebrating the Emancipation Proclamation" (81). But still missing was a large enough context for him to fully grasp Unka JoJo's story until he was introduced to geography in the formal environment of the classroom, symbolized by his third-grade teacher's "blue and green and yellow globe revolving on its tilted axis" (54). Only upon "learn[ing] to use the globe for Miss Lexine Metcalf" did Scooter "realize that [Unka JoJo] was talking about coming all the way across the Atlantic Ocean from another continent in another hemisphere" (82). "[F]rom then on," having "come into contact with [the] broader environment" that Dewey argues it is the progressive school's responsibility to provide (*Democracy and Educa-*

tion 24), Scooter "was to become a schoolboy above and beyond everything else, for all the absolutely indispensable times I was still to play hooky with Little Buddy Marshall" (54).

Scooter's reflection suggests formal schooling has a role to play that is distinct from the education one gains informally: it provides the tools and knowledge for individuals to remake or create the selves they can imagine, regardless of parents or personal history. Only what Dewey calls a student's basic "equipment" matters: "Education must take" individuals as they are, he writes; "that a particular individual has just such and such an equipment of native abilities is a basic fact. That they were produced in such and such a way, or that they are derived from one's ancestry, is not especially important" (*Democracy and Education* 86). Or, as Scooter rephrases what he learned from Miss Tee: "[T]here was no family name or ancestral bloodlines of identity and inheritance that was likely to stand you in much better stead than the also and also of the background you could create for yourself by always doing your best in school" (86–87)—a profound lesson Scooter's reordering of his story makes plain. The book reveals late that Miss Tee, the woman taken to be a family friend, is Scooter's biological mother. Who his father is remains a mystery. The lesson this reorganizing points up is that Scooter must—and can— create himself.

Reordering chronology moves us into the specifically aesthetic dimension of *Train Whistle Guitar* and to the second teacher-learner configuration: Murray as artist-teacher, readers as learners. We recall that for both Dewey and Murray, the basic stuff of art is everyday experience, and such experience becomes art once it is reworked, much like experience must be reconstructed to become educative. Restoring a relationship between the everyday and art was radical when Dewey published *Art as Experience*. Murray, however, could assume that continuity and extend it, which we see when he argues in his essays that U.S. blacks in the twentieth century have made a profound contribution to the world's "equipment for living" through the invention of a blues aesthetic, crystallized in jazz, which derives from the black community's vernacular culture. But as much as Murray values music and discursive argumentation, his bias toward such literary forms as novels and poetry rivals that of Dewey, who in *Art as Experience* claims that these forms not only have "an intellectual force superior to that of any other art," but also have the "capacity . . . to present the values of a collective life" (239–40). That bias, then, sets a tall order for Murray's fiction: there should be his fullest communication that U.S. black culture holds the aesthetic values the nation collectively needs to renew itself in contemporary times.

To see that in *Train Whistle Guitar,* let's go first to the novel's structure, which overall suggests blues-based jazz. It opens with a vamp—the short introduction that starts off a jazz tune. Devoted to the chinaberry tree, this vamp is followed by one of five italicized sections that function much like musical riffs—short musical phrases that repeat throughout a tune, typically with slight but important variations (Pearson 114). These riffs take as their focus the actual and potential of Scooter's identity—he's Jack the Rabbit of the briarpatch, or the schoolboy, or a cultural hero like Jack Johnson. Between these riffs are narrations of incidents, and in form they suggest jazz solos or ensemble playing, such as when the townsfolk gathered at his parents' fireside build a story. Within any of these—vamp, riff, solo, or ensemble—blues and jazz elements translated to literary form are also evident. For example, early in one paragraph of the opening vamp we get the AAB structure of the blues lyric stanza: From the chinaberry tree "[y]ou couldn't see the post office flag," and "[y]ou couldn't see the switch sidings for the sawmills," but you could see "the telegraph poles and the sky above the pine ridge" (2). This AAB structure is broadened over the rest of the vamp, so that a later paragraph begins, "You couldn't see the blackberry slopes," and two paragraphs later, "Nor could you see One Mile Bridge," but in the next paragraph, "[Y]ou could see . . . the sky above Bay Poplar Woods fading away" (2–3). As readers, we *experience* that structure, gradually recognizing the artifice while engaging our imaginations with the seen and unseen. In our role as students we are "fully enlisted in doing something," while Murray the artist-teacher has made sure that "the doing requires observation, the acquisition of information, and the constructive use of imagination" (*Democracy and Education* 161). But because what we experience is the stylized blues form "deliberately and fully" imposed upon the raw particulars of a landscape, it moves beyond the educative to become an aesthetic experience (*Art as Experience* 137).

For Dewey, an aesthetic experience is not a political experience. When artists set out to convey a "special message," Dewey explains, they "limit the expressiveness" of the material they have shaped (*Art as Experience* 181). Murray has long been committed to—and criticized for—that same view of art, but he extends Dewey to clarify that art nonetheless has "political significance and applicability." Yet because art is concerned with "the essential nature of existence among a given folk in a given community" (*Hero* 97), it "establishes the context for"—rather than prescribes—"social and political action" (10). Murray's artist functions much like Dewey's teacher, who, in being responsible for "supplying the conditions which insure growth" through "conjoint activities" (*Democracy and Education* 61, 48), empowers rather than dictates.

As a series of riffs and "little stories" lacking in traditional narrative links, *Train Whistle Guitar* suggests rather than announces its meaning. The connections between the stories are loose, with an element of one being picked up by the next, much in the way the instruments of a jazz ensemble respond to each other. One chapter of the book containing six little stories has as its basic theme how the sacred and secular of Sunday and Monday in Gasoline Point are intertwined. Sundays include church service, so the first vignette introduces the intensely spirited Miss Sister Lucinda Wiggins. Her church singing lends a connection to the next vignettes focusing on Monday morning chores, when the ladies in the neighborhood hang laundry while engaging in call-and-response, reminding Scooter of blues musicians. The idea of blues musicians leads to a reflection on Stagolee Dupas (fils), the juke joint piano player par excellence. Because his raucous playing often led to a preacher's Sunday sermon, Scooter recalls Miss Sister again "tell[ing] the world . . . about trouble in the land" (100) on Monday morning. The blues and Monday morning are picked up in the chapter's last little story, focusing on Blue Eula Bacote.

Let's stay with Blue Eula's story for a moment, for here Murray captures so well the "essential nature of existence among a given folk in a given community," laying the groundwork for social and political action. Childless and married to a good man who was also a gambler, Ms. Bacote has her share of life's hardships, and they can get to her: "Hello central hello central hello central ring me Western Union" (102), she can be heard saying to herself sometimes at the local honky-tonk. But she also "always used to wear high-heel patent leather pumps and spang-dangling 18-carat gold earrings . . . and used to have the best short plump brownskin strut you ever saw" (101). On Monday mornings she would clean her whole house, listening to Bessie Smith or Ma Rainey or Louis Armstrong, so that by the middle of the day, after putting her clean house back together, "it was as if she had finally gotten everything ready to make it through another week" (103). Blue Eula is the "affirmative beat [that] is always geared to the rugged facts of life" (*Omni-Americans* 141), a beat, Murray tells us, always underlying the blues.

Put another way, Blue Eula Bacote, an ordinary woman in the black South of the early twentieth century, improvises a means of coping with the " lowdown dirty shame" of her life: She has a look, a walk, and a general routine indicating not only that she has the ability to adapt, the human trait underlying Deweyan pragmatism, but that she has elevated her ability to improvise to a life style. Then by pairing her actions with the music of such jazz innovators as Bessie Smith and Louis Armstrong, Murray reminds us of the continuity between everyday experience and art that Dewey sought to restore in the 1930s. Because that reminder is made by way of a black character's experience and a style of music invented by black musicians in the United States, it also takes on political significance, serving in 1974 as a counterstatement to the lingering mid-twentieth-century view of African American culture as impoverished and degraded—since a culture that gives rise to an art style, which Murray calls "the highest as well as the most comprehensive fulfillment of culture" (*Omni-Americans* 54), can hardly be a degraded culture. But it is when we also consider how Murray has embraced Dewey's principle that the force of art is realized through the audience's experiencing of its form that we get to Murray's great achievement with the novel. To be sure, Murray indicates through Blue Eula Bacote's story that black culture has significant claim on the origins of jazz and the art style it represents. And he is adamant in his essays that that fact needs to be respected. But Blue Eula's story and the message regarding the vitality of black culture are conveyed through a form that does more than function as a translation of blues-based jazz elements into literary technique; through its improvisatory texture, it also encourages our participation as readers. The effect of this is profound: rather than claiming the style to be the exclusive property of the black community, as some have criticized Murray for doing, he invites all of us—no matter our background—to experience it as our common possession.

8

Albert Murray and Tuskegee Institute

Art as the Measure of Place

CAROLINE GEBHARD

Some years ago, Albert Murray inscribed my copy of *South to a Very Old Place*, "For Caroline—who is doing what I once did in these parts, A. Murray, Tuskegee 1935–1939, 1940–1955." This generous inscription acknowledges a bond—in this case, the fraternity of those who have taught English 101 at Tuskegee. Most important, however, Murray's inscription underlines the length of time that he spent at Tuskegee Institute—in this reckoning, almost twenty years. Surely his time at Tuskegee had a profound impact on his work. This essay will explore Albert Murray's relationship to Tuskegee Institute and how it shaped his thinking as writer and cultural critic.

Unlike his classmate, close friend, and literary confidant, Ralph Ellison, Murray was a Tuskegee insider. Although he shared with Ellison frustration over successive Tuskegee administrations, for him, Tuskegee was destiny, that is, a key destination on the path to self-realization, a staging ground for testing manhood, and a constellation of persons and places that embodied all the necessary elements for the hero to progress. For Murray, Tuskegee could not be incarnated in a single powerful leader. Indeed, unlike many representations of the school, which are so often overshadowed by portraits of Washington, Murray's representations of the institute never focus upon one figure. Instead, Tuskegee is synonymous in his imaginary with certain moments in time, landscapes, and people—especially his close companions and his beloved English teacher and friend, Morteza Drexel Sprague. In his memoir *South to a Very Old Place* (1971), the school becomes a "triangulation point," a means of taking moral and literary compass of his own bearings in the larger world. At the same time, Tuskegee, for Murray, always remains one of those places designated as "home."[1]

Like many poetic reckonings, Murray's Tuskegee dates turn out to be more metaphoric than strictly factual. As the author himself warns in his epigraph to *South to a Very Old Place,* "not everything in this book is meant to be taken literally. Some names have been changed, some not." At the age of nineteen, Murray enrolled in the fall of 1935 in Tuskegee Institute, graduating in 1939. However, the period from 1940 to 1955 was not spent continuously at the institute; he began teaching English in the fall of 1940, but he joined the air force in 1943. He returned to Tuskegee in the fall of 1946 as an ROTC instructor, teaching air science and tactics until 1955. In those years, however, he also left Tuskegee to take his first trip to Europe and to attend New York University from 1947 to 1948, where he earned his master's degree in English.

Tuskegee often helped pay for schooling or travel for select faculty and staff whom it expected to return to the school. While Ellison never received the financial aid he sought from Tuskegee and chose not to come back his senior year, Murray appears to have been one of the school's favored ones.[2] When Murray writes to Ellison on March 27, 1950, that the school had not only approved his leave but was also giving him "$300 toward expenses" for his trip to Paris, Ellison responded admiringly, with a hint of envy, "[Y]ou must be working a very smooth magic to get those boys to shell out that much dough" (*Trading Twelves* 10, 11). It is not surprising then, given Murray's long-term special relationship with the institute, that his portraits of Tuskegee differ sharply from Ellison's in *Invisible Man* (c. 1952).

Although Ellison pointedly does *not* name the school in his famous novel, the "honeysuckle and purple wisteria" in the "bee-humming air," the "forbidden road" winding "past the girls' dormitories, past the hall with the clock in its tower," and "the small white Home Economics practice cottage" clearly evoke the alma mater from which he never officially graduated (*Invisible Man* 27).[3] Yet Ellison's novel treats the campus and campus life only in passing: what takes center stage is the relationship between the hapless protagonist and Dr. Bledsoe, the school's dictatorial president. He runs afoul of Bledsoe when, instead of giving a visiting white trustee the "right" tour, he takes him to forbidden places off campus, which eventually leads to the student's permanent expulsion by a ruthless Bledsoe, whose "letters of recommendation" seal the protagonist's fate as unemployable. Ellison's fictional Tuskegee is dominated by this deeply duplicitous powerful authority figure who arouses strong and contradictory emotions that seem to have been inspired to some extent by Ellison's real feelings about Tuskegee's leadership.[4]

Yet it is clear from his correspondence with Murray that it would be simplistic to read the novel as a roman à clef.[5] Nevertheless, Ellison feared his satiric novel would bar him from Tuskegee; however, Murray reassured him that Tuskegee people "are reading the hell out of *Invisible*" and that everybody is "very very impressed" (Trading Twelves 36).[6] Murray even helped arrange for Ellison to return to give a special series of lectures as part of Tuskegee's entertainment course, an enrichment series that brought artists to campus.[7]

Although in some measure Ellison was reconciled with Tuskegee Institute, and both President Frederick D. Patterson and President Luther H. Foster turned to him for advice about the school, in his private correspondence with Murray, Ellison continues to rail against what he sees as a black academic leadership too indebted to white power and too concerned with maintaining its own power at the expense of liberal education. At one point, he even confessed to Murray that "self liquidation" might be the best answer for Tuskegee.[8] Ellison's criticism, it should be noted, also extended to other black schools.[9] At the end of his life, however, he had begun to think of Tuskegee in quite a different light. He wrote the school's president in 1988 that he now saw that coming to the school "had exposed him to the 'transcendent vision'" of its founder, Booker T. Washington (qtd. in Rampersad 552).

Although Murray, too, privately expressed disgust with more than one Tuskegee administration,[10] his literary representations of Tuskegee Institute could not be more different from Ellison's. His perspective was not that of the prickly, brilliant artist who conceived the alienated protagonist of *Invisible Man* but that of a privileged insider, a member of "Mister Baker's Talented Tenth," who had found friends and teachers who made Tuskegee for him as richly imaginative a space for an artist as "any skylight garret in Paris, as fabulous as any workshop in the Florence of Benvenuto Cellini" (*South* 109, 110). By contrast, *Invisible Man* constitutes an anti-bildungsroman that asks: What character is even *possible* for an ambitious young black man in a society that cannot even see him? Thus, Ellison's book is more a novel about the miseducation of its reluctant hero than it is about his maturation, and no institution is untouched by Ellison's merciless satire, including the black college. On the other hand, Murray's novel *The Spyglass Tree* (1991) typifies the classic bildungsroman whose aim is to portray the hero's personal growth through "the recognition of his or her identity and role in the world" (Abrams 120). Praising how Murray weaves together elements of his own life to create the hero, his homeplace, and his episodic journey to adulthood in *Train Whistle Guitar* (1974), Warren Carson concludes, "Together, these elements combine to yield perhaps the most phenomenal African American Bildungsroman written to date" (291). Carson, however, is quite critical of *The Spyglass Tree*, judging it only an "average novel" compared to the artistry of the earlier work (295). As the sequel to *Train Whistle Guitar* in charting the hero's schooling, however, the novel seems especially to fit the bildungsroman genre, which Murray himself recognized in commenting on writing *The Spyglass Tree*: "As a writer, you're trying to put together what is called a *bildungsroman*—that is, an education story, a coming of age story, a story about how a person's consciousness develops" (qtd. in Rowell, "'All-Purpose'" 400). At issue in both novels is the self-conscious way in which Murray sets out to render the hero's journey of self-discovery in *his* world—the world of Gasoline Point, Mobile County Training School, and Tuskegee Institute.[11]

Tuskegee in *The Spyglass Tree* is the chief setting for the trials the hero must undergo, yet Murray, like Ellison, never identifies the college in the novel by name. He does, however, locate it clearly through his descriptions, for example, the view he describes from a dorm room in Sage Hall: "The water tank that is probably still the first campus landmark on the horizon after you turn off U.S. Highway 80 at the city marker on your way in from Montgomery and points north or south was all the way back to the left of your window and out of sight between the new science building [Armstrong Hall] where most of the academic class sessions were held . . . and the new gymnasium [Logan Hall]." He, again like Ellison, invokes the clock tower on White Hall, one of the most prominent landmarks on Tuskegee's campus (9).

Yet Murray pointedly invents a triumvirate—a "fieldhand, a blacksmith, and a handyman" (24)—as the school's founding black fathers. This revision holds a key to Murray's vision of the school and what it means for the hero's development. Almost certainly aware of the role that Lewis Adams, a Tuskegee blacksmith, actually played in founding Tuskegee, Murray revises the famous monument of Booker T. Washington lifting the veil from the slave. And in sharp contrast to Ellison's depiction of the "cold father symbol" in *Invisible Man* that baffles the protagonist because he is "unable to decide whether the veil is really being lifted, or lowered more firmly in place" (28), Murray instead invents three bronzed men: one with a hoe, another with a hammer, and the third with an open book on his knee, but no veil over his face and no man above him helping to remove it (*Spyglass* 22). Thus Murray unambiguously depicts the school as the inspired work of cooperative black labor and not the fruit of only one man's genius.[12]

The central crisis of the book also calls for cooperative action. It involves the hero's readiness to stand with Giles Cunningham, a local black gambler and juke joint owner, when Will Spradley, a poor black man, gets himself in a jam by unwittingly enraging a white working-class man determined to force Cunningham to leave town. "Schoolboy" must be initiated into the ways of "antagonistic cooperation" (178). He begins to understand this lesson when Will appears beaten and bloody, and he sees how this particular jam eventually requires the antagonistic cooperation of the white racist sheriff, the rich white landowner, and the black tough guys who surround Cunningham to effect a peaceful resolution. He thinks that "[a] jam session, after all, is a musical battle royal, and as such it is always a matter of performing not only with hair-trigger inventiveness and ingenuity but also with free-flowing gracefulness which is to say elegance, not only under the pressure of the demands of the music itself but also in the presence of and in competition with your peers and betters" (178). In this particular "jam," Schoolboy plays his individual part flawlessly. Clearly, here, Murray alludes to Ellison's famous "battle royal" scene by way of counterstatement.[13] In return for showing courage at a moment's notice, being willing to face danger in the form of angry whites bent on revenge, the hero wins praise from Cunningham, as well as a part-time job and a bass fiddle, symbols that the hero is on his way to becoming, as Cunningham phrases it, a "real pro" (205). Instead of a young black man being utterly manipulated and shamed by powerful white men, as in Ellison's battle royal, Murray's protagonist is skillfully mentored by a powerful black man.

Murray's most subtle "counterstatement" to *Invisible Man* lies in the contrast between the dead or duplicitous father figures that loom over Ellison's protagonist and the supportive men who surround Murray's hero. Throughout Ellison's novel, the invisible man must struggle to fathom his grandfather's legacy of meekness coupled with and contradicted by his deathbed ravings that point in exactly the opposite direction. Not surprisingly, where the hero of *Invisible Man* finds a false harbor, Murray's hero finds true sanctuary. As in *Invisible Man*, much of the critical action in *The Spyglass Tree* takes place off campus, but unlike in Ellison's novel, the school itself is a refuge. It is also the scene of the protagonist's intellectual initiation through his conversations with his brilliant roommate, who pushes him beyond the class syllabus and opens up the worlds of art, architecture, and literature to the questing hero. Missing from Murray's novel is *any* sense of an oppressive administration thwarting the hero's exploration in *any* way. It seems clear that Albert Murray cannot conceive of his hero's development without Tuskegee.

Indeed, perhaps the most striking contrast between Ellison's and Murray's portraits of young black men is in the kind of male mentoring they receive. Unlike Ellison's ambiguous father figures, beginning with the grandfather in *Invisible Man*, Murray's work is populated by a host of older, wiser black men, from Luzana Cholly, a rootless gambler, in *Train Whistle Guitar* to Fred Douglas (aka "Deke") Whatley, the manager of the local barbershop in *The Spyglass Tree*. For example, the monologue on politics by Whatley astutely analyzes oppression, arguing it is more deeply rooted than one notoriously racist sheriff and predicting that even when blacks win more power, politicians will still be beholden to powerful interests.[14] Carson notes that characters like these, "whatever physical or moral weaknesses they may possess, always manage to find something positive and edifying to pass on to the Scooters of the black community" (291). Although Scooter is obviously tutored and nurtured by women in the community as well, it is significant that in Murray's fiction, as well as in his nonfiction, he highlights the "avuncular" role played by many black men, from those at the bottom of the social scale to the top. This theme of "uncle figures" runs deep in all of Murray's fiction as well as in his life. When called upon to give an address at Howard University celebrating those who had achieved academic honors, Murray projected himself as speaking in the tradition of "grownups around the firesides in the old down-home cabins of yester-year" and imparting the "hard-bought wisdom" he had heard "in the barbershops" and on "store-front benches" that "were the hangouts of such legendary uncles as Uncle Bud, Uncle Doc, Uncle Ned, and Uncle Remus, among others."[15]

The point of casting older men he'd known growing up as "uncles" and as kin to the musical and literary figures he evokes is not only to counterstate the "Uncle Tom" stereotype but also to challenge the mainstream American coming-of-age story that makes rebelling against the stifling convention of one's elders a necessary rite of passage. Instead, the challenge facing black people coming of age—especially young men of intellectual and artistic promise—is "to become the living answer to the old folks' prayers" ("Academic Lead Sheet" 18). To bring about true revolutionary change in America, Murray argues, the most "subversive" thing a black intellectual or artist can do is to strive for the most cosmopolitan, universal, "comprehensive frame of reference" possible (19–20). Yet he also makes clear that seeking worldly knowledge beyond one's background at the same time does not mean abandoning one's roots, for according to Murray, nowhere in American life is there a richer tradition to draw upon than the one that has come down to us from an enslaved people forced to craft a tough, resilient, and life-affirming culture—a blues culture. It is in this sense that he holds that "the blues statement" points a way for dealing creatively with trauma, homelessness, rootlessness, and cultural disintegration, because it speaks not only to black Americans but to worldwide crises that the planet now faces.[16]

Although Murray began work on the manuscript that would eventually become *Train Whistle Guitar* and *The Spyglass Tree* contemporaneously with Ellison's book, the finished novels would not be published until much later. Murray's most clear-cut answer to Ellison's devastating critique of black education at schools like Tuskegee in *Invisible Man* is in *South to a Very Old Place*. This distinctive book began as a *Harper's* magazine assignment to interview writers, mainly white ones, but became his own personal literary experiment testing whether one really could go home again in the course of exploring what changes desegregation had brought to the South.

Significantly, Murray opens his recounting of his Tuskegee homecoming with the memories of his freshman year and of a peer—another Tuskegee student. In a trope that he continues in this chapter, he invokes collective memory as he thinks of this classmate: "Wherever old narrow-eyed, level-talking, pigeon-toed-walking Gerald Hamilton is now he is not likely to have forgotten those days."[17] He also evokes the historic heart of campus: "the then rust-red but now silver dome of Tompkins Dining Hall, the weathered green clock tower, White Hall lawn, the Band Stand, the old Bugle Stand, and the whiteness of the academic columns as you saw them through the flat preautumnal greenness of the elms lining Campus Avenue" (105). He recalls the alcoholic drinks the male students concocted, the classes and professors, the students he knew, the clubs (frequented primarily by male students), the jazz heard at night over the radio, and "the Block"—the shops across from campus.

In *South to a Very Old Place*, Murray will insist that Ellison "will also remember those days," adding slyly, "But not as an invisible freshman" (107). He confesses, though, that memories of *that* Tuskegee will be most closely shared by Gerald "Jug" Hamilton, for there together they were introduced to "un-Mobile County Training School things such as free association and stream of consciousness" and would talk about "unheard of *avant-garde* writers such as James Joyce, Marcel Proust, Virginia Woolf, and Gertrude Stein as casually as if they were boxers, baseball or football players or movie stars" (109).

The Tuskegee that Murray builds for his reader throughout this chapter is not a place dominated by stifling authority and petty rules but a space that allowed young black men to congregate and range freely in their imaginations, engaging in intellectual "jam sessions" that made them responsive both to the "very old"—classics like Boccaccio and Chaucer—and the "very new"—the latest Hemingway story in *Esquire* magazine. It was also the place from which and through which Murray could begin to see his native South as a "very old" place, to understand his native land and himself through the lens of both Greek tragedy and Faulkner. Seeing the grand antebellum mansion that bordered the campus, now the president's house, the young Murray came to grips with his southern heritage in a new way. He credits Hamilton for the insight that "miscegenation"—that word "full of pubic hair—is something very special and very fundamental on the faulknerian landscape, like incest in Greek tragedy" (118). Later Murray himself will build on the idea that miscegenation—the mixing of races and peoples—is also very special and very fundamental to the American landscape and culture, for without it, America is not America.

Ironically, in Murray's recollection of Tuskegee, "you were like to forget that Booker T. Washington, who after all had been dead for only twenty years at that time, was of the same generation" (120) of the grandparents of himself and his peers. In his rendering, Washington is no longer a man but a legendary figure in the distant past who almost belongs to the age of Franklin and Jefferson. He tries to convey the special kind of forgetting that transformed Washington as an actual man into a figure who signified first and foremost Murray's own generation's obligation to let nothing hold them down. The famous Washington-Du Bois debate is dispensed with in a parenthetical phrase—he says that his teacher Mr. Benjamin F. Baker has already said what needs to be said about that subject: "*Booker T. Washington sacrificed too much to expediency. Dr. DuBois in his up-north bitterness spends too much time complaining. The youth of today must find the golden mean*" (122). In Murray's hands, then, Washington is not the towering authority figure ruling Tuskegee or the accommodationist that some later critics have made of him but simply, to the students of the class of 1939, a figure they affectionately associated with their own families' aspirations for them: "Hell, man, we can't be letting Unka Buka Tee down" (124).

Yet Murray's identification of Tuskegee as a "triangulation point" in *South to a Very Old Place* means more than Washington's stirring legacy, more than "the Block," with its soda fountain, "taxi cab pundits" (125), and its stores attracting "out of town sharpies, athletes and big-league musicians"(125), more than fond memories of pretty girls accompanied at twilight to dances in Logan Hall, more than jazz greats first heard late at night on the radio, more even than the special camaraderie young men enjoyed at Tuskegee: for him, Tuskegee is also the place where William Faulkner and Thomas Mann meet, where Albert Murray, incisive cultural critic and literary artist, was born. *Triangulation,* Murray tells us in *The Spyglass Tree,* is a military term that relates not only to "map making and map reading" but also to "personal adjustment" and "target practice" (61). In this novel, the term is used by Old Trooper, his roommate's great-uncle. Old Trooper's tutelage, however, has to do with being a man of the world; a retired Buffalo Soldier and prizefight promoter, he "treats" the young men to a visit to a brothel in which they are transformed, "what with our make-believe capes . . . into two elegant *flâneurs* winding our way back across fin-de-siècle Paris from Montmartre to the Left Bank" (*Spyglass* 57).[18] However, in his memoir of Tuskegee, *South to a Very Old Place,* the figure Murray finds himself celebrating the most is not the old soldier, not Washington, not his precocious roommate, nor even himself as the emergent artist. "[T]he very special dimension of tuskegeeness" he finds himself "acknowledging and celebrating above all else" (126) is incarnated in his first English teacher at Tuskegee: Morteza Drexel Sprague.

If Tuskegee itself represents a "triangulation point," a means by which all else is measured, then the "post–Booker T. Washington Liberal Arts emphasis" that "was the very self and voice" of Sprague becomes the "exact point" within this triangulation, the "benchmark" that is the point of departure and the point of return by which all other journeys, actual and artistic, are measured (*South* 126). His later voyages to Cuba, the Swiss Alps, Venice, Rome, Athens, and Istanbul were all mediated through Sprague who, by introducing him to Hemingway, Mann, Henry James, and a host of other writers, had first initiated him into the larger world of "Arts and Letters" (131). And even if he didn't literally encounter Mann until after he'd graduated, it was under the influence of Sprague that he began to understand himself as a literary brother to the German writer and to grasp that magic triangulation of time and place that literature eternally brings about: "Say you know how it always is in the early morning of hemingway's havana," or "Say, you remember how it was with Hans Castorp on that long journey" (126).[19]

Sprague was not only a gifted teacher who encouraged Murray: he also modeled for him what it meant to be an engaged intellectual whose commitment to social justice did not need to be said and whose high academic standards included a profound appreciation for the classics. He inspired students such as Ellison and Murray to see that great art was theirs, too. Though later Ellison and Murray would discuss how Sprague was perhaps not political enough in advocating for the liberal arts at Tuskegee, in this elegiac tribute to Sprague, Murray suggests that his presence was more than enough: in his "well cut gray suit" (133), strolling through campus "with a clutch of new books and current magazines in the crook of his left arm" (131) his very person bespoke an education in itself.[20]

At the beginning of the 1970s it was both poignant and provocative that Murray chose to focus upon his student days at Tuskegee. Unlike Ellison, whose memories of Tuskegee were still colored by the bitter humiliations of segregation when he began composing his novel about a young black man's struggle to make himself felt in the world, Murray was writing from the vantage of ripe middle age—his mid-fifties—and also in the aftermath of the civil rights movement. It is significant that he recalls what Tuskegee was *before* the dismantling of Jim Crow in the South. He looks back to a time when only black teachers taught at Tuskegee—a policy, incidentally, that Booker T. himself began. From this perspective, Murray can see that the official end of segregation may have brought white teachers to Tuskegee, but integration by itself is hardly the end of racism. In 1971, the campus bookstore—and clearly, Murray fears, the new curriculum—at his alma mater abounds in reading that features, in Murray's famous formulation, *"the folklore of white supremacy and the filthlore of black pathology!"* (*South* 134). In *South to a Very Old Place*, Murray takes pains to underscore what historically black schools could—and did—offer despite Jim Crow.

The Tuskegee chapter also closes with a reference to an inscription, this one by Ellison to Sprague, whom he calls "[a] dedicated Dreamer in a land most strange" (*South* 134). That most strange land of the all-black college is the place that enabled Murray to see that his own little "briarpatch" was as big as the world. *South to a Very Old Place* was not intended to be a journalistic essay on the post–civil rights South; as Murray explained, "I decided . . . I would write a book about coming to terms with yourself, with myself upon the earth, as it were, in dealing with how I came to have the outlook and the sensibility I have. . . . in *South to a Very Old Place* I tried to make a poem, a novel, a drama—a literary statement—about being a Southerner" (406). Murray's account of going back "home" to the South, to "triangulation points" like Tuskegee, deftly evokes nineteenth- and twentieth-century debates on black identity, southern history and politics, modernism and myth, and the role of the artist, all the while paying homage to what is "very old"—classic in the truest meaning of that word. It is Murray's particular genius to show how "classic" applies to tales told by bootleggers and blues singers just as much as it does to blue-ribbon anthologies, for, as he reminds us in his elegant epilogue, art is an old, old story about promise and fulfillment, about what we have come from—and through—and it is owing to the self-discipline and the commitment of the storyteller that we are able to take the true measure of any place, any life. And such is the power of art, he suggests, that even at its most unassuming, say the "good-time music" of down-home folks, it rivals Creation, sounding "like rhapodized thunder and syncopated lightning" (*South* 230).

Notes

1. In an insightful discussion of *South to a Very Old Place,* Carolyn M. Jones argues that the book is more than the author's own "Odyssean" homecoming: "it is beyond that, an interrogation of American culture as 'home' for black Americans" (60).

2. Arnold Rampersad in his recent biography paints a picture of Ellison's acute distress over his lack of money; unable to make enough working on campus and playing in the band or to count on enough support from home, he felt exploited and vulnerable, and when the State of Oklahoma finally provided its promised scholarship, Ellison used the funds instead to go to New York City (52–80).

3. Although Ellison never completed his undergraduate degree, instead dropping out of Tuskegee Institute, Tuskegee nevertheless awarded him an honorary doctorate

in 1963, and in 1988 the school awarded him a medal, recognizing him as its "most distinguished living alumnus" (Rampersad 396–97, 551). Posthumously, Tuskegee University established the annual "Ellison Lecture" in 1996 in his honor.

4. According to Rampersad, Ellison later told a close friend that he "was hounded out of college by a homosexual dean of men," whom his biographer identifies as Alvin Neely (61). Rampersad claims that Ellison felt degraded by his contact with Neely, who may have used his position to make advances to Ellison; the biographer speculates that Ellison's loathing for Neely may have also fed into his anger at William L. Dawson, notable composer and teacher, whose inaccessibility frustrated Ellison (63). It seems reasonable to conclude that Ellison's Bledsoe is an imaginative composite of his feelings about male mentors and administrative staff at Tuskegee rather than a portrait of the school's president at the time, Robert Russa Moton. Indeed, the Motons seemed to have liked Ellison especially; his circle of friends at Tuskegee included the president's son, Robert Jr., as Rampersad notes (56) and is also confirmed by my interview of Louis A. ("Mike") Rabb.

5. Making it clear there is no one-to-one correspondence between the novel and his experiences at Tuskegee, Ellison wrote Murray on April 9, 1953: "[H]e [Chauncey Eskridge] tells me that the new chaplain at Tuskegee tells him that the people there are making a game of trying to guess who I was talking about. You should set up a class of adult education down there, man, 'cause some of those cats sound too simple for pity" (*Trading Twelves* 44).

6. The full quotation of the letter, dated June 6, 1952, from Murray to Ellison reporting on Tuskegee's reaction reads: "[P]eople are reading the hell out of *Invisible* around here. The library has a waiting list of about 90 at all times and there are quite a number of private copies being passed around. The *Time* notice certainly is responsible for all that. Everybody very very impressed; you may become Tuskegee's Frank Yerby., no? I don't think you're really going to become persona non grata after all, although there are some who claim to remember when it all happened, and MOTON kicked you out."

7. The correspondence between Murray and Ellison makes clear it was no easy task to arrange for Ellison's visit—not only was Ellison worried about being remunerated properly, he was also concerned about the travel arrangements, since he avoided train travel because of the Jim Crow cars. Murray, acting as a go-between for Ellison, who admitted that he was inclined to be "oversensitive" (*Trading Twelves* 69), and an administration dedicated to cutting costs, assured him that Julius Flood, director of the entertainment course, "understands about the money part" (65). Ellison alludes

to asking "Lieut. Murray" to intercede in the arrangements so that there would be no confusion about his fee or his preference for air over train travel, adding, "I am naturally very much in favor of helping the Entertainment Course stretch its budget. As a former student I realize how important the course is to the intellectual horizon of the student body" (71).

8. On October 22, 1955, Ellison wrote Murray that though he had received "a letter from Foster requesting ideas of what [the] program of Tuskegee should be, I haven't yet written that self-liquidation is the trick" (*Trading Twelves* 99). See also his letter of August 9, 1954, in which he expressed disappointment in the new president of Tuskegee, labeling what Murray sent him as an example of Foster's thinking as "lame as the outpourings of any mushmouth who has convinced himself that his uncletomism is wisdom" (79).

9. For example, reporting on his "disappointing" visit to Howard University in a letter of April 12, 1954, Ellison criticized the faculty, singling out John Hope Franklin as the "only real scholar" and Margaret Butcher for her teaching, but declaring that the "rest seem naked before the blast of reality. Can you imagine me standing up before a group of so-called leading Negro so-called scholars and saying that they had failed to define 'Negro' except in blood terms, and have no one open his mouth? Maybe it's because they're afraid. The government has cut their funds again and there's talk of doing away with the school if integration comes and there they sit, the mask of illusion slipping down" (*Trading Twelves* 74–75).

10. See, for example, Murray's letter to Ellison criticizing then president Frederick D. "Pat" Patterson's trip to Europe and Africa, or his letter to Ellison complaining that the new administration of Luther Foster "ain't showed me much but negative so far" (*Trading Twelves* 15, 72). At another point in their correspondence, when it appears the trustees will make a disastrous choice for the next president, Murray goes so far as to tell Ellison that there "was many a cat around here with the Bledsoe Blues last week" (47).

11. Paul Devlin sees that the point of Murray's "semi-autobiographical novels" *is* the hero's self-actualization—but self-development in the tradition of Stendhal rather than of Horatio Alger: "Scooter succeeds not by making a lot of money or advancing a political program or telling the white man that he feels something is amiss, but by becoming comfortable with his own consciousness" ("Albert Murray at Ninety" 259).

12. Murray's version, perhaps because of his wife Mozelle's having grown up in Macon County, is closer to how Tuskegee Institute was actually founded. There was already a vibrant black community in Tuskegee that used its newly acquired political

power to petition the State of Alabama to provide the funds for a school for blacks at Tuskegee, and the Alabama state legislature signed the bill on February 12, 1881, establishing Tuskegee Normal School, later Tuskegee Institute (now Tuskegee University). Men and women like blacksmith Lewis Adams and his wife, Sallie Green Adams, who had been conducting informal classes in practical trades, knew they needed more qualified teachers, so Adams wrote to Hampton Institute, which resulted in the recently graduated Booker T. Washington's coming to Tuskegee. Adams became one of the school's original three commissioners, a position he held until his death in 1905; Washington, the school's first "principal," opened the school officially on July 4, 1881, and Olivia A. Davidson, who arrived that August, became the school's "assistant principal." However, both Murray's and Ellison's literary portrayals ignore women's role in establishing Tuskegee.

13. Counterstatement is a key concept in Murray's aesthetic that deserves more critical attention; in his interview with Charles Rowell, Murray makes it clear he sees his work as countering false images of the South and of being black in America; even the blues statement, he explains, is a kind of counterstatement: "[T]he musicians counter-state their problems; they counter-state the depression, despair, despondency, melancholia, and so forth. Blues music is a ritualistic counter-statement" (414).

14. This fictional monologue almost certainly refers to the real Macon County sheriff of the time, Edwin E. "Pat" Evans, known for his especially brutal treatment of blacks. In the novel, "Cat Rogers" ironically alludes to "Pat Evans" through the change of one letter in the first name and the clever play on Roy Rogers and Dale Evans in the substitution of the last name. The monologue also recalls another scene of keen avuncular advice in *South to a Very Old Place*, where Murray is treated to "unka so-and-so's monologue" on Lyndon Johnson, a change for the better only because it's time there were "some mean old crackers on our side" (178).

15. Murray revised his Howard address into an essay, "Academic Lead Sheet," for his collection *From the Briarpatch File*.

16. See also Barbara Baker's discussion of the blues aesthetic in "Turning Impossibility into Possibility." Expounding upon Murray's ideas, she shows how it is that the American blues artist who, "by studying and practicing his craft, consuming all that went before him, aesthetically identifying beyond his own community" (74–75), makes artistic statements that encompass the best traits of American identity, transcending regional and ethnic particulars to signify universal truths. I am indebted to her for first introducing me to Albert Murray and for her insights into his far-reaching claims about the importance of the blues as *the* metaphor for American culture.

17. Murray remarked in an interview that Gerald Hamilton, who figures so largely in both *South to a Very Old Place* and *Train Whistle Guitar,* was "like a roommate, not an actual roommate" at Tuskegee (qtd. in Rowell, "'All-Purpose'" 403).

18. By making Trooper a real Buffalo Soldier—an original member of the legendary all-black cavalry unit that fought Indians in the West and later with Teddy Roosevelt's Rough Riders in the Spanish-American War—Murray invests him with extra glamour. The capes here refer to the wool capes that were a part of the school's uniform required for male students since the late nineteenth century, showing how Murray's imagination could clothe even Tuskegee's antiquated uniforms in romance.

19. See Lauren Walsh's essay in this volume, chapter 6. *In South to a Very Old Place,* Murray credits Sprague for sharing with him a range of then new work, especially Mann's "*Joseph* story," noting that his teacher found it natural that a lover of Mann's work should also be a lover of Ellington's (110). In *The Blue Devils of Nada* (1996), he recalls that he discovered Thomas Mann's *Joseph* novels "in a down-home"—that is, southern—library, most likely Tuskegee's (16). He may have read Mann after he'd graduated and became Sprague's colleague in the Tuskegee English department, or it may have been someone else, another friend, who suggested he read Mann. What seems crucial here is the poetic fact that Murray consistently associates Sprague with discovering his most important literary influences, both classic and contemporary.

20. In a letter of February 1, 1954, Ellison makes clear he thinks his old teacher needed to do more to influence education at Tuskegee in favor of the liberal arts: "Mort's either going to have to make his values felt or quit. He was fine for us, but that was damn near twenty years ago and it's *now* that his qualities should be most effective. It's all right to hate ignorance in important places and brown-nosing and whatever that shit is that Walker and Davis put down, but hell, if his values aren't worth teaching to Foster—and even getting his head whipped a bit to get them across—then he's playing himself cheap. Not to mention those kids to whom he owes a responsibility by birth, by sensibility, by intelligence and by position" (*Trading Twelves* 66). Murray agreed that Sprague left the field too much to others at Tuskegee: "[W]hen things take a turn toward the stupid his first reaction is to back the hell out. So there he is on the bench pouting, while out here on the field is Fumbling Foster losing from five to ten yards on every play" (72).

9

A Conversation with Albert Murray (1996)

DON NOBLE

Don Noble: The three of your books that I know the best, *Train Whistle Guitar, South to a Very Old Place, The Spyglass Tree:* I hear them described as either quasi-fictional or quasi-autobiographical. They seem to occupy a kind of gray area in between the novel and memoir, between fiction and nonfiction. How do you think of those books in terms of fiction or nonfiction?

Albert Murray: Fiction. Fiction is the ultimate. Fiction is an attempt to order chaos. You see, I now think in terms of particles and/or waves. That's the way we conceive of entropy, which is chaos, and the one thing we have or the only thing we can do about it is to use that endowment that we have that Joyce was talking about when he referred to the "ineluctable modality" of the visible, of the audible, of the conceptual. The concept is an attempt to bring some form. Without that, you just have chaos. So you've got to have some sense of form, whether it's up, down, outside, inside, round, square, or whatever. So for me, everything is fiction. It's a matter of finding an adequate metaphor that would be commensurate with the complexities and possibilities of our surroundings. That's something we simply conceive of; so the whole thing is fiction. When a person talks about documentation, it means documenting concepts. What serious fiction tries to do is to bring the deepest, the most comprehensive insights to bear upon it. That's one answer to that type of question.

DN: There's an expression—it may be African; it may be worldwide—It takes an entire village to raise one child. Is that the way it actually was in your childhood, the way you describe it in Scooter's childhood?

AM: I think of it in terms of survival through leadership, the preparation for the hero. The ultimate heroic action is epical action. So that makes it universal and all-inclusive. There's a phrase in one of my books, and they say, Is that boy the man? Is that boy the savior? Is that boy the one? Is he the one who is going to have that special talent to be the salvation or provide the security for the group? But you get that in all cultures. It's universal culture. I have no particular interest in African culture simply because there is no great literary tradition there. I'm concerned with writing, and so I'm a writer. I'm not a spokesman. I think of myself as being an all-purpose literary intellectual. But it has to do with the validity of the metaphors that are involved. There would be a pattern, but it's what we call the epical pattern. The survival of the whole group may depend on the people in the group, or the special people in the group who have special talents. And somebody recognizes that.

DN: Your picture of Tuskegee is of a place that is really an active literary center. Speak for a moment about the creative atmosphere at the Tuskegee that you knew. Was that a place that generated writers? That generated literature?

AM: No, it wasn't. No. We were the only ones there. We just happened to really like books. There were others there, too. Ellison was two classes ahead of me and Hamilton at Tuskegee. Then there was Mr. Sprague in the English department, and there were several other people. These teachers were very, very conscientious. There was not a big interest in literature. But the library. There was a librarian there named Walter Williams who was gone when I got there. But he had built a very good collection of books. When I got there and I saw the magazines in the periodical room, I was going through all these things every week, every month, like *Saturday Review of Literature,* the *New York Times Book Review,* the *Herald Tribune Book Review, Atlantic* and *Harper's* and the *North American Review*. There was the *Southern Review* and the *King Review*. I became involved in that. It was there because a librarian was very imaginative and very much involved with liberal arts.

DN: Your picture of Tuskegee Institute is much different from the picture painted by your friend Ralph Ellison in *Invisible Man*, which I think is much more negative. What is your response to Ellison's picture of Tuskegee? Do you find fault with it?

AM: No. That's his. That's the type of guy he was. That's the way he responded, and that was his story. This is where we have to watch. If we get tricked into sociology, then you think we're making a factual report or a historical document which you think is factual. We're making it up. It's your attitude that you are documenting. He had one type of response. Then he went through a Marxist-type thing. There's a lot of rejection in that. I operate on a concept which I derived from my old friend, my late friend, Joseph Campbell, and he probably got it from Heinrich Zimmer: antagonistic cooperation. My whole blues theory has to do with that. You confront the dragon or the menace, and you work out a way to deal with it. So if you look at it and you see it as an opportunity for creativity, then you write one way. If you look at it another way, you see it as an occasion for attack, protest, a lamentation. That brings us to the Kenneth Burke notion about literary strategy. He says that we can divide literature or literary statement into two categories. Certain kinds of literary statements belong in frames of acceptance. On the other hand, you have frames of rejection. In frames of rejection, you look at the context, and the literary strategy would add up to the plaint, the complaint, the protest, the lament, the elegy. These are completely legitimate literary statements, great masterpieces among them. That's a frame of rejection. Life should not be like this. On the other hand, you have the frame of acceptance. This is the way it is. What are my possibilities? What should I do? So if you see yourself in heroic terms, then you come up with the epic. The epic comes out of accepting the necessity for struggle. So you look upon the dragon as an evocation to heroic action. You can protest it. You could mount a revolution against it. You could do a number of things. Here you look for opportunities. You riff on it. This is how I come to the blues as my containing metaphor. It looks at the facts of life. The lyrics of the blues look at the facts of life, and then the music counterstates it because the blues is not a lament. It is a matter of getting rid of despondency, despair, discouragement, getting beyond death, disaster, and these things. The title of my book *Stomping the Blues* means just that. It's a purification ritual. At the bottom of all that you have a fertility ritual. In a blues function, at a Saturday night function, what do you have? You have a purification ritual. That is, you stomp away the blues, and at some point it becomes a fertility ritual. So you've got your basic patterns of human consciousness, the basis of all aesthetic expression, that in terms of which you survive. If you don't have continuity, if you don't end up at a fertility ritual, then that's the end of the species. So you stomp the blues away. You don't stomp the blues by turning your foot into a sledgehammer. You stomp the blues by snapping your fingers, tilting your head a little on the beat, and snapping on the after-beat. The more elegantly you move when you're dealing with the blues, the more effective you are. That's art.

DN: Where one person sees protest, you see catharsis.

AM: That's a point of view. That's what I'm saying. It's his point of view. If he sees it in that light, he sees it. If something goes wrong, I don't look for sin. I don't look for the devil. The dragon is not evil any more than an earthquake is evil or a tidal wave is evil. A monster is not evil. A snake is not evil. Any of these destructive things, alligators or what not, they are not evil. It's just the way life is. So what you have to do is develop that creativity, resilience, ability to swing, ability to riff that will enable you to live because you're not going to destroy them. It's entropy. That's the one thing that is not going to be destroyed. That's what the blues symbolize for me. They are going to be there the next day. If you get Louie Armstrong, or if you get Duke Ellington, or you get Dizzy Gillespie, Charlie Parker, Thelonius Monk, they're going to hold the blues at bay, just as Bach and Mozart and Beethoven did. And if they're very good, they'll hold them at bay time and time again. But the blues is going to be back the next day. When you wake up, they'll be all around your bed. So it's an ongoing battle. The pit hole for me in that is if you get into evil, you get into crime and punishment. You're running a big risk of self-righteousness. Do you want to kill somebody because you think they are guilty? You decided. You haven't checked it all out, just what you received. You say, "Well, yeah, guilty." I can't do that. Where I am in my conception of life, I know that destructive conduct has to be controlled in some way or other. But I'm beyond conventional conceptions of crime and punishment, good and evil, retribution, sin and redemption. It's about actually addressing individual problems of equilibrium, that is, of point of view, and giving the person a more adequate outlook on life, on the possibilities. Protest is not my mode. What good would it do you to protest? I just don't believe I was put on this earth, that the meaning of Albert Murray, that I was put on the earth to complain that some people don't like other people. I was put on the earth to find out how I could survive, and if somebody doesn't like me, either I could make them like me, or I could destroy them. Or I could keep them from hurting me. But just to protest that they don't like me seems to me pretty futile.

DN: Campbell taught us that dragons have to be dragons. Dragons have to behave like dragons. They partake of dragoness. But how do you persuade other people to stop complaining about the dragon and start adopting a heroic, epic attitude toward the dragon?

AM: You go back to the basic thing as to why you are a writer and you try to create an adequate image of human behavior and outlook and possibility that will be attractive. And they will prefer to see themselves in heroic terms rather than in terms of victimization. That's become very, very fashionable now. It's worse than it's ever been since I've been around. People have gotten into that. These categories, those frames have always existed. You've had plaints; you've had complaints. You've had all the different literary statements that come out of that particular frame of reference or that particular intellectual or emotional orientation. But on the other hand, you've also had those epics. Life is rough. You go over there and fight ten years, and then you've got ten years getting back home. You've got the Cyclops. You've got the Sirens. You've got Circe. You try to get back home. But you want to be able to measure up to that type of perseverance. That is what my emotional orientation leads me to.

DN: I know Hemingway is a great model for you and had a lot of influence on your writing and thinking. How did Hemingway—especially early Hemingway like *The Sun Also Rises* and the early stories—how did early Hemingway affect your worldview?

AM: My master's thesis was a comparative study of *The Wasteland* and *The Sun Also Rises*, symbols of sterility and fertility, the prose as an extension of the poem. As I continued to study it, what I realized was that Hemingway's approach was much more profound than T. S. Eliot's. As wide as Eliot's influence was, it was downright superficial once you accepted Hemingway's *The Sun Also Rises.* The big image, the quest, you come up on the wasteland which is ruled over by Fisher King, the implication there is that there was once a golden age, and through some type of transgression, some type of misfortune, they fell upon evil days and barrenness symbolized by the womb of the king who is sitting fishing. You've got all these possibilities of poetic symbols of fertility and continuity. That's good. But it implies that there was a golden age. Hemingway's confrontation was more like the blues. Life is a low-down dirty shame that shouldn't happen to anyone—futility. All is futile. I appropriated that in my interpretation of the blues. You come back to this, and it's not nihilism, and it's not despair, and it's not hedonism. It's a sober recognition that you have so many bars, and the more you can make them swing, the better. Then when you're gone, it doesn't matter.

DN: Let's change directions for a minute. You're a creative writer. You're used to working in your room alone. But you had the experience of writing Count Basie's autobiography, a long collaborative effort. How was that? How did you feel about it, and what did you learn from it?

AM: I really answered that in another essay which will be in *The Blue Devils of Nada* that's called "Comping for Count Basie." That means accompanying Count Basie. So I got the job as a result of writing *Stomping the Blues.* I was invited to work with Count Basie on his autobiography. He asked me, "Where do we start?" and I said, "Well, why don't we start like the Greek plays started, in the middle of things, maybe some crucial turning point in your life."

He said, "That sounds okay. Where do you think is a crucial turning point in my life?"

I said, "Everybody knows you as the apotheosis of Kansas City music, the stomp style, the Kansas City 4/4, velocity of celebration and all, walking bass. But I know you came up in Redbank, New Jersey, and coming up there, at that time, you started out as a stride piano player (which is eastern ragtime) and you took that and went into show business, a showbiz piano player traveling with a vaudeville troupe. I would think that the turning point in your life was when you decided to be a jazz musician rather that just a general musical entertainer." I said, "When did that happen?"

He said, "When I heard the Blue Devils out from Oklahoma City." That was a territory band.

I said, "Okay. That's good. We'll start there."

DN: Well, then, where was the crucial turning point in your life?

AM: I'm trying to discover that every time I write. It's hard for me to say exactly when I wanted to be a writer. I suppose that's what you mean. It was there when I left high school. I had a choice between a scholarship in physical education or one in liberal arts and education. When I got to Tuskegee I realized that physical education was not for me. When I'd see coaches come in, forty-five- or fifty-year-old coaches, they were beyond certain things. So somewhere in college with all the books and so forth I was just moving toward writing.

DN: You were in the United States Air Force for twenty years. What part does that have in the development of your intellectual and social life?

AM: Well, it does fit in. You make everything fit in. You have to make it fit in. If you're interested in enough things, then you say this is the time for this and this is the time for that. Great writers have been interested in the military and lived on military time, so I could identify. Hemingway was writing about things like that. That was fine for me. Faulkner was fabricating all kinds of stuff about his military experience which he didn't have. Tolstoy was very much involved with that. Stendhal. So it was in the literary examples.

DN: Let me tell you what prompts the question. You're known as a highly autobiographical writer. Here's a long stretch of your life that doesn't appear in your works. Now, you have a right, of course, like any creative artist, to choose your own metaphor. But the metaphor of war, the whole military metaphor, seems not to appear in your work and in a sense, it is glaringly present by its absence.

AM: Right, because my metaphor is the blues. It depends on how you use it. It's a matter of how you adjust to it and what you learn. But you turn it into your major image. You could do that. That's my territory. When I looked around, this is what it is. In *The Seven League Boots,* which is the third volume in the Scooter sequence, the type of mobility both social and geographical that I could have used in writing a story about the military, I could use writing about a jazz band.

This interview is from The University of Alabama, Center for Public Television *Bookmark* Interviews 1996.

10

Albert Murray's House of Blues (1997)

ROY HOFFMAN

> You can take the "A" train uptown from Forty-second Street in mid-town Manhattan and be there in less than ten minutes. There is a stop at Fifty-ninth Street. . . . But after that as often as not there are only six more express minutes to go. Then you are pulling into the IND station at 125th Street and St. Nicholas Avenue, and you are that many more miles north from Mobile, Alabama, but you are also, for better or worse, back among homefolks.
>
> —Albert Murray, *South to a Very Old Place*, 1971

New York

Natty in velour hat, tailored sports jacket, and knit tie, Albert Murray, son of Mobile, resident of Harlem, prepares for an outing in Manhattan. Although eighty now, the novelist and blues historian is, as always, on the go. His calendar is packed with readings at Yale, Vassar, and the Library of Congress. For his books, ranging from the analytical *The Omni-Americans* in 1970 to the fictional *The Seven League Boots* in 1995, the National Book Critics Circle celebrated him as a "national treasure." In May 1997, he is being inducted, along with Studs Terkel and select others, into the prestigious American Academy of Arts and Letters.

An American writer—"I am not African American," he says testily, "I am 100 percent American"—he shows a visitor the view from his eighth-floor apartment window: the edges of Central Park several blocks south, the spires of midtown Manhattan farther away.

To what Murray wearily calls the "conventional" mind, it may seem like a far piece from little Magazine Point, just outside downtown Mobile, to vast Harlem. But to Murray, a self-described "cosmopolitan," literal time and place offer few restrictions.

As he slides out two small, dim snapshots of his home on the Mobile River and the foster parents who reared him in the 1920s—the father, he points out, "looks like William Faulkner"—it's as though he is a boy again. He remembers the boats in the Port of Mobile, the hubbub on lower Government Street, the activity at Bienville Square, the streetcar that ran to Magazine Point.

Although most people, he admits, look at the literary section of a paper "like they're looking at the obituary page," and "pass a bookstore like they're walking by an undertaker's shop," he relished the literary page, and bookstores.

He also loved sports, recalling one World Series: "It was October 1927 and I was ten years old and I realized I could read the *Mobile Register* by myself and could figure out the box scores, the baseball lineups."

"I was in touch with a pretty cosmopolitan atmosphere," he says. "When I got to the third grade and had a geography book, I could see it. It wasn't like I was outside of the world. I was a part of the world."

Part of that world was the honky-tonks along the Mobile River. The music Murray heard there took hold in his imagination. His trilogy of novels set in Gasoline Point—a fictional Magazine Point—and his several nonfiction works, most notably *South to a Very Old Place,* are charged with musical rhythms. "My prose tries to be the literary equivalent of jazz. You do that by reading the greatest books where the language is being used. You can't do that unless you read Pound, unless you read Eliot, unless you read Mann, Hemingway, and Faulkner. That's what a musician would do."

Little wonder that Murray writes his works longhand, then dictates them to a computer operator, carefully tuning the sounds of his prose as he goes. In the apartment filled with books by world authors, photographs of two of Murray's heroes, Duke Ellington and Louis Armstrong, look sweetly on.

"Albert Murray is the greatest living Alabama writer," contends Pulitzer Prize–winning journalist Howell Raines, a fellow Alabamian who puts Murray's accomplishments ahead of even Harper Lee's. From his office as editor of the *New York Times* editorial page, Raines speaks with delight of Murray's *South to a Very Old Place,* recalling "its jazz inflections, the riffs on language, the invocation of the smell of fish frying in his boyhood home near Mobile. It's like you could play it on a trumpet."

"It's interesting, but not surprising," Raines adds, "that he writes about Gasoline Point, Alabama, from Harlem because a lot of southerners, particularly a lot of Alabamians, find they're closest to home, in a literary sense, when they're away."

> The official name of that place (which is perhaps even more of a location in time than an intersection on a map) was Gasoline Point, Alabama, because that was what your post office address was, and it was also the name on the L&N timetable and the road map. But once upon a time it was also the briarpatch, which is why my nickname was then Scooter, and is also why the chinaberry tree (that was ever as tall as any fairy tale beanstalk) was, among other things, my spyglass tree.
> —Albert Murray, *Train Whistle Guitar,* 1974

On Albert Murray's writing desk are his "reference books": mythology by Joseph Campbell; novels by Ernest Hemingway, William Faulkner, and Thomas Mann; world histories. Among the "references" are Mother Goose, "Uncle Remus," and a collection of fairy tales. Odd choices for sacred texts?

"If you can't write a fairy tale," he says with mild annoyance—a recurrent mood—"you can't write a novel. If it's got five hundred pages you're trying to make it something as meaningful to a sophisticated reader as a fairy tale. A fairy tale you never outgrow. Journalists' minds are so screwed up with sociology and economics that they don't see you're talking about fairy tales. They spread confusion."

Murray intends to make his literature accessible, and clear. In doing so he returns, time and again, to the geography of his youth, and to heroic characters like Dr. Benjamin Baker, his beloved teacher and principal at Mobile County Training School.

The neighborly street corners of his youth have long been bulldozed over to make way for paper mills. The Magazine Point he knew endures in his imagination. The voice of Scooter, the fictional narrator of his novels, keeps the place alive for others.

"When you deal with your consciousness it's got to have a real base, a point of departure. The meanings begin there. This is where literature turns into romance. The facts are nothing unless they become legend."

Does Murray feel any connection to another black southern writer of his generation, Richard Wright, author of *Black Boy* and *Native Son?* "I don't think a novelist should be telling the reader how to vote," he complains. "It feels better to me to be going somewhere with Hemingway than going somewhere with any number of other writers. Certainly going somewhere with Richard Wright, who's depressing to me. With Hemingway I would see the landscape; I would see the streams; I would see the sun; I would see the people; I would hear the language. That's what being alive means to me. That's the earth. You've got to go through race if the guy's talking about a bottle of wine?"

In fact, Murray bridles at being called "black," preferring the term "colored." In America, he argues, black and white are no longer accurate, nor are they valid as distinctions. He explored the nuances of race and identity in his first book, *The Omni-Americans.* "We don't know who's Negro and who's white," he says. "You don't know who's passing, and nobody cares. People no longer care if a guy's a black second baseman. They care if he's a good second baseman."

Twenty-five years after publication of *The Omni-Americans, Newsweek* is on the newsstands with an article titled "In Living Colors," proclaiming that "for this multiracial generation, hip isn't just black and white."

Murray just smiles and laughs wisely when being told he is ahead of his time. "People are born out of date," he explains. "A kid who was born yes-terday, does he know as much as you? A kid who's fifteen, does he know as much as you? Twenty? Thirty? He's still trying to catch up to all kinds of fun-damentals. I don't see why people can't get that straight. I've been there for almost eighty-one years. I haven't been anywhere else. All this stuff that was happening"—he chuckles—"I was here when it was happening! Take a guy who's never even heard of a 78 rpm record. To me, he's ignorant. He doesn't know that the CD came after the LP. See what I mean?"

> The blues as such are synonymous with low spirits. Blues music is not . . .
> Not only is its express purpose to make people feel good, which is to say in high spirits, but in the process of doing so it is actually expected to generate a disposition that is both elegantly playful and heroic in its nonchalance.
> —Albert Murray, *Stomping the Blues,* 1976

Albert Murray's wife of fifty-six years, Mozelle, kisses him on the cheek good-bye as time comes to tour the city with his visitor. Mozelle and Albert met as students at Tuskegee Institute. While at Tuskegee, Albert befriended an upperclassman from Oklahoma who also had a passion for books: Ralph El-lison, who would go on to author the great novel *Invisible Man.*

Long before he became a famous writer, though, Ellison was a camera buff. Photos taken by Ellison of an intense, young Albert and a fetching, youthful Mozelle fill one of the Murrays' many picture albums. In the albums are also affectionate photos of their daughter, Michele, who went on to be-come an Alvin Ailey dancer.

The names Mozelle and Michele appear in all of Murray's books on the dedication page.

In their early family life together, Albert, Mozelle, and Michele lived in Tus-kegee, California, Paris, and Morocco. The reason is simple: before becoming an author, Murray spent a career in the air force, retiring as a major in 1962, then moving his family to New York.

At fifty-four, an age when many men and women are biding their time until retirement, Murray started phase two of his life: he wrote *The Omni-*

Americans and launched his literary career. His literary sensibility "had been operating" all along. He had taught literature at Tuskegee and had completed a master's at New York University between periods.

The Omni-Americans was reviewed prominently not only in publications like *Time* and *Saturday Review,* but also in *Air Force* magazine. Willie Morris, then editor of *Harper's,* soon sent him on the journey back to Mobile that resulted in *South to a Very Old Place.*

Murray the exuberant New Yorker is now hurtling downtown in a taxi. Before back operations made it difficult to walk, he zipped around town from high culture to low, Lincoln Center to honky-tonks, a familiar presence in cafés and nightclubs.

He still takes on New York with zest, directing the driver to the Gotham Bar and Grill in Greenwich Village. He is right at home dining with his visitor where publishers and financiers, all around, deal-make and gossip.

Over lunch he explains how blues and jazz are an "American art form." He tells how his book *Stomping the Blues* and his passion for music helped launch "Jazz at Lincoln Center," one of Lincoln Center's constituent arts organizations. Trumpet genius Wynton Marsalis, its artistic director and a family friend of the Murrays, has helped jazz take its place in a world of classical music, opera, and ballet.

With Murray at the event were Michele and Michael James, Ellington's nephew. Michele reminisced about the time she was nine years old and was awakened in the middle of the night to meet a friend of her daddy's, Duke Ellington.

Ellington once wrote: "Albert Murray is a man whose learning did not interfere with understanding." He called him "the authority on soul from the days of old."

After lunch, Murray and his visitor head to Strand Bookstore. He sidles up to the employees' side door, knocks, and is welcomed like a long-lost celebrity. "Hey, Albert, where you been!"

Around him are "eight miles of books," as the store claims—towering stacks, crowded tables. Bibliophiles roam down endless aisles of used books, remaindered books, hard-to-find books.

One of the clerks hands him sparkling water and a bar of chocolate. "If they see me," Murray teases, "they say, 'We got to keep the old guy from drying up.'" He takes a bite of chocolate. "Keeps me kissable," he says, grinning.

Murray the philosopher and heady, contentious author is now Murray the bon vivant, the back-porch neighbor. People come over to him, shake his hand, ask him to sign a book. "He's like my dad," one woman says.

He swivels in a chair. "This might as well be Mobile."

"Albert's been coming here for ages," says Fred Bass, owner of this literary cornucopia. "The thing I like about Albert, he's interested in so many things. And he's got an up attitude."

A book clerk carts over a stack of tomes held aside for Murray: Montaigne, Pascal, Emerson, Hemingway. "These are like a reprimand," Murray says, shaking his head at so many books, so little time. "Like you should read Bury's *History of Greece*."

It is as though he is a boy again, thrilling to discover a book under the organ lid at home in Magazine Point, or walking into Mobile County Training School, wide-eyed at the intellectual exuberance of Benjamin Baker.

But he is in New York City, the crossroads of international letters, and another clerk brings him a copy of *South to a Very Old Place* to show him, a first edition priced at $90.

Murray turns his head in wonderment: two million books. Even Shakespeare would feel small in this ocean of words. "I can't figure out," Murray says, meditating on the endless worlds waiting to be explored, "why anybody would want to remain stupid with this stuff around."

In general, black Mobilians are considerably less polemical than New Yorkers on the subject of black heritage. But after all, black teachers in Mobile, like perhaps most others throughout most of the South, have been observing Negro History Week (the week in February that includes Lincoln's and Frederick Douglass's birthday) for decades.
—Albert Murray, *The Omni-Americans*, 1970

Among Albert Murray's many enduring friendships—with artist Romare Bearden, novelist Robert Penn "Red" Warren, composer Duke Ellington—was a lifelong connection to Ralph Ellison.

New York Times editorial writer Brent Staples, author of a memoir, *Parallel Time: Growing Up in Black and White,* wrote of Ellison: "With his friend and rival, the critic and novelist Albert Murray, he fought a lifelong battle against black separatism, arguing that blacks were not just deeply American but the most American people of all."

Back in his apartment, Murray lets a visitor catch a glimpse of a stack of typewritten letters to him from Ellison. He is working with the Ellison estate concerning publication of this correspondence. He does offer a postcard from Ellison typed to Murray. Dated May 14, 1951, it begins: "Dear Albert, You are herewith warned that I have dropped the shuck."

When his visitor asks what that means, Murray shakes his head. "Don't you know anything?" He smiles, translating: Ellison had finished the manuscript of *Invisible Man.*

After Ellison's monumental success with *Invisible Man,* though, he labored on another. Murray recounts the sad story of how that second novel in progress, an original, handwritten draft with no copy, burned up in a house fire. One of the few people who'd heard portions of it read aloud was Murray. Ellison turned to Murray to help him remember those sections. Ellison died in 1994, having never published the manuscript.

Murray takes out a treasure: a first edition *Invisible Man* inscribed by the author. He says a collector recently offered him $30,000 for the book. Murray declined. He says there is nothing he wants now that money could buy—except, maybe, a swimming pool. In Ralph Ellison's green pen, the inscription reads: "For Albert Murray, My friend who was schooled in the same briarpatch to confound the squares, bears, and fools thereabouts. Passion is his, and with it consciousness, but best of all self-acceptance and self-respect. In his my voice becomes richer for his love and knowledge of the experience we both share. Sincerely, Ralph Ellison. Tuskegee, 1954."

This piece, courtesy of the *Press-Register* © 1997 all rights reserved, was reprinted with permission in Hoffman's *Back Home: Journeys through Mobile,* U of Alabama P, 2001.

Michele Murray in *Masekela Langage*, Russia, 1971. Courtesy of Michele Murray.

11

An Interview with Michele Murray

LAUREN WALSH AND PAUL DEVLIN

Understanding Albert Murray's relationship to dance is crucial to understanding his work. It will help to explain his emphasis on the blues as dance music as well as shed light on why Scooter, the hero of his tetralogy, gives up music in order to (aside from becoming an academic) write the biography of the legendary tap dancer Royal Highness. Toward the end of *The Magic Keys* (2005), for instance, Murray has Royal Highness paraphrase a theory central to the work of the great musicologist and dance historian Curt Sachs (1891–1959). Royal Highness refers to "some old professor in Germany or Switzerland or somewhere over there" (i.e., Sachs) who told him his idea that "people started dancing before there was any music to dance to. So dance comes first and then music." He goes on to note that "them professional cats over there got theories about everything" (182). The books by Sachs that Murray relies upon most are *A World History of the Dance* (1937) and *Rhythm and Tempo: A Study in Music History* (1953).

Michael James frequently noted that Murray was one of the finest dancers on the jazz scene and that Murray's relationship to jazz was mediated through dance. In fact, Murray's interests in dance, as well as his knowledge of it, are essential to his literary output. It is in this context, but also in the biographical context (of both Michele and Albert's biography), that we interviewed Michele Murray, Albert and Mozelle's only child. Michele reached the pinnacle of the dance world as a star with the Alvin Ailey Company just when Ailey was taking the world (dance world and otherwise) by storm. Murray encouraged his daughter's luminous career both practically and theoretically. After her career as a dancer, she remained connected to dance and continues to be involved with Ailey, the New York Public Library for the Performing Arts Library at Lincoln Center, and the Schomburg Center for Research in Black Culture, in addition to spending a great amount of time devotedly caring for her parents.

In what follows, Michele talks to us about her background in dance, the role of music in her upbringing, and a childhood surrounded by books. Through Michele's voice, and aided by her incredible memory, one sees that Albert Murray's artistic interests do not play out only in the literary sphere but are integral to his family life and parenting as well.

Lauren Walsh: Perhaps you could start by talking about when you joined Alvin Ailey.

Paul Devlin: And then perhaps work backwards from there.

Michele Murray: I joined Alvin after I left Juilliard. I was only there for two years. I'd met Alvin in Boston. I knew about Alvin in California, when I was going to high school. When I came back to the East Coast after finishing high school in California, my dad was already here at Hanscom Air Force Base in Massachusetts and he was asking me, "Where would you like to go to school?"—for dance and so on. I already had mentors at Tuskegee who told me what to watch in film, musical comedy. I collected all of them; I got the tapes. The reason I chose Juilliard, as opposed to the Boston Conservatory, was because Gwen Mitchell went to Juilliard.

LW: Who was Gwen Mitchell?

MM: She was a friend of mine from Tuskegee. She lived across the circle from us. The circle was where the faculty lived. She went to Juilliard when Miles Davis went there. She didn't stay long.

PD: A lot of students don't stay the whole time, right? Like Wynton—didn't stay the whole time.

MM: That's right! And those seem to turn out to be the best people! [laughing] Anyway, I met Alvin up in Boston at this dance studio where Dad used to bring me on the weekends.

PD: So you and your dad got to know Ailey by taking you to the studio?

MM: Yeah, but not only that. When we were in L.A., there was a dance studio where Alvin, Carmen de Lavallade, and James Truitt used to rehearse. They had been written about in a dance magazine that Dad subscribed to for me. Alvin, Carmen, and James were all in that musical, *Carmen,* with Dorothy Dandridge, so I already knew who they were. After that, they got opportunities on Broadway and came east. They came to City Center with Roscoe Lee Browne and Geoffrey Holder. He was married to Carmen. Dad knew Maya Deren: she did the ceremony for them.[1]

PD: She did the marriage ceremony?

MM: Yes!

PD: I didn't realize that she was uh . . .

LW: Ordained!

[laughter]

MM: I'd seen her film at the Whitney.

PD: You mean *Divine Horsemen: The Living Gods of Haiti?*

MM: No, the one with Talley Beatty in it, *A Study in Choreography for Camera* . . . where he jumps . . . into a whole different place. Incredible. Maya was well read. She knew a lot about literature. Dad might've met her when I was four years old and he was going to NYU.

PD: I think he met her through Joseph Campbell.

MM: That's possible, because his wife was a dancer.[2]

PD: She was with Martha Graham.

MM: Exactly. I had such *wonder* about Martha Graham. When I came to Juilliard, they wanted us to take everything. In your second year you could pick what you wanted to major in, so I picked modern dance, Martha Graham technique. I'll never be sorry I did that! She was an amazing woman, she was just amazing. When I was in Juilliard, on break, I would go to the Graham School.

LW: How did Ailey get started?

MM: Robert Tracy was the archivist for Ailey. He came and interviewed me—and Dad—for this book he was doing on Ailey, from the beginning. When

Alvin started he was working with these Broadway people, black people on Broadway, and he said, you know, we need to get a dance company for all these black people who are so talented. The first performance was at the Ninety-second Street Y.

LW: So Tracy interviews both of you, and I understand why he interviews you, because you have a background in dance, but how much does your dad know about dance?

MM: He knows a lot about it! He talked to Maya Deren! He talked to Joseph Campbell's wife.

LW: So he was surrounded by all these people, seeing their performances.

MM: Right. So then, I joined Alvin, and Dad knew Alvin from Boston, because he took me to see him. Dad took me to see Carmen de Lavallade at the outdoor festivals. She is an amazing woman. She's not just a dancer but an actress. She taught up at Yale, and she worked with movie actors, you know, some of the top actors. So, I'm following all this at the time and it's sinking in: *This is what I want to do.* I went to Paris to work with her and Geoffrey Holder. I remember doing Asian-inspired dances. That's where I rejoined Alvin.

PD: How long were you in Paris?

MM: About a year and a half.

LW: So you left Alvin and then rejoined?

MM: Right, I rejoined in Paris. When Alvin was just beginning he didn't have steady work, so I was gigging. For example, I was doing nightclub work at Birdland, where Charlie Parker, Miles Davis, and Dizzy Gillespie had played. They were gone by the time I got there. When I was working there it was a famous R&B club. I was in this chorus line of dancers.

PD: I remember around the time James Brown died you mentioned seeing him . . .

MM: He came there, that's right. James Brown, Marvin Gaye, Wilson Pickett, Flip Wilson, all of them. The choreographer was a friend of ours. He was dancing with Donnie McKayle, who was one of my teachers at Juilliard. He was one of the first black dancers in the Martha Graham Company. Like I said, I had left Alvin.

PD: When you left Alvin, was this before you danced with the company in the USSR?

MM: Yes! This was before. I left and auditioned for the World's Fair, in Queens.

PD: Oh! So this is '64; the USSR tour was not until '71.

MM: That's right! I remember in Russia we did a dance by Alvin called *Masekela Langage,* inspired by Hugh Masekela.

LW: What kind of dances were you doing at the World's Fair?

MM: At the World's Fair I was in the Texas Pavilion. It was the largest stage ever made. I went there every other day by train. They had this moving stage. I had my own dressing room; it was unbelievable. We would do dance routines from the films of the thirties, forties, and fifties.

PD: You mean like *West Side Story?*

MM: No, we didn't quite get up to that. Now Jerome Robbins, he knew my friend Louis Johnson. Louis was one of the first black dancers in New York. He was the one who hired me to teach at Howard University, to work with actors who wanted to learn how to dance. The reason I wanted to do that is because that's what Martha Graham did. Katherine Dunham also. Marlon Brando learned from Katherine. A lot of white actors wanted to know how to dance. Katherine Dunham started out in Chicago. Her teacher wanted her to be the first black girl to be a ballerina. One of her teachers, I think it was at the University of Illinois, told her to check out anthropology. That's how she got into all these dances connected to so-called black people. African, Caribbean; she knew all about it. That's how she got her company together and came to New York and blew everybody's mind, because they never saw anything like it. That's how Balanchine got to know her. Turns out, she was choreographing for *Balanchine!*

LW: And you knew Katherine as well, didn't you? How did you and she meet?

MM: I think I met Katherine for the first time when I worked with Talley. Talley was one of her main dancers. He was in *Stormy Weather* with her.

PD: What were some of the dances you performed?

MM: Oh there were so, so many. With Alvin, *Icarus, Wade in the Water,* . . . *Metallics* by Paul Sanasardo.[3] He was a lovely man.

PD: Did you ever meet Balanchine?

MM: Once I was on the bus going downtown. I saw Arthur Mitchell and

I got off the bus and ran across the street to Lincoln Center—and Arthur introduced me to Balanchine! Of course, that blew my mind—I mean, who has ever been introduced to Balanchine? [laughter]

PD: I guess that's one of those things that could happen in New York at that time.

MM: Being in New York was incredible. I've always known about New York since I was four years old, living in Bedford-Stuyvesant when it was a nice place. We lived in Compton when it was a nice place. In Bedford-Stuy my mom put me in daycare and that was the first time that I saw snow!

LW: Since I had a totally different experience, I'm wondering what was it like for you growing up with a dad who was a writer. I had a businessman father who went to the office each day. I imagine you had a very different experience.

MM: I never knew myself without books around. Have you seen that picture?

PD: Do you mean the one where you're sitting on the floor in front of the wall of books? It's in *Trading Twelves.*

MM: That's right! Growing up he always gave me books as gifts.

LW: Did you like that? Because kids don't always want to get books.

MM: Oh, absolutely! And music, he gave me music. I remember my little record player.

LW: Was he giving you children's books . . . or Mann and Malraux? [laughter]

MM: Oh, yeah, children's, but a little higher: science books . . . and later on, dance books. In my room, I have all the books about dance that Dad gave me over the years.

PD: When you were growing up was there a lot of music in the house?

MM: Oh, yes! Definitely. Duke Ellington came to the house. He came to the campus. Dad was in charge of bringing people to Tuskegee and he brought Duke Ellington. He brought Sugar Ray Robinson.

PD: Wow!

LW: So, you never had to learn the music, you just grew up with it.

MM: Yeah!

PD: Your dad was a good swing dancer, right?

MM: He taught me how to dance!

LW: Was your mom a swing dancer also?

MM: Yeah! And then when we came to New York—I'm sure he told you about the Savoy.

PD: He took you to the Savoy?

MM: Yeah!

PD: Was it unusual for a kid to be taken to the Savoy?

MM: Oh, I don't remember. I was just so thrilled to be at the Savoy.

PD: While we're on the topic, let me ask you another question about Duke Ellington. What is the exact connection between your dad, Ailey, and Duke Ellington? Is it correct to say your dad put Ailey and Ellington in touch for what became *The River?*

MM: No, it's because I was in the Ailey company.

PD: So you're the connection . . .

MM: Exactly.

PD: Was your dad involved when Ailey and Ellington were working together?

MM: He came to where we were rehearsing, talked to everybody.

LW: Before we conclude, let's talk about another member of your dad's artistic circle. You've lived with two writers: of course your dad, and then actually you lived with Ralph and Fanny Ellison for a little while when you first attended Juilliard. Were your dad and Ralph similar in their work habits or very different? Was one, for instance, messy and one neat?

MM: They were different because, number one, Fanny was like a secretary. She had been working; she has her own history before she met him.

PD: She worked for Dr. Seagrave, the Burma surgeon.

MM: Right. Michael [James] told me, *You should read her obituary.* Incredible! You could see why Ralph was impressed. And she was an excellent cook. She knew Asian food.

LW: Fanny and your mom were good friends.

MM: Fanny and Ralph just *loved* my mom—I mean, everybody does, and did. Ralph took beautiful pictures of her.

LW: Michele, thanks for talking with us. You have an incredible memory and are so well versed in your field. I feel like you could talk about dance for hours and hours. Did it ever occur to you to write something?

MM: People have brought that up recently! Several friends have said, "You should try it." I just say, "Turn on the mic!"

LW: You and your dad are both the sort of speakers who, when taking questions, think very far ahead in giving your answers. You work through those questions and respond with so many ideas. It's a tremendous skill.

MM: Inherited! [laughter]

Notes

1. For more on Albert Murray's friendship with Maya Deren, see *Trading Twelves*, 24–25, 27, 80. Deren is listed in the index of the book under "Maya." Deren wrote a long and funny dozens-style inscription in Murray's copy of her book (later it became a film) *Divine Horsemen: The Living Gods of Haiti* (1953).

2. Campbell's wife was named Jean Erdman. Her 1962 dance *The Coach with the Six Insides* is based on James Joyce's *Finnegans Wake.* Albert Murray recalls attending the premier.

3. Anna Kisselgoff wrote in the *New York Times* (April 14, 1969): "[T]he lithe and dynamic Michele Murray enhanced Paul Sanasardo's 'Metallics.'"

The interviews were conducted on March 7 and June 5, 2008.

12

Conjugations and Reiterations

An Interview with Albert Murray (2003)

BARBARA A. BAKER

Barbara Baker: We're absolutely delighted to have you here in Alabama with us to receive the Distinguished Artist Award from the Alabama Council on the Arts. I hope you're happy about that. It's certainly well deserved. The poems that you just read from *Conjugations and Reiterations*—I think I told you on the phone that I think this book of poems is like the strawberry on top of the whipped cream on top of the exquisite sundae that your work taken in sum is to me and to many, many other people. I wonder if you would just talk for a minute about where you conceived the poems, when you conceived the poems, and why you decided to publish them when you did.

Albert Murray: I have been playing around with verse, since I play around with words in all of my books, and I don't want to draw a line between poetry and prose when I'm writing. I've always been interested in poetry since my freshman year when I discovered the Louis Untermeyer anthologies of modern American and modern British poetry when I took on this whole thing of Eliot, Pound, and e. e. cummings. It got me away from folk poetry and then led me into what was happening in those required courses. So I would jot down verses every now and then. But when I published an episode from what became *Train Whistle Guitar* I bought a fancy leather notebook, and I kept it, and I put things in it I wanted to write about. From time to time I found myself scribbling verse. My literary sensibility is informed by all of the formal courses that you take in American education, but contemporary literature is my specialty. I wanted to see what I could do with that and see how what I knew about the blues could be used as a basis for literature, for one big metaphor, and then you put all these images and so forth around, and how you can deal with the circumstance that that metaphor sets up. So I would keep notes on the side and every now and then I would play. Of course I would read poetry. By the time I started writing I was also under the influence of W. H. Auden, Spender, and Day-Lewis. They came after Pound and Eliot and cummings and people like that. Auden sounded so much like the brightest schoolboy you ever heard of. You could see through his poetry to the books he had read and that he had digested, and he could play with them, you see. So I did a little play on the side as I worked at the prose, at the fiction and at the nonfiction, which was aesthetic theory, most of the time, or cultural theory. So when I sold this first episode to *New World Writing* and I got about $300 for this at that time, I think, I put some of it in a hi-fi set since music was a basic, and I bought a very expensive leather-back notebook, not the full-size notebook but the next size. And I would scribble poetry, and I would work on things, and I would play around with how the words would go.

BB: Do you still have that notebook?

AM: I have it. It's a beat-up book, you know, and it dry-rotted. But I hate to throw it away. From time to time I would add something.

BB: It must have been a significant moment when you bought the notebook because I noticed that you mentioned in the letters to Ellison that you bought the notebook.

AM: That's the notebook. I forgot about that.

BB: And you were talking to him about the hi-fi set, too, at the same time.

AM: I began to think of writing poetry on the side, but meanwhile I was bootlegging all kinds of poetry in that other thing. Because *South to a Very Old Place,* when I read it, and people frequently ask me to read it, to me it's poetry. The swing is on another beat.

BB: As a matter of fact I wanted to ask you something about *South to a Very Old Place.* Last time that I saw you was when you came to Tuskegee to give the Ellison lecture and you read from the preface [of *Trading Twelves: The Selected Letters of Ralph Ellison and Albert Murray*]. We stood outside the door, I and Kathryn Dufer, who you remember, and we sold *South to a Very Old Place* to the audience. And a lot of your friends and cohorts and people who knew you came by and they picked up the book and they started thumbing through the book looking for their names. They were very amused looking for their names. But it struck me when I reread it last week that it's such a complex book. In a way, I think this question that I'm going to ask you would be like asking Joyce: "When you wrote *Finnegans Wake* who was the audience?" because how many people read all the way through *Finnegans Wake* and really understand it? So I was wondering who you thought would be reading *South to a Very Old Place?* When you were writing, who were you thinking of as the reader?

AM: When I write anything I'm aiming at the most sophisticated writer or reader that I can think of. I know the average person—they're not interested in that. They haven't read *The Wasteland* and all this stuff. I thought Robert Penn Warren would think it was a good book.

BB: His name's in it, too, isn't it?

AM: Yeah, he was involved. See, this is what happened. Willie Morris, who is a Mississippi boy, was the editor of *Harper's* magazine at that time, and they were doing a series on going home in America. We had become friends, and of course I was a friend of Ellison's, and he was a big friend of Ellison's, always talking about Ellison, but he spent a lot of time with me, much more time, because Ralph was busy trying to finish the unfinished book. So Willie and I were very close, and he got a lot [of information] about New York from me. My literary interests were more abstruse than his. So he sent me south to talk to some white intellectuals, newspapermen and so forth. And before going I talked to Robert Penn Warren at Yale, and C. Vann Woodward at Yale, and I make a whole metaphor out of the whole thing. The first metaphor is you can go south by going north from where I was at that point, Forty-second Street, and go uptown and you're going down-home. You see, you go back down to Forty-second Street to Grand Central Station and go up north, and you go down-home because Robert Penn Warren and Cleanth Brooks and these people are teaching at Yale. So the South is up there, but they are sophisticated southerners and literary southerners, which is in my context. They were the most impressive critics. They were the founders of New Criticism and all that stuff. That's who I write for. I mean, if I were a boxer I would be trying to get in Madison Square Garden or whatnot. If I were a ball player I would be thinking about being the one who took Alabama to the Rose Bowl. So it was always the highest or most sophisticated reader I could think of. These others have teachers like you to tell them what it was about.

BB: That's a good segue into my next question because I wanted to ask you something about your own career as a teacher. You say in *The Hero and the Blues* that good writing always instructs, and I always think of you as the consummate teacher. I know a lot of other people think of you as a teacher. Roberta [Maguire] thinks of you as a teacher, and other people. I wonder if you could reflect for a moment on your teaching, particularly when you taught at Tuskegee Institute—if you remember anything about what it was like to be in the classroom and to teach there, if you have any thoughts you would like to share with us.

AM: Well, it goes back to when I was a student, I suppose. I had a favorite teacher whose name was Morteza Drexel Sprague who did a lot of things that were not in the textbooks, and could follow interests that you had beyond the textbook. At that time I was so impressed with the library at Tuskegee. We had books that I had only read about because I couldn't get them. And then the big, sophisticated magazine for guys who thought they were really hip, really cosmopolitan, was *Esquire* magazine. And at that time Hemingway and F. Scott Fitzgerald, Dos Passos, a number of these people were writing for *Esquire* magazine. Hemmingway was being serialized in *Scribner's* magazine at that time. So, all these books were at the Hollis Burke Frissell Library. Some of them were in the racks. The first time I saw Faulkner it was at the circulation desk—*These Thirteen. Absalom, Absalom!* was on the board of new arrivals and all this. And my buddy, a guy named Gerald Hamilton, who was from Detroit—he had read everything: Byron, "Maid of Athens," we'd get down to the last line, and he would read it in Greek: "Zoë mou sas agapo." We were reading François Villon. He was reading Rostand's *Cyrano de Bergerac*.

He was the big challenge because he knew all these things; he went with all the magazines and so forth. So he was actually more my mentor than Mr. Sprague. Mr. Sprague had the academic authority, and he was open. He was from Hamilton College, which was a very fine college, and we knew that Alexander Woollcott, who was a radio commentator on the arts at that time, and who else but Ezra Pound himself had gone to Hamilton.

So, all this stuff was coming to me. I wanted to put it in the context of what it was about, where it came from, what type of person I was. And with Hamilton, he used to be one of the smartest guys in class. That was just a habit I got at Mobile County Training School, part of the dynamics of the talented tenth that the administration down there was working toward. But then I was open, you see, to the influence of Hamilton and then the authority of Mr. Sprague. So that's really what set my goals in terms of literary statement. I was interested primarily in writing plays when I came [to Tuskegee]. I was a good actor. I was a debater. And Mr. Baker insisted on elocution, thinking on your feet, debating. All these things are part of what you're supposed to do. It came together with the library, with the reading. By the time I finished, I knew that was the field I wanted, and I was so fascinated by the Louie Untermeyer anthologies of modern poetry. But it made sense, all of the required surveys of English literature and so forth, and even the Latin that I had and all these names. It just came together, and that's what I thought education was, that aspect of education.

BB: Sometimes when you go in the [Tuskegee University] library now you see the dustcover from a book by Albert Murray hanging on the board. That must be a good feeling to know that you made it. The students can go now [and see that].

AM: I wondered if ever something like that would happen.

BB: It does happen. As a matter of fact, I teach your stuff when I get the opportunity to. Usually if I'm teaching a freshman course I like to teach "Academic Lead Sheet" from *From the Briarpatch File,* and I usually assign the Tuskegee section from *South to a Very Old Place,* which is pretty challenging for freshmen. In an upper-level class *The Hero and the Blues* has got to be required. *The Hero and the Blues,* I think, is a definitive, complete statement about aesthetics.

AM: You know, people who overlook that miss something. They have to work out a number of things themselves and they might not make it. Whereas, at this point, I was really trying to pull together what my conception was, and then I finally hit upon what was going to be my metaphor, that is, my basic approach to what life is. It's the second law of thermodynamics, which adds up to the blues, the tendency of all phenomena to become random. In other words, ain't nothing nothing. So what makes it something? Metaphor, whether it's prose or whether it swings all the time like poetry. The idea is to make the prose swing like the poetry swings. It's a matter of articulating the blues, not the blues that gets confused with an art song, but a confrontation with the nothingness of the universe. In this last book I was talking about what I mean by the blues. Go to a planetarium and sit there and look at the planetarium, and then think of the people, the lies they've told and so forth. [Sings] "It don't mean a thing 'cause it ain't got that swing." Because swing is elegance, and elegance is what makes human life worth having. Some people confuse it, think it's sex, it's this, it's drink, it's that and whatnot, but I think the most legitimate one is sex [laughs] because it affirms, it's also about keeping the species going. Maybe they can be taught something. Do you see what I mean?

BB: I sure do.

AM: But you go back to all the things that you are taught. You see Mr. McCarmack teaching physics and so forth, I'm going to get the third law of thermodynamics and put it into literature. But there it was. I think of the second floor of the academic building, and I remember Mr. Fuller's math class and Mr. McCarmack's physics, and the chemistry department, all these things. And I said: This all comes together at some point. But when I was a mature enough intellectual, I could see their poetry, that is, the metaphor, is what really humanizes all the scientific data and gives it some type of purpose. So it's a story. If you don't get a metaphor for the story you might as well not. See, where there is no good story there's always a bad story, because there's going to be a story. So the whole idea of teaching English is to give them a good story, a fructifying story, an enriching story, an overreaching story that bespeaks continuity. This is worth doing, and the only thing that makes it worth doing is those moments when you can achieve at the height of aesthetic experience. That's where ecstasy comes in. Of course, at the juke joint at that time when someone really hits the groove and everybody really gets into the groove, they say, "Lord, am I born to die?" That means: Why shouldn't this happen over and over forever? My problem as an individual writer is how to take all these idiomatic folk-level things, all local things, and try to process them into literary statement that has universal appeal. Well, to do that you ought to know all of the best writers of your time and see what you could do that will approach them. So if you stay on that level you have a chance, I think. Even if you fail, you don't really fail. But that's why Faulkner's always saying you're not going to get it right, but it's worth trying.

BB: You're working on *The Magic Keys* right now, and I hope it's not a secret, but Scooter's going to go to graduate school, right?

AM: Oh, yeah, it's the next step that's implied in the one that precedes it, *The Seven League Boots.* The whole idea of traveling with the band is that he wants to supplement his graduate school study. I mean, he has this award, and so he gets this part-time job, all of which is in *The Seven League Boots.* Now that's playing with the metaphor, always playing with the metaphor. *Train Whistle Guitar* is the evocation to heroic action. You want to go somewhere, but you've got to have a purpose for going. So Scooter is boxing the compass. He knows the world. Then you go to *The Spyglass Tree.* It's a chinaberry tree. You raise yourself above the ordinary and you have a richer perspective on what the community is about. By the time he's doing that, he's in the third grade, he's discovered world geography. So he knows what the whole world's about. So now you take this kid and he walks into the Hollis Burke Frissell Library. There's all the stuff; there's more stuff than was in the third-grade geography book that he's never seen. So that novel, which is a college novel, is called *The Spyglass Tree,* that's the chinaberry tree, the tree of knowledge. So the spyglass tree takes him right back to when he didn't have binoculars, but he was something because he just walked in [Murray holds imaginary binoculars to his eyes]: north, north-northeast, northeast, east-northeast, east, east-southeast, south-southeast, south. That's imagination. I bring that forward because that metaphor can be expanded. So the campus is the spy-glass tree. You see more from there. But the real spyglass tree is the library. The whole campus is that, but the symbol of it for Scooter would be that. So when he comes out he knows more about where he's going. So he has a better stride. So what do we call a better stride? *Seven League Boots.* He goes back and forth to the castle. But the epigraph of *The Seven League Boots* says, "The castle hill was dark, shrouded in cloud and mist. Nor was there any sign that a castle was there." Isn't that something? See, if you read poetically, if you read poetry, then you get all these things, and you say, "Wow, yeah." So I get a four-hundred-and-some-page novel out of that. He's not going to the castle; there's no castle. It's a metaphor. In other words, you discover your-self. That's the great quest.

See, Auden, all of a sudden he would go back to all that academic stuff and it would be stuff he'd play with. Of course he was playing with Eliot, Pound, all of them just like that. He sounds so much like a guy who just came out of school. Do you know that poem that's at the end of *The Double Man?* One of the first ones of his that struck me was "September 1, 1939."

> I sit in one of the dives
> On Fifty-second Street
> Uncertain and unafraid
> As the clever hopes expire
> Of a low dishonest decade:
> Waves of anger and fear.

He talks about [how] the skyscrapers use their full height to proclaim their power of collective man. He plays around. That really knocked me out. But then he wrote the epilogue to *The Double Man;* only a college boy could do that with all that stuff from Eliot, Pound, and so forth. Here's a guy in the next generation: "returning each morning from a timeless world / the senses open upon a world of time. . . . After so many years the light is / Novel still and immensely ambitious." And then he goes on like that [as] only a guy who has taken all those courses and really knew what they meant [could]. [Murray quotes:]

> outside
>
> its chartered ocean of perception
>
> misshapen coastguards drunk with foreboding. . . .
>
> Now an Autumn cold comes on the water,
>
> as the lesser lives retire

all kinds of stuff like that. I said, oh boy, this is for me, but I want to build the American thing out of it. So that type of stuff is in the prose as much as it's in the fiction. It's a conception of literature that I've developed, and it's all my own. I'd read magazines and I would look for that. Who comes after Eliot and Pound? Auden, Spender, and Day-Lewis.

BB: So when do we get to see *The Magic Keys?*

AM: I have no idea. That's what we were dealing with. We dealt with *The Spyglass Tree,* where we get the long-range vision. And then *The Seven League Boots,* then you sneak in the castle, then the epigraph. Then you get *The Magic Keys.* Doesn't Jewel say something about that in the previous novel? She says, "And I do hope you find the magic keys. . . . some sharp, some flat, some natural." Those are keys, too. Some gold, some silver, some platinum, some an alloy that has not been discovered yet. So you play with a large number of the applications or dimensions in a literary statement. Like it says in the poem ["Epic Exits"], there are no magic keys, except everything is a magic key. You make the most of all these things, and then some of the other things that are involved with the image of the questing hero. So if you say magic keys, that'll mean you're still looking for the castle, or as Henry James would say, "the great good place," or as they said around the fireside, "Philamayork." So if you had a question on your test that said, "What does the author mean by Philamayork?" you'd say "the great good place," or the castle, or the achievement. But it's a very relative thing.

Recorded at Auburn University in Alabama, May 2003.

13

Murray's Mulatto America

MAURICE POGUE

The year 1970, in the aftermath of the American civil rights movement and in the midst of black nationalism, Albert Murray published his inaugural book, *The Omni-Americans.* No description of the events that influenced Murray to write *The Omni-Americans* is more explicit than his own words: "The essays, commentaries, and reviews out of which *The Omni-Americans* has been built, are all intended as counter-statements and restatements in the generic sense. . . . to race-oriented propagandists, whether white or black, the title of course makes no sense: they would have things be otherwise. But the United States is in actuality not a nation of black people and white people. It is a nation of *multicolored* people. There are white Americans so to speak and black Americans" (emphasis added). It is important to note that the subtitle on the cover of *The Omni-Americans* differs from that within the text itself. The subversive *Some Alternatives to the Folklore of White Supremacy* articulates Murray's polarizing counterstatement by framing race in terms of the difference between whiteness and blackness. Though Murray reiterates race as black-and-white, he also acknowledges the United States as a nation of multicolored people; he pulls no punches in his commentary:

But any fool can see that the white people are not really white, and that black people are not really black. They are all interrelated one way or another. Thus the title *The Omni-Americans* is, among other things, an attempt to restate the problem formulated by the Report of the National Advisory Commission on Civil Disorders by suggesting that the present domestic conflict and upheaval grows out of the fact that in spite of their common destiny and deeper interests, the people of the United States are being mislead by misinformation to insist on *exaggerating* their ethnic differences. The problem is not the existence of ethnic differences, as is so often assumed, but the intrusion of such differences into areas where they do not belong.[1] Ethnic differences are the very essence of cultural diversity and national creativity. (3)

Interesting here is Murray's gesture toward multiculturalism via diversity, a gesture that resists a full articulation because it focuses exclusively on blacks and whites. Contrary to what his words might suggest, Murray's ideas are not necessarily limited to this binary. After all, one must remember the times and circumstances in which he wrote. In a newly desegregated America—of course "with all deliberate speed"—people continued to reevaluate questions concerning the so-called fundamental differences between blacks and whites, including those of economic, educational, and social practices. Questions regarding differences that should have been addressed by equal opportunity were often answered with implications of empirical evidence that blacks remained dysfunctional in American society.

In *The Omni-Americans* Murray signals his approval of the Kerner Commission's conclusion of 1967, but Daniel Patrick Moynihan's infamous *The Negro Family: The Case for National Action,* known as the Moynihan Report, received no more mercy from Murray in 1970 than it does today from contemporary intellectuals. Murray's first book still stands as a seminal text in many contemporary discussions of racial issues because, like Du Bois before him, he predicted that race in the United States would be the most pressing issue in the twentieth century and beyond.

Murray's *The Omni-Americans* boldly subverts polemics of racial authenticity through the recuperation of the trope of the mulatto in an American idiomatic identity. According to Murray, "American culture, even in its most rigidly segregated precincts, is patiently and irrevocably composite.[2] It is, re-gardless of all the hysterical protestations of those who would have it other-wise, incontestably mulatto" (*Omni-Americans* 22).

Understandably, some may have an aversion to the term *mulatto*. After all, its etymology is rooted in white supremacist ideology with an intended impact on racial identity—namely, maintaining the purity of the (white) race and of (white) women by reifying interracial taboos.[3] The term also appears to reify race as a black-and-white affair, pejoratively signifying the union of the two. However, I believe that by using *mulatto* unabashedly, well aware of its immediate and historical circumstantial weight, Murray attempts to re-invigorate and recover the term from its original insinuations and thus make identity politics in the United States *idiomatic*—that is to say, he attempts to affirm how our identity as a people is inextricably bound up with our unique history, both in how we think about race and also in how we orient ourselves in this conversation.

In an interview, Louis Edwards asks Murray to elaborate on how *The Omni-Americans* came about within the political and literary climates of its time. Murray responds: "[*The Omni-Americans*] had to do with what I thought was basic—that is, the question of identity and who these people were and how they saw themselves in the actions that they were participating in . . . so I wanted to define what it meant to be an American, and how we fit into it, and I came up with the idea that we're *fundamental* to it—that you can't be an American unless you're part us, just as you can't be an American unless you're part them. I came up with the concept of a culture that as a context makes for, literally and figuratively speaking, a mulatto culture" (78).

When Edwards later suggests the idea of an "omni-America" as a micro-cosm of an "omni-humanity," Murray agrees: "Yes. Absolutely." He con-tinues: "We're looking for universality. We're looking for the common ground of man. And what you're doing when you separate the American from all of that, is you're talking about *idiomatic* identity . . . so what you enter into to make sense of things are patterns and variations in culture. What you find are variations we can call idiomatic—idiomatic variations. People do the same things, have the same basic human impulses, but they come out differently" (79). Murray is not necessarily opposed to difference, and in fact indicates that diversity is actually an essentially positive facet of Americanness. After all, America's most outstanding cultural uniqueness lies in the fusion of differences that make it an emblematic amalgam of culture. The problem arises when, as Murray indicates in the introduction to *The Omni-Americans,* black life is unjustifiably juxtaposed with the expectations of white "traditional" standards, especially given the fact that white people have not been subjected to the negative baggage that accompanies the legacy of slavery or the subsequent discrimination and segregation. In Murray's formulation, this legacy manifests itself in the folklore of white supremacy and a fakelore of black pathology that results in biased assumptions such as "Anything that black people do is abnormal. If it's good, it's still abnormal" (80). Conscious of the Moynihan Report as a particular source of muddled polemics that marginalize the black experience, Murray is dismissive of critical gazes from those who occupy positions of privilege with the ability to distort historic truths with empirical "facts" (also often recognized as *statistics*).

While the Moynihan Report, for example, situates black women as responsible for illegitimacy, the emasculation of the black man, and matriarchy, Murray says that a more accurate representation of the Negro family may be "a cycle of illegitimacy, matriarchy, and female victimization by gallivanting males who refuse to or cannot assume the conventional domestic responsibilities of husbands and fathers" (*Omni-Americans* 30), justifiably indicating these misogynist accusations. Moreover, Murray does not say that black men fail to be *men* or otherwise responsibly maintain the domain of their household through domination; instead, he charges those responsible for the abuse and neglect of their families. Nevertheless, in the context of the primary argument in Murray's project and this discussion, Robert Staples in *The Black Family* offers insights that Moynihan vindicators may have overlooked.

According to Staples, "recent evidence has indicated that the post-slavery Black family structure was essentially similar to that of White Americans of that period, 1865 to 1925. About 75 percent of all Black families were what [we] would call 'simple nuclear families'" (18). Staples goes on to imply that the Great Migration—practically a necessity considering the lack of work available to black men in the Jim Crow South—contributed greatly to what appeared to be the disintegration of the black family. Additionally, Staples finds that in 1992, 60 percent of black births were out of wedlock; concurrently, 22 percent of white births were out of wedlock, with 26 percent of white women heading families.

Dorothy Roberts finds that the birthrate for single young white mothers has doubled since 1980, while the rate for black women has risen only 7 percent, adding that "many Americans see unwed teen pregnancy as a black cultural trait that is infiltrating white America" (113). She cites Charles Murray (practically an antithesis to Albert Murray), who "observes that the white illegitimacy rate of 22 percent is dangerously close" to the "black pathology" precedent established by the Moynihan Report. Considering that Moynihan found 23.6 percent of out-of-wedlock black births problematic in 1965, Staples asks in 1999, "What [do these new findings] say about the White American family in 1992?" (19). Murray's earlier analysis, however, suggests a lens for Americans to view each other across racial boundaries in more amicable ways than those relating to danger and disease. For, as his pithy subtitle reminds us, the line between folklore and fakelore is slippery, and to implicate blacks as "pathological" is to implicate simultaneously white oppression as responsible for such pathology.

Omni-Blues

Beverly Bateman's interview "Albert Murray: Up Tempo or 'The Velocity of Celebration'" comments on *The Omni-Americans* as an appropriate counterstatement to both black separatism and the misguided ethics of social scientists at the time. In the interview Murray says, "It's the quality of the dialogue at a given moment. We can look at it as a jam session. When I wrote *The Omni-Americans,* I took a voice, literally the mask, of a piano player. And I said all these guys are blowing those solos and they've forgotten what the basic chords are. You know, what is the nature of humanity and experience? What is the nature of American experience? I want affirmation. The artist is concerned with the terms on which he will survive as a human being" (21). Perhaps the metaphor of the jamming blues musicians is applicable to contemporary racial debaters: are these soloists—the Moynihans, the Limbaughs, the O'Reilleys, and the Baisdens, Joyners, and Smileys—curious about what the "other" is playing? Put another way, are they—if we identify them as intellectuals—truly invested in the interests of the members of the marginalized sectors that they critique, or is Murray's contestation of their professional analysis accurate, in that they may have forgotten the real reasons for their conversations? The point of emphasis here is essentially the question of inclusiveness, and the idea of a *mulatto America* is contingent upon comprehensive American participation. In other words, America can only be "incontestably mulatto" if its multi*racial,* multi*cultural* inhabitants contribute to American art and aesthetics.

So, how do these two figures—the artist and the intellectual—truly participate in as well as represent an American "idiomatic" identity that is in keeping both with their own individuality and with the larger "mulatto" nation of which they are a part? Still within the bounds of his blues motif, Murray explains, "The function of the artist is to create images or the musical equivalents thereof that are commensurate with the complexities and the possibilities of life in our time. Whereas the intellectual or the so-called thinking person has a responsibility to formulate questions, issues, and definitions that adequately reflect the problems of the times and thus form a basis that adequate specialized technicians can build on" (*From the Briarpatch File* 19). Murray suggests that intellectuals who want to make aesthetic contributions must parallel artistic contributions. He conflates art and criticism in much the same way that his theories attempt to fuse identity and blues. This confluence is as fundamental to American idiomatic identity as it is to the blues. Thus the blues idiom statement is the ideal metaphor for idiomatic identity that is best represented as "mulatto America," a place of coalescence rather than polarization, and also a place where the American can reject either or both of those terms (*mulatto* or *American*) in his or her self-identification.

It may seem as though idiomatic identity aligns with the American "melting pot" trope. On the contrary, Murray deploys the blues idiom as an evolutionary gesture—he is interested in the blues as fine art rather than folk art. This differentiation between "folk" and "fine" indicates the sophistication of the banal. Above all, this trope suggests that *mulatto-ness* happens passively and amicably, while idiomatic identity distinguishes itself by acknowledging the chaos that must ensue before blacks and whites can begin concentrating on their similarities rather than their "differences." Murray calls this process of requisitioning chaos and the emergence of those who will quell it "antagonistic cooperation": "The writer who deals with the experience of oppression in terms of the dynamics of antagonistic cooperation works in a context which includes the whole range of human motivation and possibility. Not only does such a writer regard anti-black racism, for instance, as an American-born dragon which should be destroyed, but he also regards it as something which, no matter how devastatingly sinister, can and will be destroyed because its very existence generates both the necessity and the possibility of heroic deliverance. The firedrake is an evocation to the hero" (*Hero* 49). In short, antagonistic cooperation is an artistic feat that incites heroic action. The writer in Murray's anecdote, or an artist such as Murray himself, does more than just point the blaming finger at the dragon, the metaphorical representation of life as a struggle against inequality and injustice. She or he acknowledges the dragon as a necessary evil that provokes humanity into evolution, and I am not talking about Darwinism but rather the human capacity to write, to think, and even to love one's fellows. This is the essence of idiomatic identity—the simultaneous conquest over the basic struggles plaguing the human condition alongside the progression of the art that captures for all times this persistent struggle.

In *Blues Ideology and Afro-American Literature,* Houston A. Baker Jr. provides a functional definition of the blues idiom that is germane here. He says that the blues "translate[s] music of American junctures into practical scholarly benefits" (200), validating Murray's examples of the roles of intellectuals such as those he describes in *From the Briarpatch File.* One can think of the blues as a guideline for living life in often unfavorable circumstances, whereby both the problems and the people circumscribed by them endure, yet the endurance affects the souls and struggles of future generations. If Jim Crow racism terrorized blacks in the first three-fourths of the twentieth century, then glass ceilings and institutionalized forms of racism haunt the descendants of Jim Crow victims. The blues that were inflected by racism *then* maintains relevance *now* because the struggle remains—but, like its adversary, it too takes different forms. Considering the functionality of the blues idiom in this way complements Baker's personal objective and challenge to the reader: "Do what you can to decode what Albert Murray so astutely refers to as the American 'and also'" (202).

Of course, the blues idiom itself is incontestably American. What is of interest here, though, is a consideration of what components make up "the American" and the "and also" in Baker's challenge. The "and also," or those marginalized peoples who are un- or anti-American, appears to be a subtle reference to America's status as "incontestably mulatto," because, as I have argued, usage of *mulatto* infers a negative stigma that is placed upon the products of miscegenation, and in an expansion of racial exclusion it operates here secondarily as a reference to other nonwhite marginalized people. If whites interested in maintaining their racial dominance once used the term to underscore the blackness in a racially ambiguous person under the shadow of the one-drop rule, then how could the term *American* in Baker's referencing of Murray mean anything other than *white*, while the "and also" implies all others? If America is incontestably mulatto, then of course so are its inhabitants and cultural capital *also*, thus, they are idiomatic in how Americans are represented and represent themselves.

Idiomatic Identity

"Idiom" can be defined as the various forms of expression that are particular to a distinct nation, and those include art forms such as music, art, language, and writing. I propose that the process of producing expression is culture, and the product of this process is identity, generated idiomatically.[4] The production of culture is idiomatic in itself, and artists *inscribe* identity before intellectuals *ascribe* it.

The blues idiom is a universal statement (*Blue Devils* 12), and as Edwards observes, it also serves to illuminate an "omni-Americanness" that suggests an "omni-humanity," which can be applied to the whole of the human condition. As Murray says, "I don't know of a more valid, reliable, comprehensive, or *sophisticated* frame of reference for defining and recounting heroic action than is provided by the blues idiom, which I submit enables the narrator to deal with tragedy, comedy, melodrama, and farce simultaneously. . . . I hear the music counterstating whatever tale of woe (or worse) the lyrics might present for confrontation as part and parcel of the *human condition*" (14–15; emphasis added). Here Murray emphasizes the improvisation at the core of heroic action and suggests that it is both a heroic and a creative response to traumatic situations. The result of this heroic, creative improvisation is art, and art ultimately contributes to the production of culture. As Murray explains to Bateman, heroic scrapping with the proverbial dragon can take many cultural—as well as social and political—forms:

> [Bateman]: There's the dragon of political injustice.
> [Murray]: It's a challenge, it would seem to me. You know, I'm not primarily a political commentator. . . . The hero concept can be translated into anything. Someone has to confront the political circumstances and spell them out. I was concerned about that sort of thing in my first book, *The Omni-Americans*, because I saw misdefinitions and I knew that the policies for corrective action would be inadequate. Counterstatement does not have to be simplified into just protest, polemical protest.
>
> Murray's powerful counterstatement was an affirmative battlehymn sung against the misdirected shouts of black separatists and the inept moanings of social scientists. Ralph Ellison, among others, called the work "indispensable." (Bateman 20–21)

If the controversial affirmation of "race difference" is a source of chaos that a hero might encounter, triumphing over it creates the possibility of omni-American art and the subsequent idiomatic American identity that accompanies it. Furthermore, America's precondition to antagonistic racial categories has, in theory, provided the ideal staging ground for an amalgamation that is beyond racial categories.

Polemics of Multiculturalism

As I have stated, the term *mulatto* itself only constitutes the union between two: a black person and a white person. Of course, Murray's theoretical *mu-*

latto America presents a paradox in the face of a racially multifaceted one. But he recognizes that this is not his paradox alone:

> No one can deny that in the process many somewhat white immigrants who were so unjustly despised elsewhere not only discover a social, political, and economic value in white skin that they were never able to enjoy before but also become color-poisoned bigots. Indeed, an amazing number of such immigrants seem only too happy to have the people of the United States regard themselves as a nation of two races. (Only two!) Many who readily and rightly oppose such antagonistic categories as Gentile and Jew, gleefully seize upon such designations as the White People and the Black People. But even as they struggle and finagle to become all-white (by playing up their color similarities and playing down their cultural differences), they inevitably acquire basic American characteristics—which is to say, Omni-American. (*Omni-Americans* 21)

Murray refers to Irish, Italian, Jewish, and other people who have historically faced ethnic conflict after immigration to the United States in the middle and late nineteenth century. He goes further in insinuating that they *passed* into the collective term *white* in order to assume the privileges that they could not acquire at "home,"[5] particularly upward mobility, often at the cost of the denigration of "Black People." Though we often think of passing in terms of a mulatto transgressing the racial threshold, this type of passing deeply entrenches other people who might otherwise be classified as "minority" under the guise of whiteness.

It is undeniable that racial dynamics in the United States are rooted in the white/black binary. But what of people who identify as both in an era when the one-drop rule is obsolete, and neither whiteness nor blackness fits into the mulatto American paradigm? Returning to Murray's attempt to revamp the term *mulatto* in an idiomatic sense, his nuanced usage expands to incorporate those who feel or attempt to place themselves outside of the black/white binary, and even to amplify its effect upon those "who would think otherwise," such as non–Anglo-Saxon immigrants who wish to merge or pass for white, so that they too can *feel* their blackness. Remember that idiomatic identity is unifying through the blues idiom. As long as an American of any lineage creates art—which can be as simple as a personal story—then he or she too contributes to an idiomatic identity.

Praxis

Rhythm and blues is an appropriate contemporary venue to demonstrate Murray's conception of an American idiomatic identity. It can be said that the blues has been dominated nearly exclusively by black artists throughout its existence. The music derived from the folk blues, of course, has seen its fair share of white artists—perhaps most notably Elvis Presley. But within the past decade, the current flavor of blues-derived rhythm and blues has seen a resurgence, as several successful white artists have broken into the mainstream in this genre. Justin Timberlake, Robin Thicke, and Nelly Furtado are three artists who have appeared high on the Billboard Top R&B recently. Two of these artists are also known for their success in other genres: Timberlake was first known for his participation in the boy band 'N Sync, and Furtado is noted for her pop- and folk-sounding albums *Whoa, Nelly!* (2000) and *Folklore* (2003). Through Timberlake's *Justified* (2002) and *FutureSex/Love Sounds* (2006), Furtado's *Loose* (2006), and Thicke's critically acclaimed *The Evolution of Robin Thicke* (2005),[6] their work demonstrates that white artists can *legitimately* participate in the jam sessions that Murray talks about in "Albert Murray: Up Tempo or 'The Velocity of Celebration,'" particularly the "nature of humanity and [American] experience." They are not the "soloists" or so-called social commentators with whom Murray takes offense. Instead, they contribute their "idiomatic variations" by lyrically (and visually through music videos and live performances) conjuring the complexities of human life, including struggle and triumph, heartbreak and love.

Using the term *legitimate* or even *authentic* is certainly problematic, given the distinctions between fine and folk art that Murray draws. But even within the tropes of omni-Americanness and idiomatic identification, there are still territories that remain impassable to some without a "navigator." Conscious of my own skepticism toward BET, I point to the network because unlike a similar network, MTV, BET fails to feature genres of music (among other phenomena in popular culture) dominated by white artists, such as rock and alternative, while MTV is more inclusive, though MTV's discriminatory practices (with the exception of artists such as Prince and Michael Jackson up to the early 1990s and its simultaneously apologetic yet exploitive circulation of *Yo! MTV Raps* within the same time frame) is duly noted. Although BET primarily targets black audiences, it now appears that because Timberlake, Thicke, and Furtado invest their work in a predominantly black genre of music, their productions are "allowed" to appear on this so-called black network. Timberlake and Thicke have even won awards and performed for live audiences during BET and Soul Train awards shows (2003 and 2007, respectively).

Appearing on BET is by no means *the* definitive marker denoting omni-Americanness. However, these white artists are in many ways validated in the R&B genre through their collaboration with the likes of the Neptunes and Timbaland. Nonetheless, at this juncture one might consider the danger of accepting concepts of collective identities wholesale. Besides money, what influences MTV's decision to represent a musical cornucopia, while BET fails to do the same? If answers narrow down to the distinction between "white folks music" and "black folks music," as I often hear mostly older Americans say, then given Murray's meta-inclusive, omni-American statement about Americanness, there is a semireflexive resistance to it, since the R&B contributions of white artists are asterisked; blacks jovially recognize and approve of derivatives of *their* art, which is only considered derivative because of the appearance of those creating it. It is not coincidence that the genre neo-soul, or the transcendent expression of the experiences that Murray talks about in the blues idiom, also practically exclusive to black artists, has risen to the fore alongside the emergence of white R&B artists within the same time frame. It is as if blacks are willing to acknowledge that whites can jam, too, but not like blacks do. We have seen this before with the dialects and folktales of Joel Chandler Harris and Thomas Nelson Page juxtaposed with those of Paul Laurence Dunbar and Zora Neale Hurston;[7] put in this way, oddly, these dynamics represent a sort of subverted minstrel show wherein whites perform like blacks with black endorsement.

Yet this practical example of idiomatic identities or omni-Americanness expressed in a derivative of the blues that Murray and other contributors to American culture discuss is somewhat paradoxical given the centrality of universality in Murray's ideas. It is also instructive in how the efforts toward achieving universality in America become idiomatic as a result of the various ways in which Americans pursue sameness; moreover, in the example above, I find that idiomaticness itself suggests the type of difference that underscores separatism rather than universality.

Nevertheless, recapitulating one of Murray's primary purposes in writing *The Omni-Americans,* I reiterate his claim, "Ethnic differences are the very essence of cultural diversity and national creativity." From the beginning of his writing career, in *The Omni-Americans,* Murray established the permanence of his contributions to American literature in general, and perhaps his concern for the human condition and his acquiescence to an "omni-humanity" could serve as the initial impetus for an idiomatic identity that expands beyond American borders and nearly exclusively Western ideologies and epistemologies, even if we are aware of the persistent though conquerable subliminal influence of racialist sentiment.

Notes

1. President Lyndon B. Johnson chartered the report, chaired by Illinois governor Otto Kerner Jr. in 1967, to investigate the causes of race riots in cities such as Atlanta, San Francisco, Oakland, Chicago, and New York City. The Kerner Commission, as the report is called, suggests that the conflict's catalysts include poor living conditions and lack of job opportunities for blacks and concludes that separate is indeed unequal.

2. The subtitled section of the book is "E Pluribus Unum"—one out of many. It means that people are interwoven, and they represent what Constance Rourke calls a "composite" (Edwards 79).

3. The word is derived from the Portuguese adjective and noun *mulatto.* It is interesting to see how the fluidity of this term develops over time, juxtaposed with the creation of "race" and all of its stigmas during the transatlantic slave trade. In the sixteenth century, *mulatto* referred to "a person of mixed race" and, later, "young mule." The eighteenth century brought "dark color" (*Oxford English Dictionary*). Of course, the eighteenth-century reference brings us closer to why contemporary sentiments toward the word align with negativity. Miscegenation laws (active up until 1967) assumed that the sexual union between people of different races (specifically, white and black—even more specifically, a white woman and black man) resulted in genetically defective and psychologically unstable children (Foreman and Nance 547).

4. Even Murray himself says that identity is best defined in terms of culture. He continues: "[T]he culture of the nation over which the white Anglo-Saxon power elite exercises such exclusive political, economic, and social control is not all-white by any measurement ever devised" (*Omni-Americans* 22).

5. Considering slaves, exiles, and expatriates, especially through a postcolonial lens, I cannot help but think of questions concerning "home." Pertinent at the time of writing this essay is the question of "home" in a globalized world, sans the clichés. Where is "home" for the noncitizen, the black slave in nineteenth-century America, or the illegal immigrant in 2009?

6. Robin Thicke, unlike the other two artists, has always worked within some derivative of the blues genre.

7. I have Shelly Eversley's *The Real Negro: The Question of Authenticity in Twentieth-Century African American Literature* in mind when I make this statement.

Chinaberry tree in Alabama. Courtesy of Scott Thigpen.

14

Chinaberry Tree, Chinaberry Tree

BERT HITCHCOCK

To complement (or to counter) moonlight, mockingbirds, and magnolias—those most stereotypical, romantic emblems of the American South—I wish to propose another iconic trio. Also (if variously) alliterative and much more widely appropriate are (1) blinding, blistering summer sun; (2) crows; and (3) chinaberry trees.

Once so common a sight as to be practically emblematic of the region, chinaberry trees appear often in imaginative southern literature of the twentieth century. No writer has done more than Albert Murray to manifest this tree's historical import and symbolic value—its embodiment and ultimately unification of the lives of diverse races and social classes and its function as a privileged agent of inspiration. In observing simply, on one hand, that "there was a chinaberry tree in the front yard" and asserting, on the other, that "the chinaberry tree . . . was ever as tall as any fairy tale beanstalk" (*Train Whistle Guitar* 1, 3), Murray traverses a vital gamut of human experience, and especially African American human experience, in his native South.

What is this thing called chinaberry tree? Most students at my southern land-grant university today do not know.

Scientifically it is *Melia azedarach.* In English, besides chinaberry tree, it is also called the Persian lilac, paradise tree, white cedar, umbrella tree, bead tree, syringa, hoop tree, China tree, and pride of India (Schmutterer 605). Other objective data can be gleaned from common botanical reference sources. A member of the mahogany family, the chinaberry is a medium-sized deciduous shade tree growing especially rapidly in the first several years after seed germination; in four or five years it is likely to be twenty feet tall with an equal spread, and in maturity it will reach thirty to fifty feet high. It has dense, fernlike, dark green, three-compound pinnate leaves two to three feet long with numerous one-to-three-inch leaflets. In the spring, fragrant lavender-lilac flowers, each three-fourths of an inch across, appear in five-to-eight-inch panicle clusters at the ends of its branches. In the summer come the berries—smooth, eventually golden yellow, one-half to three-fourth inches in diameter. Inside each berry is a large pea-sized bony seed pit. In the autumn the leaves turn a bright yellow and fall early. The berries, which are very green and very hard at first but which become wrinkled and sticky as they ripen, remain in clusters on the bare tree into the winter. Chinaberry trees grow in a wide variety of situations in which other trees fail—including hot full sun, dry soil, and alkaline soil (Gilman and Watson; Dean 239; Crockett et al. 128, 153).

In addition to scientific description, social and cultural facts about the chinaberry tree are also readily referenced. The heartwood of the tree, though brittle, can be used for cabinetmaking and, because of its resistance to termites, is employed in some larger building purposes as well; its leaves have been utilized as an insecticide and as fish poison (Schmutterer 608). The chinaberries themselves are said to be poisonous to humans and other animals—pigs, for example. Birds, however, can and do eat the berries, though not without effect sometimes (Crockett et al. 128). "The fermented berries," it has been observed, "are attractive to the jays in springtime[,] giving them a wild 'tipsy' feeling" (Dean 129). Also reported, for humans, is that "during the American Civil War the [chinaberry] fruits were used as a source of alcohol (10% by weight obtainable)" (Schmutterer 608). Historically, the greatest human use of the chinaberry is indicated by the widely used label of "bead tree." The stones or pits of the berries are large fluted drupes that are easily pierced and dyed to make beads for necklaces and rosaries (Dean 129; Schmutterer 608; Crockett et al. 128). "In Persia, India, Ceylon, and Malaysia, where the chinaberry is considered to be holy, the berries are strung into garlands and draped over altars" (Crockett et al. 128). In the U.S. South, chinaberry necklaces and bracelets were commonly worn ornamentally by females young and old. For youthful southern males the chinaberry provided fine ammunition for homemade slingshots, peashooters, and popguns.

Evaluative judgment or personal opinions about the chinaberry tree are also to be found in reference sources. One "illustrated encyclopedia" opens its entry on *Melia azedarach* by calling it "[a] scourge over much of the South" (Dirr 229). And under "General Information" in a kind of question-and-answer format in a University of Florida Cooperative Extension Service publication there appears this memorable entry for the chinaberry: "*Outstanding tree: no*" (Gilman and Watson 3).

The hard historical fact is that the chinaberry tree has not fared too well in the United States. Horticulturally, its reputation has suffered a near-fatal decline.

"Originally a native of tropical Asia" (Schmutterer 606), the tree has "been cultivated in England since the sixteenth century" (Grant) and was introduced in a big way to southern colonial America in the eighteenth century. A French immigrant botanist and nurseryman, André Michaux (1746–1802), receives the most credit for this introduction; it was, says one horticulture historian, Michaux's "most noteworthy" such achievement despite the fact that Michaux was also responsible for bringing the azalea and crepe myrtle to America (Hedrick 193). China trees were planted at Mount Vernon by George Washington and at Monticello by Thomas Jefferson. In many southern communities (Charleston and Savannah, for example) it was planted in large numbers along city streets—the beautiful, shady, and ornamental public-avenue tree of discriminating civic choice (Grant).

Passionately opposed to the slavery that brought the plantations and flourishing port cities of the South into being, Harriet Beecher Stowe was positively passionate about the China tree. In chapter 32 of *Uncle Tom's Cabin* she makes it the supreme example of natural and moral beauty among terrible ugliness, a natural representative of the vitalizing world of spirit as opposed to the consumptive world of human materialism. When Uncle Tom arrives at Simon Legree's plantation, "[t]he wagon rolled up a weedy gravel walk, under a noble avenue of China-trees, whose graceful forms and ever-springing foliage seemed to be the only things that neglect could not daunt or alter,—like noble spirits, so deeply rooted in goodness, as to flourish and grow stronger amidst discouragement and decay" (369). Later, as Legree rides toward the slave quarters on "a superb moonlight night," "the shadows of the graceful China-trees lay minutely penciled on the turf below, and there was that transparent stillness in the air which it seems almost unholy to disturb" (419).

Ironically, the chinaberry tree's fall from horticultural grace began just about the time Stowe's best-selling novel appeared. Writing to the editor of the *Natchez Daily Courier* in October of 1854, Thomas Affleck was "among the first horticulturists to bash the ever-so-common Chinaberry with the written word: 'The perpetually recurring Pride of China tree, beautiful though it be, to the exclusion of the scores of magnificent trees, native and introduced, is, to say the least of it, in very bad taste. It is a filthy [yard] tree, too . . . when compared with many others'" (Grant).

Today it is hard to find any favorable professional word for the China tree. "In the United States the chinaberry has fallen into disrepute," it is said, "because its seedlings tend to spring up like weeds" (Crockett et al. 128). Indeed, it is now labeled a "weed tree" and negatively categorized as "invasive" (Gilman and Watson 3, 10). The berry itself, eventually very messy, is regarded as an especial problem. The tree's "fruit," notes one source, is "scary in their abundance" (Dirr 229), and more than one authority comments sympathetically but in resigned forlorn hope, "It would be nice to find a 'fruitless selection'" (Dirr 229; Gilman and Watson 4). Today, according to the Florida Cooperative Extension Service: "You will not find anyone recommending planting this tree" (Gilman and Watson 3).

In twentieth-century American literature it was a different story. If only by virtue of specific mention of the chinaberry, modern writers of and about the South followed the example of the author of *Uncle Tom's Cabin.* For some of them the tree is simply a firmly planted fixture in their realistic presentation of the region. For others it becomes more than just accurate backdrop or scenery prop. It grows to become an objective correlative, to blossom into a significant symbol.

In its literary fiction as in actual southern landscape in the earlier twentieth century, one is most likely to encounter a chinaberry tree around the humble houses of backcountry black families. Economically not well to do, members of these families often, however, "do well" in other respects. Here, for example, is how William Faulkner describes the home of admirable Parsham Hood, "Uncle Possum," in *The Reivers:* "It was a dog-trot house, paintless but quite sound and neat among locust and chinaberry trees, in a swept yard inside a fence which had all its palings too and a hinged gate that worked, with chickens in the dust and a cow and a pair of mules in the stable lot behind it, and two pretty good hounds . . . and an old man at the top of the gallery steps above them—an old man very dark in a white shirt and galluses and a planter's hat, with perfectly white moustaches and an imperial" (167).

A chinaberry tree also graces the yard of the home of Joe and Missie May in Zora Neale Hurston's "The Gilded Six-Bits," a short story that begins: "It was a Negro yard around a Negro house in a Negro settlement that looked to the payroll of the G. and G. Fertilizer works for its support. But there was something happy about the place" (985).

Eudora Welty's story "Livvie" concerns another poor rural black couple. In it the title character, the unhappy young wife of an old and ailing husband, is nostalgically, transportedly reminded of "Chinaberry flowers!" by the fragrance of some lipstick that a traveling cosmetic saleswoman is trying to sell her: "Her hand took the lipstick, and in an instant she was carried away in the air through the spring, and looking down with a half-drowsy smile from a purple cloud she saw from above a chinaberry tree, dark and smooth and neatly leaved, neat as a guinea hen in the dooryard, and there was her home that she had left. On one side of the tree was her mama holding up her heavy apron, and she could see it was loaded with ripe figs, and on the other side was her papa holding a fish-pole over the pond, and she could see it transparently, the little clear fishes swimming up to the brim" (234).

Typically, then, the literary chinaberry tree appears in the domestic domain of rural and small-town southern African Americans. In fact, the chinaberry is often seen as a denominator of and a demarcation for such locations or communities. In Madison Jones's *A Cry of Absence,* for example, oaks and pecans and boxwoods are associated with the old-plantation "big house," while in back there were "four log cabins across the field in a stand of chinaberry trees" (89). And it remained the same in the 1950s town setting of Jones's novel: "at the north edge . . . where the interstate would come through, . . . the run-down houses with their chinaberry trees and the little green oasis that was . . . [a] spring where the neighborhood Negroes still got their drinking water" (109).

Occasionally the tree occupies an intimate place in the lives of whites, but whites whose hardships and social status place them in the spiritual company of southern blacks. From west Alabama actuality via Truman Capote's childhood memories, and loaded with magical evocative possibility, an easily climbable, double-trunked China tree supports the centrally important tree house of Colin Fenwick and Dolly Talbo in *The Grass Harp.* As did no one else, says Capote, these two alienated, outsider characters were aware that this China-tree tree house was really "a ship," "that to sit up there was to sail along the cloudy coastline of every dream" (16).[1]

A merging of black and white racial worlds, with the chinaberry tree playing a central assimilative and humanizing role, is manifest in Jessie Fauset's 1931 novel *The Chinaberry Tree.* In her foreword, Fauset says that this work, subtitled *A Novel of American Life,* is "the story of Aunt Sal, Laurentine, Melissa, and the Chinaberry Tree" (ix). D. Kaye Campbell's synopsis of the work is as follows:

> *The Chinaberry Tree* contains three stories, of three successive generations of women who must each find a way to deal with the issues of race, gender, and class that have made them what they are. The first story, of the [biracial] love between Sarah Strange (Aunt Sal) and . . . Colonel [Halloway] is told in retrospect only. The second, of the effects of that love on their [illegitimate] daughter Laurentine, is the core of the novel. The third story follows Melissa, who is treated by Laurentine more as her daughter than as the younger cousin she is . . . [and who] very nearly meets disaster because she does not know the truth of her own illegitimacy.

The title tree, Campbell goes on, "is the physical and emotional focus of the house and grounds given to Sarah by Colonel [Halloway]. The Southern tree is out of place here in Red Brook, New Jersey; but it is the symbol and container of Sarah's one true love and becomes a haven for Laurentine and later for Melissa" (198).

The first paragraph of Fauset's novel, then, describes another African American woman's home, this time not in the rural South but directly reflecting a southern white lover's deep and genuine personal devotion: "[A]bout the trim dwelling lay miniature grounds extending for perhaps a tenth of an acre, beautifully laid out and beautifully kept. It was a lovely place sweet with velvet grass and three or four varieties of trees. In the spring there were crocuses and, later on, lilacs and peonies. In summer the place was lush with roses. Gladiolas flamed in the fall and prim, hard, self-reliant asters. There was a grape arbor and a vine with giant roots. . . . But what the three women loved most in that most lovely of places was the Chinaberry Tree" (1).

And here is the ending of Fauset's work: "But Laurentine and Melissa, so widely different, were thinking on none of these things. Caught up in an immense tide of feeling they were unable to focus their minds on home, children, their men. . . . Rather like spent swimmers, who had given up the hope of rescue and then suddenly met with it, they were sensing with all their being, the feel of the solid ground beneath their feet, the grateful monotony of the skies above their heads, . . . and everywhere about them the immanence of God. . . . The Chinaberry Tree became a Temple" (341; ellipses in the original).

With this kind of lyrical presence flowering in the fiction, it is not surprising to find the chinaberry tree as also, literally, the subject of poetry. Andrew Hudgins in "The Chinaberry Trees" writes from the perspective of a white boy who goes to the "colored" part of town for an experience that he is still striving to understand:

Under the flowering chinaberry,
we parked, and drifted on the tide
of hot scent ebbing toward a dream
we shied from. Mystified,

we gave ourselves to fragrance, eyes shut
to barrel fires and wicks
flickering in smoky shacks.
What was there to fix

our eyes on—purple flowers hidden
in the leaves and the leaves in darkness?
We didn't have to understand
what we had witnessed. Fragrance

numbed and suspended us among
then-the-past and then-
the-future, and then, which was the now
we levitated in.

I've never been so far transported,
as I was there, under trees
I wouldn't have on my green lawn.
....
Azalea, redbud, cherry grace
our lawns. (34–35)

To Turner Cassity (also white), in his poem "The Chinaberry Tree," it also clearly seems, at least, the Tree of Knowledge:

Its shape uncertain in the bloom that scrims it,
Purple, and itself a haze of gnats,
The tree that will be knowledge, or what seems it,
Beckons in the rising heat and waits.

Its shade will feather, and be serpent: there,
Instinct to take the field and meet the beast,
Are bound, already bargainers, a pair
On whom the subtleties will all be lost. (189)

The chinaberry holds such a place in James Applewhite's mind and re-membrance that he produced "Ode to the Chinaberry Tree." His poem's last section reads:

Chinaberry tree, our separate country,
We tenanted your green imagining.
From our flight of mind that aimed too
High, we arced in descents
You cushioned with your cotton swing.
Above the coal pile's kingdom of ants,
Your shadow and sun disguised the pure blue.
In your skin of shade, it was childhood and
morning. (37)

While many writers, then, have traveled chinaberry country, no one has tenanted its green imagining so consistently and fully as has Albert Murray. For him the flight of mind cannot aim too high: ascent, not descent, is what he emphasizes. The childhood and morning of his chinaberry tree get ex-tended into the whole of life, where the pure blue sky becomes a destination and, rather than a separate country, there is a blending of worlds. Only Zora Neale Hurston may rival him in associating the real-life chinaberry tree of childhood with seeing and seeking the far horizon. Hurston, however, cred-its her mother for the admonition "to 'jump at de sun,'" and the tree and the concept do not get so extended or so artfully transformed in her writings as they do in his.

In such essential ways does the chinaberry tree reflect the African Ameri-can experience—uprooted from its native place and brought from overseas to become first an object of value and then an outcast—that it is poetic justice—if no other kind—that this tree came to be so directly and physically a part of that experience in the Deep South. A tree that grew rapidly and could grow most anywhere, it became a high centerpiece of rustic home and gar-den landscaping; here it offered relief from a relentless sun and was a natu-ral family entertainment center, creating a shady place for storytelling and music-making, and providing raw material for jewelry as well as effective missiles for limited combat. Eminently climbable, it also offered a view of what lay beyond this home and its confined grounds. It was a reminder of the past and a fact of the present, but especially, as Jessie Fauset writes, "The Chinaberry Tree and the future were inextricably blended" (9).

For Murray, a chinaberry tree in the front yard of a three-room, shingled-top house in Magazine Point, aka Gasoline Point, Alabama, became the *spyglass tree.* There would be other, later physical heights he would give this designation to, but he is on his way out of actuality into metaphor from the beginning—it is "where[ever] you go to look out, to learn, to expand your consciousness of the world." This is what a writer does, says Murray: "to put together . . . a story about how a person's consciousness develops. That's what it's all about, and those various contexts are extensions of the original contexts. . . . As a writer, then, you try to find poetic images for the expansion of consciousness and the deepening and enrichment of insight. You have to have something concrete, because you deal with these big abstract questions in terms of idiomatic particulars (that is, concrete details) that you actually experience" ("All-Purpose" 169).

It is this particular tree that began it all and to which all subsequent experience in some way returns. "Gasoline Point, Alabama," asserts Murray, "would always be that original of all fixed geographical spots (and temporal locations as well) from which (properly instructed as to its functional and thus tentative absoluteness) you measure distances, determine directions, and define destinations, all of which are never any less metaphorical than actual. . . . The benchmarks of your original perception and conception of horizons and hence aspirations in terms of which everything else makes whatever sense it makes" are "irradicable" (*Magic Keys* 49).

In *The Seven League Boots* Murray writes:

The original out of doors benchmark and mercator projection school map triangulation point of all of which was the chinaberry spyglass tree in the front yard of that sawmill quarters shotgun house in Gasoline Point on the L & N Railroad outskirts of Mobile, Alabama, from which the North Pole was due north beyond the Chickasabogue horizon and Nashville, Tennessee, and Louisville, Kentucky, and Cincinnati, Ohio, and Chicago, Illinois. Which make Philamayork north by east up the Southern and Seaboard route to the Pennsylvania Railroad. So San Francisco, California, and Seattle, Washington, were north by west as the eagle flies, whereas Los Angeles, California, was west to the Pacific from New Orleans through the deserts and plains and across the mountains. Due south beyond Mobile Bay and the Gulf Coast was the old Spanish Main of the historical romances followed by the boy blue adventure stories about derring-do and the seven seas. (341–42)

"Scooter"/"Schoolboy" Murray would get to those actual cities—and journey beyond to important, more abstract destinations.

It is not too much to see the chinaberry tree as the botanical equivalent of Albert Murray's blues idiom. In the very nature of its existence—its cyclic seasonal life and linear cultural history—the chinaberry is the quintessential "adequate image" that provides the all-important and enduring "representative anecdote" (Murray, "Regional Particulars" 4). Both bloom and doom, gloom and glow are in its branches. There is ravishing fragrance and repulsive stink, captivating beauty and sickening rottenness. The hard and the squishy, the full and the bare, the poisonous and the playful, the glorious and the opprobrious—all are here.

How can anyone consider Albert Murray's writing without slipping into rhythm and rhyme? For some reason the old "Ladybug, ladybug, fly away home" nursery rhyme re-sounds in my head, but to make it apt for Murray it needs to say:

Chinaberry tree, chinaberry tree
Fly *me* home,
And fly me away from home.

And, also and also, to improvise on a song that Murray himself made use of:

Oh, omni-Americans,
Oh, don't you cry for me,
For I come from Alabama,
With a wondrous chinaberry tree.

Note

1. While Capote's extraordinary tree is located just inside the woods just outside of town, Eudora Welty's childhood memories of the chinaberry were as a sidewalk tree in the upper-end neighborhoods of her native Jackson, Mississippi. She uses it thus in her short story "A Curtain of Green," but she makes this botanical choice for a very artful reason, I think. In this story, Mrs. Larkin had become an alienated, psychologically unstable recluse as the result of an "incredible" accident, an occurrence that defied all reasonable explanation. The life of her young husband had been taken away right in front of their house as she gaily awaited him one sunny summer day, watching in shocked disbelief as he was crushed in his blue car by the fall, with "no warning," of "the enormous . . . fragrant chinaberry tree" (109). In multiple respects, from scientific fact to typicality to pleasant traditional associations, no other credible species of tree could so well have created such dramatic incredibility—the depth of human incomprehensibility and coping challenge that Welty's sensitive story demands.

15

Scooter Comes Home

Jay Lamar

Any which way you turn Albert Murray he is ours, that is, Alabama's. And we are his. He has helped us see and understand ourselves in ways we never saw or understood ourselves before. In his very act of naming the places, people, plants; the sounds, smells, tastes; the habits and expressions that originated here, he has revealed their capacity for meaning and imagination, their capacity for signifying and being signified on. That capacity may always have been there—surely it was—but it was Murray who called it out, applied his technique, and followed the Bossman's directions to play it with soul: "Talking about the rhythm and tempo of life as *the folks* came to know it and live it in the *down-home* U.S. of A." (*Magic Keys* 29). Murray has done nothing less than give us a world, enlarging and potentializing, for the whole multicolored lot of us.

For his epic task, the context is important. If you had cast the fortune of a Negro child born in the early part of the twentieth century in a tiny south Alabama town, not even the most audacious prognosticator might have had the vision to see through that thick hedge of time and place. Race, culture, location, timing—everything should conspire to grow up a thorny barrier behind which the boy, like Sleeping Beauty, was kept numbed, if not asleep.

But it turns out that prickly hedge exactly suits our hero, who says, "My name is also Jack the Rabbit because my home is in the briarpatch" (*Train* 4). Novelist, essayist, biographer, poet, and critic, Murray has bounded again and again into the places where more fearful folk hesitate to tread, urged on in his quest by a sense of destiny planted early by his favorite teacher, fictionalized as Miss Lexine Metcalf, who asked, "Who if not you? Who if not you, my splendid young man, who if not you?" (*Magic Keys* 20).

Just as Miss Metcalf asked her questions of Scooter and then sent him on his way to "go where you will go and find out what you will find out" Murray, too, headed out (*Magic Keys* 20). By the 1930s, he found himself at Alabama's renowned Tuskegee Institute (now Tuskegee University). He walked the same halls and sat in the same classrooms as his longtime friend and companion on the quest, Ralph Ellison, whose *Invisible Man* found its first and most perfect reader in Murray. Murray's most recent novel, *The Magic Keys,* and the decade of his correspondence with Ellison collected in *Trading Twelves* show two men vitally engaged in and by the world. Edison, Murray's fictional portrayal of Ellison, sums up their work aptly: "Man . . . I'm trying to take chitlins to the Waldorf. And I suspect you're also up to the same caper" (144). Together, these Tuskegee writers brought the black underpinnings of the southern sensibility to the literary world.

While at Tuskegee, Murray and Ellison both pursued what would be a life-long habit of reading widely and deeply—Murray consciously checking the library slips to note where the upperclassman Ellison had gone before. Murray learned that "[r]eading's the liberating device because it makes the world yours. . . . How can you segregate a guy who's coming to terms with the whole world?" Hemingway, Mann, Auden, Freud, Faulkner, Proust, Malraux, Burke, the *Iliad* and the *Odyssey*—for Murray, literature is basic equipment for living, because, he says, "without a sense of form, without a sense of purpose, middle, and end, what we have is insanity" (qtd. in Thometz).

With the publication of *The Omni-Americans,* Murray staked out a bramble-filled territory. In his first book, he asserted that race matters tremendously in America, but it is not a simple bi-tonal composition of black and white. In terms both more and less complex, Murray found both races partners complicit in creating the culture and atmosphere of the twentieth-century United

States. Murray has suggested that people have a choice in their disposition toward circumstances: one can be a race statistic, or one can use all the tools of art and intellect to enlarge the scope, and therefore the potential, of the larger scene.

Throughout his career, Murray has seen in music the potential for enlarging and understanding the world. Believing in the heroic capacity embodied in the blues, in his subsequent novels, he gives his autobiographical protagonist, Scooter, his "very first legendary hero in the flesh," guitar-playing Luzana Cholly, whose sporty limp is a "downright epical statement" (*Train* 15). The American icon Count Basie is the hero of *Good Morning Blues: Autobiography of Count Basie (as told to Albert Murray),* and perhaps it was the hundreds of hours Murray spent with the Count that helped him hone the uniquely American musical languages of jazz and blues, and create an authorial voice that captures "the rhythm and tempo of life as *the folks* came to know it and live it in the *down-home* U.S. of A." All of his cultural critiques, *Stomping the Blues, The Hero and the Blues, The Blue Devils of Nada,* and *From the Briarpatch File,* sing in Murray's own brand of Alabama-born blues language that relies on the technique, feeling, improvisation, and the pulse of the blues to inform, explore, and transcend. The "fully orchestrated blues statement" best serves his artistic paradigm of "acknowledging the fact that life is a low-down dirty shame and for improvising or riffing on the exigencies of the predicament." The beat Murray hears in the fully orchestrated blues provides him a means to turn "a low-down dirty shame" into affirmation, for as he says, it is "likely to be as affirmative as the ongoing human pulse itself" (*Blue Devils* 15). Murray as hero of the blues has found a means to make the down-home blues speak beyond itself to the very core of the human condition.

For our questing artist, everything depends on the "regional particulars," the "idiomatic details, the down-home conventions, the provincial customs and folkways" (*Blue Devils* 11). The people, landscapes, images, sounds, and sights of Alabama create the backdrop in the novels that draw extensively on Murray's own life—*South to a Very Old Place, Train Whistle Guitar, The Spyglass Tree, Seven League Boots,* and *The Magic Keys.* The "chinquapin thickets" and "blue poplar trails to Mobile County," the "thin gray, ghost-whispering mid-winter drizzle," Stagolee and outlaw Railroad Bill, the sound of freight trains headed to Meridian, the chinaberry tree and the briarpatch, the language of real people in a real place—these are his regional particulars. Murray writes, "Gasoline Point, Alabama, would always be that original of all geographical spots (and temporal locations as well) from which you measure distances, determine directions, and define destinations, all of which are never any less metaphorical than actual" (*Magic Keys* 49). The corner of Dauphin and Royal in Mobile, where "you used to stand . . . waiting for the trolley car, with Checker cabs and chauffer-driven Cadillacs and Packards and Pierce Arrows passing," with "so many different kinds of people and . . . many languages all around you because there were ships flying flags of all nations docked at the foot of Government Street . . . and newsboys chanting the headlines against the background of the empire state tallness of the Van Antwerp Building [and] you knew very well that where you stood was the crossroads of the world" (*South* 216–17).

Alabama is a point of departure and destination. It is home not only in the sense of a place with people, landmarks, and place-names, but also as "the very oldest place in the world . . . somewhere you are likely to find yourself remembering your way back to" no matter how many miles north by east from those "chinquapin thickets" and "old crepe myrtle blossoms" you might go (*South* 3). These are the "regional particulars" Murray stylizes into universal statements because, for him, beneath "the idiomatic surface of your old down-home stomping ground, with all of the ever-so-evocative local color you work so hard to get just right, is the common ground of mankind in general" (*Blue Devils* 12).

If circumstances create heroes, those that Alabama presented to our hero helped create Albert Murray. He says, "[H]ow I felt about the socioeconomic and political circumstances in the Alabama in which I grew up during the 1920s and the 1930s added up to me thinking of myself as having to be as the ever nimble and ever resourceful mythological Alabama jackrabbit in the no less actual than mythological Alabama briarpatch" (*From the Briarpatch File* 4). As he proceeded in his quest for the magic keys, "some golden, some silver, some platinum, and maybe some of some as yet undiscovered alloy" or maybe "some sharp, some flat, and some natural," he discovered that "we do not receive wisdom, we must discover it for ourselves, after a journey through the wilderness that no one else can make for us, that no one else can spare us, for our wisdom is the point of view from which we come at last to view the world" (*Magic Keys* 113, 20). Down-home U.S.A. is Murray's starting point, and ultimately, the center of his worldview. As he says, "All of this is nothing if not down-home stuff. . . . [I]t is precisely such southern 'roots' that will dispose and also condition my protagonist to function in terms of the rootlessness that is the basic predicament of all mankind in the contemporary world at large" (*Blue Devils* 17). His novels illustrate the writer's circumnavigation from Alabama to the farthest reaches of the imagination and back: "[W]ithin this many Alabama miles north by east from the outskirts of Mobile and the river and canebrakes and cypress swamp moss and the state docks and the bay and the Gulf Coast beyond the storybook blue and storm gray horizons of which were the old Spanish Main and also the Seven Seas and the seven storybook wonders of the ancient world" (*Magic Keys* 186).

Although they are informed by his down-home roots, his "stories are really about what it means to be human." They are concerned "with the life of human feeling" (Murray, "Regional Particulars" 3). Through his work he peels back the layers of individual history, character, and voice to reveal, in the form and intent of our own original music, an American mythology. Not a make-believe cartoon, but a mighty story of human existence and potential that finds a narrative, a code, and a hero in the blues.

As an Alabama writer he shares a sense of place with the other native sons and daughters who preceded and are contemporary with him. Even the most casual reader—if such exists for Murray—will see that the place forms a bass line to all his compositions. Like almost every serious Alabama writer, he takes its measure, grapples with its contradictions, loves its loveliness, and rages against its failures. What he also does is enlarge our understanding of it by showing it in its profound fullness and by helping us to see it in the context of the universal, bringing to literature a vernacular that is unique but undeniably genuine and, in its fundamental realness, as old as humankind itself.

Interestingly, "vernacular" comes from the Latin word *vernaculus,* which refers to a slave born in the master's house, or a "homeborn slave." Truth be told, Murray is the master of this house and we the ones born in it. Our sense of ourselves as part of a unique place, and the art and literature that express that, can never really be the same after him.

In short, we take our measure of the world of Jack the Rabbit, the Scoot-about man. We proceed in his spirit, following him as he goes on telling us what he tells us, including "the also and also of all of which," and we can join him in saying we are "still trying to keep it swinging, maestro. Still trying to keep as much of it together as we can, still trying to find out how much else we should be trying to get together" (*Magic Keys* 96–97).

Reminiscences and Appreciations

Albert Murray. Photograph by Carol Friedman.

16

Wynton Marsalis on Albert Murray (2001)

ROBERTA S. MAGUIRE

Roberta Maguire: How would you characterize your relationship with Albert Murray?

Wynton Marsalis: Back in 1982, when I met Albert Murray—he was in his mid-sixties and I was twenty—it was familiar. That's the best way to describe it. It was like talking to my grandfather, except Al knew about music. So right away he was more than a mentor, because he was like family, like my grandfather. And like my grandfather, he would be giving me information, except Al was helping me understand things: he helped me understand that jazz musicians had objectives. I didn't know that. Before meeting Al, I thought that if you could play, you just played. But from Al I learned the importance of knowing your whole tradition, so as a musician you wouldn't be one-dimensional; you'd be able to deal with a whole range of forms.

I remember when I first went to Al's apartment in Harlem. I went over with Stanley Crouch. I had on some sweatpants, and Stanley said, "Man, where are you going?" I said, "We're going to Murray's." Stanley said, "You aren't going to Murray's dressed like that. You better put some pants on. Do you know who Albert Murray is? You better act like you know." And then when we got to his apartment in Harlem, I saw all those books! Al just started talking and pulling some books off the shelves and turning the pages. I had never seen anything like it. That's not to say I didn't think scholarship was important before then, because I always made good grades; I liked to study and learn. But Al is somebody you can hardly believe exists. He knows so much.

Albert Murray gave me an education that no amount of money could buy. If you had $2 million and you said, "I'm going to pay for this education," you wouldn't have gotten what I got. He was willing to talk with me day and night. He'd suggest books for me to read, and I'd read them, then call him, maybe at 10:30, 11 o'clock at night. "You up?" I'd ask. "Yeah, man, I'm up," he'd say. "Come on over." I'd go over, we'd sit down, I'd pull out my notepad, and he'd start talking. We'd talk about interpretations of poems. Thomas Mann's *Joseph and His Brothers:* "A blessing is also a curse." Or *Doctor Faustus:* "Do you know of any emotion stronger than love? Yes, interest." The function of education. Or Harold Cruse's *The Crisis of the Negro Intellectual.* Or mythology: he had me read Heinrich Zimmer, Joseph Campbell, John Kouwenhoven's *Made in America* and *Beer Can by the Highway.* If I asked him a question over the phone, by the time I got to his apartment, he'd have five books laid out to help explain the answer.

But our relationship wasn't only about studying. It was more familiar, like family. We'd talk about so many things, all of it interconnected. I remember once we were talking about Picasso, and I was saying, "Man, you know I love Picasso." I had read John Richardson's biography of Picasso. "But what I can't figure out is why none of the people in his paintings are ever smiling." To me that took away from what he was doing. So you know how Al is. He started talking about smiling and what it means in terms of human emotions and the depth of emotion. I just told him that I like to see people smiling. That's the sort of quirky conversation we would always have. But even there, his genius would be undeniable.

He always has something to tell me that I need to know. And he's honest. I don't do anything serious unless I get his perspective on it. I didn't know if I wanted to go up to Lincoln Center because I had my own band. I was working. I was making good money. Going to Lincoln Center I knew would mean making much less money, having much less freedom to do what I wanted to do while dealing with a lot more people and having to work within the constraints of an institution—things I didn't necessarily want. This was a very serious decision for me. So I went to see Al. I sat down with him, and we talked for four or five hours about it. And he was just laying it out for me, what the meaning of an institution is, what you can do, how. He just laid out the whole thing that made me really understand what was happening because he put it in a context. That allowed me to make a decision the next day. He didn't tell me what to do. He gave me clear information. "You can do this or you can do that. This means this and this means that. And this came from this and that became that." He gave me historical references. He's so rich with that information.

When I started with Lincoln Center, there wasn't really anything to be on board with. It was just three concerts I was asked to do in the summer. But Al developed the intellectual foundation of what was to become Jazz at Lincoln Center. He said, you all should have four components: curatorial, archival, educational, and ceremonial. That foundation came from him.

But that doesn't mean he likes everything I do there. He treats me like family, he tells me stuff, and I listen to him. But I do what I have to do because I'm the one who has to do it. That's a point he also makes—that being in the ring is not like being in the corner. You need a corner man to tell you something, but you've got to be in the ring. He knows I need to do what I have to do. But he's extremely supportive of me. Extremely. And he has given me a lot of love.

I could talk about him all night. Albert Murray, I love him.

The above is excerpted from an interview with Wynton Marsalis conducted by Roberta S. Maguire on October 9, 2001, at Lawrence University in Appleton, Wisconsin. Mr. Marsalis and the Lincoln Center Jazz Orchestra played there as part of a forty-six-city "United in Swing" tour.

17

Albert Murray's Du Bois Medal Citation (2007)

HENRY LOUIS GATES JR.

I have known Albert Murray for thirty years now, and it is a tremendous honor to present him with the Du Bois Medal for his contributions to the arts, culture, and the life of the mind. He has been my friend, my teacher, and my model, and he is a scholar and a thinker who has contributed immeasurably to the African American arts (Wynton Marsalis, who is joyfully present today, is more than a protégé of Al's—he is a disciple). We present Albert Murray with the Du Bois Medal today to let him know that his life's work is not only valued, but also recognized as vital and central to our intellectual and artistic tradition.

To write this citation, I have been revisiting Al's major writings: *The Omni-Americans* (1970), *Stomping the Blues* (1976), his Count Basie autobiography (1985), *The Blue Devils of Nada* (1996), and his trilogy of autobiographical novels, published between 1974 and 1996. I was struck once again by the independence and ferocity of his voice. This is a man who, at the height of the Black Power/Black Arts movement, had the nerve to argue in *The Omni-Americans* that Black Art was a constitutive part of American culture, not separate from and outside of it at all, but indispensably and definitively American. This is a man who, like his friend and soul mate Ralph Ellison, extolled art and cultural creativity as nothing short of salvific for black people. (I nearly wrote "for the black community"—but that rings too sociological, and Albert Murray fought long and hard to strip black intellectualism from its sociological moorings and cast it squarely into the realm of art and aesthetics.)

This is a man who made the claim—galling to some and glorious to others—that "American" means "black" and not "white," as was, and still is, the prevailing cultural presumption on which our nation's artistic life is built. But, as he showed to such great effect in *Stomping the Blues* (and, in fact, to the greatest acclaim he achieved in his career), it is the improvisatory nature of the blues that underlies the American national character. He gave the name "vernacular imperative" to the black artist's drive to create. This "imperative" leads the black artist, in Murray's words, "to process (which is to say stylize) the raw native materials, experiences, and the idiomatic particulars of everyday life into aesthetic (which is to say elegant) statements of universal relevance and appeal."

Since Al wrote this, I have never been able to think in terms that are more descriptive or more apt. I have never honestly felt the need to.

Albert Murray came up from Magazine Point, Alabama, through the Tuskegee Institute and the United States Air Force, to New York, where he has presided over black cultural life for several decades. He spurred Ralph Ellison's thinking for decades (and sparred with him as well), and sharpened the "narrative" of Romare Bearden's gorgeous art. Today, Stanley Crouch and Wynton Marsalis still labor under his dictates, and I do, too.

It is my great honor to present the Du Bois Medal to Albert Murray, in recognition of his outstanding contributions to the arts, culture, and the life of the mind.

Originally given as a speech, June 3, 2007, at the presentation to Murray of the Du Bois Medal at Harvard University.

18

At the Bar and on the Avenue with My Pal Al Murray

SIDNEY OFFIT

Soon after I met Al Murray at a PEN reception, circa 1970, I signed on as friend and fan. We swapped books, ideas, and lessons: Al as discreet teacher and mentor, I the appreciative apostle.

In May 1972 Al agreed to the reprint of an excerpt from *South to a Very Old Place* in *Intellectual Digest,* a magazine I helped to launch and edit. "Albert Murray is at war with abstraction be it the jargon of the sociologist or the rhetoric of the race dialogue," we blazed as introduction to his lines. "The poetry and truth of the American experience is his quarry."

Selections from Isaac Bashevis Singer, Cyril Connolly, J. B. Priestly, Ralph Vaughan Williams, and even Herman Melville shared the contents page, but it was Al Murray's essay that inspired the most admiring responses.

Not long after, Al and I were among a select group of writers, musicians, artists, and other lunchtime party boys who gathered at a midtown social club for conversation, only conversation, never networking and no autographs. Among our revered tipplers, including Drew Middleton, Charley Collingwood, Ralph Ellison, Matt Clark, John Chancellor, and Charles Rembar, was John

Hammond, sometimes identified, but not only by Al, as "the man who discovered jazz."

It was John's conviction that our bar snacks, cheese crackers and salted peanuts, needed company. So, the self-anointed caterer hand carried a cup of dry-roasted peanuts that he discreetly offered to members of his choice. Al and I made the cut, but Al insisted upon the fair and square. It was Al's suggestion, offered in a gentle but commanding voice, that instantly persuaded our benefactor that the dry-roasteds would be more "democratically" distributed with the cup residing on the bar, available to all.

Al's intuitive grace and manners, qualities he sometimes referred to in others as "refinement," were also expressed in his assumption that you, his friend or student, knew as much as he did, so he leveraged an observation about literature, jazz, the visual arts with profound references to history and the classics.

From time to time after our bar call and late lunch, Al and I would amble up Fifth Avenue to talk ourselves out and see the sights. On one of those jaunts we encountered Anatole Broyard, my New School faculty colleague. I'd known Anatole since the early sixties when I began my run conducting writing workshops at the Village's adult education temple. We'd spoken frequently about approaches to the craft and Anatole's conspicuous talent for attracting muses of distinctive style and beauty. There was no question about who was the star when I spoke to Anatole Broyard until that moment on Fifth Avenue when Anatole encountered me in deep and animated conversation with Al Murray.

When Al assured Anatole that he and I routinely lunched together, Anatole was so impressed he called me that evening to find out what Al Murray and I talked about. Did our agenda include riffs about music? Jazz? Anatole's suspicion was on the mark. Although Al did talk to me about his friendships and impressions of Duke Ellington, Count Basie, and Wynton Marsalis, I had nothing to contribute to his enlightenment other than that my neighbor Siggy Shapiro had collected early blues and jazz recordings from a shop on Pennsylvania Avenue, Baltimore, Maryland, circa 1945.

I didn't confess to Anatole. I dared to suggest that "Al and I talk about everything. How could we not discuss jazz?" Anatole was sufficiently impressed, or suspicious enough, that he suggested we meet for lunch. I managed to avoid the date because I knew I was unable to live up to the high expectations due a friend of Al Murray, the Olympian critic and scholar who so well understood the soul and beat, beat, beat of our country.

19

My Beginnings with Albert

Louis A. "Mike" Rabb

Albert Murray was and is a valued friend of mine—one possessed of a delightful personality. During his days at Tuskegee he was knowledgeable on a wide range of topics and expressed comments on issues with confidence and in depth, which indicated awareness and thoughtfulness about current events and goings-on.

Albert was friendly—but serious. No-nonsense—a thinker with wit. His personality had a touch of brilliancy. He was proud. He was determined and he was always so confident.

Albert possessed a sharp mind and a remarkable intelligence. During his days at Tuskegee, some of his acquaintances who may not have known him very well felt intimidated by his superior intellect and sometimes considered him to be pompous. Maybe, on certain occasions, he could have shown more concern about a person's feelings when he made comments. I don't know.

Obviously concerned about his appearance, Albert was always attractively attired. I believe he maintained good relationships with his students in his English classes.

He and his good friend, Ralph Ellison, went about the campus all the time with several books under their arms—an unusual occurrence, generally, among the majority of the students in those days. Albert had a close personal relationship with Mort Sprague (his name was Morteza) the librarian, who encouraged and urged Albert and Ralph to read the classics. And they did.

I was impressed that, to me, Albert always seemed to project a fierce determination, early in his educational career, that he wanted to become the gifted and talented writer that he is today.

I graduated from Tuskegee several years before him and Ralph. When I think back about my relationship and friendship with them when they were students and after I began my employment at the school, I was always surprised—and very pleased—that, considering their studiousness and their educational focus, they spent so much time associating with me while I was a student and after I graduated and began my employment at Tuskegee. I am proud to have six autographed copies of Albert's books that he sent to me.

Albert and his wife, Mozelle, have always been good friends with me and my wife, Marianna. (She passed recently.) I'm sure that Albert will remember that when he would return to Tuskegee to visit, he could always count on having the use of my car for his transportation while he was here. We were just good friends.

To show you how he may have felt about me, here are two of the comments that he made in autographing his books. He said in one, "To Mike and Marianna, Two of the finest people I have ever known." And in another book he wrote, "To Mike, One of the best investments Tuskegee has ever made." I was naturally very pleased to have him say that.

20

The White Man Between Albert Murray and Stanley Crouch

SANFORD PINSKER

I have written about Albert Murray on a number of occasions, always balancing a deep respect for his work with an equally deep affection for the man. The afternoons I spent in his Harlem apartment, drinking single-malt scotch and listening to him freely range over the cultural landscape, are some of my fondest memories. Paying rapt attention (how could you not when Albert got up a good head of steam), I learned more about literature, and about life in the United States, than I ever did in graduate school decades ago.

So far, so good, but a line from Henry Louis Gates Jr.'s multilayered profile of Murray entitled "King of Cats" (see chapter 2 in this volume) has been lodged in my mind ever since my first meetings with Albert Murray and Stanley Crouch: "[T]he rift made things awkward for would-be postulants like me." Gates was describing the chasm that developed between Murray and his slightly older Tuskegee classmate, Ralph Ellison. According to Gates, the friendship, as developed in the postwar years in New York City, was so filled with bright talk about discipline and craft, culture and context, that it was often hard for outsiders to know where Ellison's ideas left off and Murray's began.

Ellison, who published his magisterial novel, *Invisible Man,* in 1952, had become famous much earlier than did Murray. According to many of their friends, this caused tension: a certain amount of envy (which Albert vigorously denies) is usually factored into Murray's side of the equation; on Ellison's side was a nagging feeling that Murray was riding his coattails.

I was not included in those who wagged their tongues as Ellison and Murray presumably snubbed each other at the prestigious Century Club, but I felt much the same awkwardness watching the divide separating Murray and Stanley Crouch widen. On the face of it, the two men share a great deal: both were instrumental in the development of Jazz at Lincoln Center, both wrote about culture with insight and panache, and both were prominently featured in Ken Burns's PBS *Jazz* documentary.

But as was the case with Ellison and Murray, a certain amount of jealousy has seeped into the relationship of the two black intellectuals I most admire. Albert makes no bones about the fact that he believes Crouch, twenty-nine years his junior, is largely responsible for the negative information that found its way into Gates's profile, originally published in 1996. "Lies, all lies," Murray would insist every time Crouch's name came up: he did not have a falling-out with Ellison, nor did he sidetrack his career with a long-delayed biography of Count Basie. (Interestingly enough, Crouch seems to be doing the same thing with his long-delayed biography of Charlie Parker.)

Stanley knew that I often went to visit Murray a day before or a day after our meetings; I tried to keep Murray in the dark about this, but since I reviewed books by both men, he probably suspected. And when Albert grew frail and confined to a hospital bed in his apartment, I tried to convince Stanley that he should patch up their differences before it was too late.

As a white man in the middle, I knew I risked a good deal by telling Stanley to do *anything,* much less apologize to a man whose novels he deplored ("No jazz band was ever so trouble-free as the ones in Murray's books. How could you give them good reviews?") and whose ideas struck him as warmed-over Ellison. I don't know if Stanley ever gave Albert a call or made his way, as he should have, up to Albert's Harlem apartment, but I hope he took my words to heart, and did.

21

On Michael James and Albert Murray

PAUL DEVLIN

Michael James (1942–2007) was Duke Ellington's nephew. His mother, Ruth, was Duke's sister. Mike was a unique, and in his way unmatched, authority on the history and aesthetics of jazz and was extraordinarily well read in many fields, especially American political and literary history. Perhaps his friend Hakim Hassan of the Museum of the City of New York said it best when he called Mike "New York's premier underground intellectual."

Albert Murray and Mike James met circa 1958 when Mike was traveling with the Ellington band and Murray was an air force officer stationed in Long Beach, California. By this time, Murray and Duke were friends, and Murray used to hang out with the band and attend recording sessions. Murray was first introduced personally to Ellington in the winter of 1947, just before Ellington's Carnegie Hall concert of that year, through an army air corps buddy who was Harry Carney's cousin. As fate would have it, Mike would remind Murray very much of Carney in his calmness, seriousness, and devotion to Duke. (Murray noted this in his statement, dictated to me, for Mike's memorial service at St. Peter's Evangelical Lutheran Church in New York on October 1, 2007.)

I do not know exactly when Murray and Mike became the close friends and sounding boards that they became for one another, but I believe, using several anecdotal guidelines, it was in the mid-1970s. Mike and the man he affectionately referred to as "the Professor" or "Professor Murray" (though in person he called him Al) were around each other regularly starting in the 1960s: at concerts, studio recording sessions, and jazz clubs. They also had many mutual friends, Jo Jones in particular. Mike was fond of saying that back then, it would not be strange to see Murray in any corner of the city, at any hour of the day or night. Mike might see Murray catching Duke's show at the Rainbow Room in the evening, then at an after-hours joint downtown, and then on a subway platform in Harlem first thing in the morning. They were both night owls par excellence. As an old Irish admonition says, "You're a long time dead in your grave"; so get the most out of life.

I was friends with Mike for the last several years of his life. He was famous among his wide circle of acquaintances for his marathon late-night phone sessions. I was on the other end of the phone probably hundreds of times. Often these conversations would range across a vast intellectual expanse, but they always returned to his profound love for "the Professor" and his work. Mike was divorced and did not go to a job every morning, so there was no incentive for Mike, as Murray would wryly note, not to talk until 4 a.m.

From what I could gather, it was in the 1980s and 1990s that their telephone sessions became multihour rituals a few late nights a week. Murray would read to Mike from works in progress, and they'd discuss the latest reviews and essays in a variety of periodicals. Once, while I was shopping with Murray at Tower Records, we saw that *The Trumpet Kings at Montreux* (Dizzy Gillespie, Clark Terry, and Roy Eldridge) had been released on CD. Murray said to me, "We'd better each buy a copy. Mike will be calling!" (Mike was very close to Roy Eldridge and Clark Terry.) They'd talk current events and nineteenth-century events; they'd speculate, philosophize, and sometimes argue. A frequent argument they had was over Tolstoy and Dostoyevsky, with Murray taking "the Count" and Mike taking the side of "the Prophet." For both of them the discussions were essential. They'd see each other at various events, perhaps at Lincoln Center or elsewhere around the city. If Murray was speaking or on a panel, Mike was sure to be there. Mike would also make the trek from his Upper East Side apartment near Sutton Place to Harlem once in a while. In person, Mike and Al were electric and dynamic together. Around one another they knew they could really talk jazz with someone to whom nothing they knew—none of the aesthetic judgments or obscure details—was foreign.

Mike was also a great champion of Murray's writing, as evidenced by a letter to the editor of the *New York Times Book Review* in which he defended Murray's latest novel against the criticisms of, in Mike's estimation (and in my estimation as well), an improperly qualified reviewer. In his letter of June 2005 he wrote that having a pop music critic review *The Magic Keys* was "an insult to a writer of Murray's stature" because according to Mike, Murray "is the most original stylist and technical innovator in American fiction since Hemingway and Faulkner." He continued, saying that through Murray's novel "for the first time in American fiction the heroism in black America is revealed. This sets Murray apart from Richard Wright, James Baldwin, and Toni Morrison. Murray has relieved fiction of victimization so popular among white critics. In reviews such as this, the real racism and condescension from white intellectuals comes in—whether from radicals, liberals, or conservatives." Although the *Times* didn't publish Mike's letter to the editor, that he wrote it and sent it illustrates his sincere appreciation for (and understanding of) Murray's literary objectives as well as the depth of friendship between them.

In the weeks before his sudden and unexpected passing, Mike was excited about an essay he was going to coauthor with Annie Kuebler for Cambridge University Press on Duke Ellington and his relationships with his musicians, but he was even more excited about collecting his thoughts on Al Murray for his recollection for this book. Mike passed only about four weeks after finding out about the recollection section for this book, and he had yet to put pen to paper. If he had, I'm sure he would've made it swing, so that he could present it to Murray with his trademark greeting, "Yeaaah, Al!"

22

Michael James on Albert Murray

GREG THOMAS

Greg Thomas, host of *Jazz It Up!:* We are sitting here with Mr. Michael James, who is a close friend of Albert Murray's, and, I'm proud to say, a close friend of mine. What is the importance of Albert Murray's thought to American thought?

Michael James: Mr. Murray has continued the Constance Rourke paradigm. In her classic study called *American Humor: A Study of Myth, Traditions and Rituals,* Constance Rourke claimed that the taproots of American culture were part Yankee, part backwoodsman, Indian, and part Negro. Mr. Murray has taken that paradigm and extended it to all Americans—when they arrive by boat or plane, your latest immigrants, whether they know it or not, become part Indian, part Yankee, part Negro, part backwoodsman. Even when they are color-poisoned bigots, they can't help but become part Negro, part Indian, and part Yankee, wherever they come from. That's one aspect.

And then Mr. Murray has defined the American Negro for himself, and to himself, to a degree and with a depth that had never been presented before. We've had many great leaders and spokesmen, mostly dealing with civil rights, because of the racism and folklore of white supremacy (really the *fake-lore* of white supremacy). Most of the intellectual energy of the group had gone into achieving their basic rights. W. E. B. Du Bois made some stabs at it. Dr. Alaine Locke made some stabs at it, [as did] James Weldon Johnson, Frederick Douglass, and Booker T., to one degree or another, but the definitive statement was first made by Ralph Ellison, and then extended, elaborated, and even refined by Albert Murray.

So his and Ellison's contributions are twofold. They revealed the American to himself. Now, most Americans are yet to become acquainted with all of this, because we've had great historians, black and white, who have documented the history, but nobody had said what all this *means* culturally, until Ellison and Murray came along. And perhaps Murray has taken it the furthest. So that, I would say, is the major contribution. And that, as Mr. Murray would say, has universal significance for the world, given the position of American culture.

23

Greg Thomas and "the Professor"

GREG THOMAS

"Why are you putting me with those guys?" an incredulous Albert Murray exclaimed to me, a confused young black intellectual who also happened to love jazz. With fear and trembling, but with the exuberance of youth, I had called Mr. Murray back in the early nineties to ask him to participate in a book project. I envisioned a work in which I would interview him, Lerone Bennett Jr., and John Henrik Clarke, and detail their influence on black American thought.

For me, the three men reflected varying streams in Afro-American intellectual life: Murray, the pro-American aesthetic philosopher of jazz and the blues; Bennett, a black historian, editor of *Ebony* magazine, and political theoretician; and Clarke, the Black Nationalist folk historian, beloved in Harlem. While these descriptions may have some accuracy, in actuality, I later realized, I was prompted to pose such a project as a way to better clarify how jazz, the blues, black American history, and Black Nationalism (or a variant called Afrocentricity) were to be resolved within myself.

According to my dearly departed friend Michael James, my state of intellectual confusion at the time can in part be attributed to the era of my upbringing. I was born the year of JFK's assassination and was a small tyke during the civil rights and Black Power movements. I came into my intellectual awareness during the 1970s, a decade not known for scintillating intellectual achievement in the United States. I became conscious of the work of Albert Murray only after graduating from Hamilton College in 1985, but had been enamored with jazz since high school, when I began playing saxophone in my sophomore year after hearing my high school's stage band perform a concert that moved me greatly.

By the time I began studying Mr. Murray's work (as well as the oeuvre of his friend and fellow Tuskegee student Ralph Ellison), I had been an avid listener of jazz for about a decade. But I was also intrigued by Black Nationalism as a source of pride in the face of the horrific legacy of slavery and Jim Crow. My love of the playing of white jazz saxophonists such as Phil Woods, Paul Desmond, and Zoot Sims precluded my ever becoming a racist, but I still flirted with notions such as the black roots of ancient Egypt, and Egypt being the fount of Western civilization. I even visited Murray once wearing a jacket with an African print. Bad move.

He ribbed me mercilessly. "Man, don't you know that when Nelson Mandela comes to the United States, he wears a Western suit?" "I'm the one who got Stanley Crouch out of his dashiki!" "Don't you know that we follow Greenwich Mean Time?" After hearing and thinking about such comments, I slowly began to realize what time it really was.

As a longtime college professor, Mr. Murray put up with my confusion and spent many hours with me in person and on the phone because he knew I adored jazz, was a serious student of black American culture, and was a budding writer. During one of these conversations, he referred me to his number one protégé. "You should contact Michael James. He'd kick your ass. Unlike some people masquerading as jazz critics, he actually knew these people." Mike sure did. As Duke Ellington's nephew, he hung out and traveled with the Ellington Orchestra back in the late fifties as a teen. Johnny Hodges was his godfather. He was in the studio for Duke's recording with John Coltrane. He seemed to know *all* of the legends of jazz. But not only that: he was extremely well read on American and world history and literature, and was a lay specialist in black American culture to boot. Mike did kick my butt intellectually on many an occasion—oftentimes referencing and pulling out quotes from the work of Murray, the man he called "the Professor"—yet somewhat more gently than Murray would have!

Murray taking time with me to explain his profound aesthetic philosophy (which he calls "Cosmos Murray") and introducing me to his dear friend Michael James were two of the gifts that he has granted me over the years. Refining my fuzzy thoughts on the meaning of history and culture was another bequest he bestowed.

I recall once sitting in his Harlem "spyglass tree," his living room lined with hundreds of books. With Murray facing me from his desk, I told him that I had heard Wynton Marsalis (yet another protégé) speak on a television program. He asked me what I thought. When I gave a weak, ambiguous answer, Murray boomed: "Man, how *precise* was he? That's the key: precision." On another occasion I asked him what he thought about the infamous Tuskegee syphilis experiments. He asked me, "What do you know about that?" I gave him a basic journalistic summary. He said, "No, that's a poor reading. Here's what happened"—and proceeded to give me a fifteen-minute history lesson.

Murray is fond of giving impromptu dissertations on a wide range of subjects, but he's not interested just in hearing his own voice. He will often ask what you know about a topic and use your response as the basis for perspicacious displays of knowledge and wisdom, which he shares freely. Considering the fact that he had dealt with and resolved many of the issues with which I had been grappling sixty or more years before our conversations, his accessibility and patience remain a wonder to me. At heart, in addition to being a great American writer of poetry, fiction, and nonfiction, and an aesthetic theorist of the first order, Albert Murray is a great teacher.

I've learned so much from him personally, and through his books, that I'll be forever indebted. Through Albert Murray, I not only took off my African garb (which is for many little more than a fashion statement), but replaced a misguided focus on African origins with a much deeper appreciation for the cultural and historical context of my own land, America. Through Murray, I know that the triumph and meaning of jazz and the blues in the twentieth century are as monumental as the building of the pyramids in ancient times.

24

Life and Literature Lessons Learned

GAIL BUCKLEY

In *The Omni-Americans,* one of the most important books about America ever written, Albert Murray writes of great African Americans like Sojourner Truth, Harriet Tubman, and Frederick Douglass, who were legends in their own lifetime, in what he called "that golden era of national synthesis"—the mid-nineteenth century.

A century or so later, in a distinctly ungolden era, in what almost seems to be a time of national disintegration, some of us are lucky enough to know Al Murray—another African American legend in his own lifetime. Granted, his name may not resound in as many households as did his nineteenth-century counterparts, but Al is a living legend, as well as friend and mentor to at least two generations of African American writers, musicians, and artists of all sorts. Al may not be a household name, but his ideas are in wide distribution— although not wide enough, as long as some African Americans stress their African heritage over their American. Certainly, Truth, Tubman, and Douglass stressed their right to an American identity.

I am lucky that Al was my writing mentor as well as my friend. He urged me to see American history for the drama it is, with all its cast of characters, and to place African Americans where they belonged. He taught that history went right along with literature, music, and painting. He gave personal seminars on Twain, Faulkner, and Louis Armstrong. He advised me to make my own writing less "uptight." (I knew what he meant.) And he explained the real difference between Booker T. Washington and W. E. B. Du Bois. Thank you, Al, for life and literature lessons learned, and for your lovable kindness and fabulous sense of fun. And thanks to your wonderful family, Mozelle and Michele, for letting us share you.

25

A Giant in Heart and Mind

Elizabeth Mayer Fiedorek

Albert Murray and I met in the early 1990s when I was Wynton Marsalis's guest at a Lincoln Center Jazz rehearsal. I had just helped Wynton put Romare Bearden images on CD covers, since I was a representative for the artist's estate at the time with ACA Gallery in New York. I knew that Albert Murray owned a number of Romare Bearden works and was his close friend and collaborator. Albert was presiding over the rehearsal, and we struck up a conversation. I asked him if I could see his art collection and possibly take some shots of the view from his apartment, where Romare Bearden's famous work *The Block* (owned by the Metropolitan Museum of Art) was inspired. This led to many more visits over the last seventeen or so years.

I have taken many photographs of the handsome, charismatic, erudite Albert Murray, and we have shared many in-depth conversations about fine art, both at his apartment and at museums. Albert is as well versed and knowledgeable about painting and sculpture as he is about literature and music. His insights and his enjoyment of fine art have made our time together truly unique and memorable.

Yes, there is much to learn about art (and music and literature) from Albert Murray. But there is much more to learn about life and about being from him.

He is truly rare in his character and admirable qualities. His physical stature is small, but he is a giant in heart and mind. He is open, brilliant, dignified, tolerant, humorous, and possessed of total confidence: all elements worthy of great admiration and emulation.

Albert is someone people go to, like a prophet or an oracle, to find the right meaning, to find the words to express an idea or thought. This has been his history with great artists and musicians as well as with students and friends. When my mother died, Albert was the first person I went to. We spent the day reading poetry, and I found the words to speak at her funeral.

Albert has been unusually important to me as a friend and as a touchstone in my life. We have connected through our photo shoots at his apartment, our discussions about his art collection and the history therein, and our visits to museums to discuss art. As a photographer, I was able to shoot a close-up portrait of Albert in his library that was published in the *New York Observer* in 1996. As a conversationalist, he taught me much about the European masters, with whom he is particularly conversant. His years in Paris coincided with a very exciting and dynamic time in the art world.

All of these were our ways of connecting, but it is Albert himself and his absolute joy of life and knowledge that make time with him most precious. He is magnanimous and one of my most precious blessings. Albert Murray is a gift to us all.

26

My Travels through Cosmos Murray

Eugene Holley Jr.

I was introduced to the work of Mr. Albert Lee Murray through the music and liner notes of Wynton Marsalis and Stanley Crouch during my college years at Howard University in Washington, DC, in the early eighties.

A year older than Marsalis, I'm a Philadelphia-born, Delaware-reared, solidly middle-class African American, raised with some degree of nationalism. So I was initially put off when Crouch and Marsalis were describing jazz not only as black music, but also as American music! When they cited the influence of this mysterious Albert Murray, I went to the Martin Luther King Library in downtown DC to see why this black man was talking about being an American in an age where we were defining ourselves as black, Afro-American, and African American.

I checked out the paperback edition of Murray's *The Omni-Americans*, and it hit me like a thunderbolt. What immediately grabbed me was his overriding conviction that *"American culture, even in its most rigidly segregated precincts, is patently and irrevocably composite"* (22), and how that theory applied to black and national identity. You see, I didn't completely buy into the rigid, either/or paradigms of the Black Nationalism curriculum taught to me in grade school, the raised fists, dashikis, and Swahili language courses.

But I didn't know how to articulate that ambivalence. In the pages of *The Omni-Americans*, Murray provided for me the Rosetta stone that unlocked the hidden inventions and dimensions of my identity. Riffing on Paul Valéry's concept of *homo Europaeus*, that the European is part Greek, Roman, and Judeo-Christian, and Constance Rourke's idea of *homo Americanus* as a citizen who is "part Yankee, part backwoodsman and Indian, and part Negro" (16), Murray wrote that Americans were—in some cases racially and on a larger scale culturally—"part Negro and part Indian" (21). That idea was a liberating new way for me to view myself in the world. And from that foundation, I delved into the other subjects Murray tackled in that book: the Black Arts movement, socialism, Africa, police brutality, education, the third world, the Moynihan Report, and the racist implications of social science. Not to mention his insights into the complexities and contradictions of Richard Wright, James Baldwin, Claude Brown, and other writers.

From *The Omni-Americans* I proceeded to *Stomping the Blues*, his erudite and down-home cultural history of jazz and the blues, written from his participant observations during its golden age, from the thirties to the mid-sixties. Free of the sociological jargon that portrayed blacks as downtrodden, perpetual victims of racism, *Stomping the Blues* was the one book that looked at both musical idioms as a mutually enriching continuum that enhanced American and world culture.

Good Morning Blues: The Autobiography of Count Basie was the next stop in my "Murray graduate studies," and two years after its publication in 1985, I took my first steps toward the world of professional writing, buoyed not only by Mr. Murray but also by the local influence of DC writers William A. Brower and A. B. Spellman, the author of *Four Lives in the Bebop Business.*

Fast-forward to the spring of 1992: I was producing an NPR-distributed documentary series on Dizzy Gillespie, and I also served in an unofficial capacity as an assistant in the embryonic stages of the network's series *Making the Music*, hosted by Wynton Marsalis. It was in that capacity that I first met Mr. Murray at an outdoor concert at Lincoln Center, where Marsalis and the Jazz at Lincoln Center Orchestra had performed. At the conclusion of the gig, I spotted Mr. Murray. Of course by this time I recognized his face, but I was surprised to see him using a walker. I didn't know that he had back and hip problems. But in a way, his physical difficulties seemed to enhance his status as an elder statesman. With a copy of *South to a Very Old Place,* his Homeric travelogue/memoir, in my hand, I walked up to him and introduced myself. He looked at me like he had known me all of my life, shook my hand, and asked me if the band was swinging. (Of course it was.) He signed my book, and I mentioned that my father also came from Alabama, which he acknowledged with a sly smile. I was immediately taken by his *southernness,* and how his voice, with its feathery yet firm high-tenor timbre, had the finesse of a down-South Shakespearean actor and the fluidity of Lester Young's sax solos.

A year later, when I moved to New York to work at a music library, I lived on Convent Avenue in the Sugar Hill section of Harlem, a twenty-minute walk from Mr. Murray's apartment, which is just across from the Schomburg Center for Research in Black Culture. My late neighbor Larry Barron, a member of the famed WWII all-black 555th Parachute Infantry Battalion, aka "the Triple Nickels," knew that I was a writer, and he offered to take me to Mr. Murray's apartment. A few days later, Barron and I showed up at Murray's apartment complex on 132nd Street and took the elevator up a few floors to his door. His wonderful wife opened it, and I saw him sitting on his couch with a kind of rehearsed poise, as he was yet again preparing to initiate a green, but brown-skin, young man into the ways of the briarpatch.

And what a briarpatch it was. It's been said that Mr. Murray's home is an adjunct to the Schomburg Center. That's no hyperbole. From the minute I entered his home, I was in the presence of a human being who is intellectually at home with the whole world. I saw rare, irreplaceable editions of the works of Hemingway, Thomas Mann, and W. H. Auden and a first edition of Ralph Ellison's *Invisible Man,* as well as numerous works on science, literature, geography, and many reference dictionaries. I recall how Mr. Murray and Barron lovingly spoke to each other, with me interjecting in respectful interludes, mindful of my father's age-old command to be quiet among grown folks.

My second sojourn to Mr. Murray's home took place at, to use Ornette Coleman's term, the "Change of the Century." I had an assignment to interview Mr. Murray about his collection of letters with his lifelong friend Ralph Ellison, published as *Trading Twelves,* for the Web site *The Black World Today.*

He answered my questions about the letters and dropped some serious science on me about his relationship to Ellison, his alma mater, the art of Romare Bearden, "the ancestral imperatives" laid down by his high school principal Benjamin Francis Baker, and the primacy of jazz and blues. He also showed me old reviews of his works, some incredible photographs of Tuskegee, Ellison, his wife, and his daughter Michele in Europe, and read some poetry from his then soon-to-be-released *Conjugations and Reiterations*. Without any explicit instructions, Mr. Murray provided me with the essential equipment not only for writing but also for living. I left his home with the fuller understanding of his embrace of the "universal particulars" required to create great and lasting art, which inspired me to investigate the works of John A. Kouwenhoven, Thomas Mann, Alain Locke, James Weldon Johnson, and Zora Neale Hurston.

With that equipment, I see how the twenty-first century is the fulfillment of Mr. Murray's omni-Americanism. Yes, Americans are part black, indigenous, and white. But they are also part Asian; part Islamic, Buddhist, West Indian, African, and East Indian; part computer geek, and backpacker, and any other hybrid that our American reality demands. It was Albert Murray who taught me to see the world, not just in black and white, but also in black, brown, and beige. If Ralph Ellison's *Invisible Man* spoke to us on "the lower frequencies," Albert Murray's grand vision sees us through the higher harmonics of our shared humanity.

27

Afternoons with Murray

Heart and Soul in the Key of Swing

Carol Friedman

Once you have had the pleasure of meeting Al Murray, if you have any smarts at all and are lucky enough to be invited, you sign on for life. Grateful for my good fortune, I have, for the past decade, taken the #2 subway up to 135th Street to spend Saturday or Sunday afternoons with Murray in the book-filled living room of his Lenox Terrace apartment. These visits are marked in summer by brutal non-air-conditioned heat and the din of whirring room fans; in winter by red wine and plenty of bittersweet chocolate; and perennially by the splendid view of the Lenox Avenue row houses as they fall into darkness. Not once did I leave before nightfall.

There are not many things more seductive than listening to Murray on the coming-of-age of Murray. That you already know of his boyhood from his series of novels—through the voice of Scooter—only adds color and context to these firsthand tales delivered by this urban, omniscient version of him. Stories take form in a rollicking oratory, in an idiosyncratic rasp that places you squarely in the time and place of wherever he lands. One wishes that all of Murray's readers had the reference of the sound and cadence of his voice.

Riffs on his formative years in and around Magazine Point, Alabama, abound: of Creoles and Cajuns and schooners and sailboats; sawmills and streetcars and the L&N railroad. I would learn that there was a fantastic array of churches, and that if you were local, you knew the sounds of all the different bells: "You'd hear the tolling and know that somebody from that particular church had passed—oh, that's Yorktown, that's Hopewell, that's Union Baptist, that's Pinegrove." And that showing up at the scene of accidents of any kind were social rites of passage for boys: "If someone got killed—got murdered, got their throat cut by a jealous guy—or if there was a train wreck, four, five miles away—we went over and looked at it." And that his discovery of geography in the third grade forever changed him. "That was one of the most liberating things; getting that geography book was like moving into puberty—that you could put the other books across the geography book and you *strap* that *way* and put it on your shoulder and you were a bigger *boy.*"

What is evident about young Murray is his unstoppable curiosity, his perfectly aligned innocence and sophistication, and his rock-steady self-image. Now ninety-two, he has not changed, apart from a century of information that he now dispenses with relish.

After a generous aperitif of Alabama yarns, I would be dispatched to Murray's superhighway of bookshelves to retrieve one book and then another, usually from the MVP fourth-row shelf that holds Joyce, Mann, Kafka, Malraux, Hemingway, and Faulkner. There are hundreds of books here from floor to ceiling, but he is partial to those titles he read in college, in the Tuskegee Library, from 1935 to 1939, and in particular those by the three authors who would forever alter and elevate his perspective: Hemingway, Faulkner, and Thomas Mann.

"Go to the fourth row down, all the way on the left, to Thomas Mann. *Joseph and His Brothers.* You see it? Black spine, tan letters? Now go all the way down to the right to André Malraux. Bring me *Man's Fate.*" And so on. Then he would read aloud or direct me to do so. His handpicked passages sometimes underscored something under discussion, but more often than not were lead-ins to the next topic he was ready to jump to. From James Reese Europe to the morality of Hemingway's hunting to Ella and Sarah and Jack Johnson to his intolerance for "activist rhetoric" to the components of

Kansas City Swing to the origins of conflict to fashion; from Harris Tweed to denim—"Blue railroad overalls became *denims* because they were made from fabric imported from Nimes . . . *de Nimes*"—to xenophobia versus exotica to the progenitors of commerce—"Who do you think it was *selling* the tools needed to those who were digging for gold?"—to Zane Grey cowboys and the *Wild West Weekly* to the marketing of Africa—"If it was relevant, the Japanese tourists would be there"—to the nature of power: "A crude way to get to elegance." And so it would go. Another afternoon of Murray musings that cover the waterfront, mixed and mastered with heart and soul and always in the key of swing.

Works Cited

Primary Texts

Murray, Albert. "Academic Lead Sheet." *From the Briarpatch File: On Context, Procedure, and American Identity*. New York: Pantheon, 2001. 14–23.

———. "An All-Purpose, All-American Literary Intellectual." *From the Briarpatch File: On Context, Procedure, and American Identity*. New York: Pantheon, 2001. 167–95.

———. "Aubades: Epic Exits and Other Twelve Bar Riffs." *Conjugations and Reiterations*. New York: Pantheon, 2001. 1–26.

———. *The Blue Devils of Nada: A Contemporary Approach to Aesthetic Statement*. New York: Pantheon, 1996.

———. Foreword. *Mitchell and Ruff: An American Profile in Jazz*. By William Zinsser. Philadelphia: Paul Dry, 2000. vii–xi.

———. *From the Briarpatch File: On Context, Procedure, and American Identity*. New York: Pantheon, 2001.

———. *The Hero and the Blues*. St. Louis: U of Missouri P, 1973.

———. *The Magic Keys*. New York: Pantheon, 2005.

———. "Of the Blues: Romare Bearden." Catalog Essay. *Of the Blues: Romare Bearden*. New York: Cordier and Eckstrom Gallery, 1975.

———. *The Omni-Americans: New Perspectives on Black Experience and American Culture*. New York: Outerbridge and Dienstfrey, 1970.

———. "Premier Cru U.S.A." *Conjugations and Reiterations*. New York: Pantheon, 2001. 43–44.

———. "Profiles/Part II: The Thirties." Catalog Essay. *Collages: Romare Bearden*. New York: Cordier and Eckstrom Gallery, 1981.

———. "Regional Particulars and Universal Statement in Southern Writing." *Callaloo* 38 (1989): 3–6.

———. *The Seven League Boots*. New York: Pantheon, 1995.

———. *South to a Very Old Place*. 1971. New York: Random House, 1991.

———. *The Spyglass Tree*. New York: Random House, 1991.

———. *Stomping the Blues*. 1976. New York: Da Capo, 1989.

———. *Train Whistle Guitar*. New York: McGraw-Hill, 1974.

———. "William Faulkner: Noun Place and Verb." *Conjugations and Reiterations*. New York: Pantheon, 2001. 48–52.

Murray, Albert, and Ralph Ellison. *Trading Twelves: The Selected Letters of Ralph*

Ellison and Albert Murray. Ed. Albert Murray and John F. Callahan. New York:
Modern Library, 2000.

Secondary Sources

Abrams, M. H. *A Glossary of Literary Terms.* 5th ed. New York: Holt, Rinehart and
Winston, 1988.

Applewhite, James. *Ode to the Chinaberry Tree and Other Poems.* Baton Rouge:
Louisiana State UP, 1986.

Baker, Barbara A. "Turning Impossibility into Possibility: Teaching Ellison, Murray,
and the Blues at Tuskegee." *White Scholars/African American Texts.* Ed. Lisa A.
Long. New Brunswick: Rutgers UP, 2005. 68–77.

Baker, Houston A., Jr. *Blues Ideology and Afro-American Literature: A Vernacular
Theory.* Chicago: U of Chicago P, 1987.

Bakhtin, Mikhail. *Speech Genres and Other Late Essays.* Austin: U of Texas P, 1986.

Bateman, Beverly. "Albert Murray: Up Tempo or 'The Velocity of Celebration.'"
Conversations with Albert Murray. Ed. Roberta S. Maguire. Jackson: UP of
Mississippi, 1997. 19–24.

Bearden, Romare. "Rectangular Structure in My Montage Painting." *Leonardo* 2
(1968): 11–19.

Boisvert, Raymond D. *John Dewey: Rethinking Our Time.* Albany: State U of New
York P, 1998.

Borshuk, Michael. *Swinging the Vernacular: Jazz and African American Modernist
Literature.* New York: Routledge, 2006.

Campbell, D. Kaye. Rev. of *The Chinaberry Tree and Selected Writings,* by Jessie
Fauset. *MELUS* 23.1(1998): 197–99.

Capote, Truman. *A Capote Reader.* New York: Random House, 1987.

Carson, Warren. "Albert Murray: Literary Reconstruction of the Vernacular
Community." *African American Review* 27.2 (1993): 287–95.

Cassity, Turner. *The Destructive Element: New and Selected Poems.* Athens: Ohio UP,
1998.

Crockett, James Underwood, et al. *Trees. The Time-Life Encyclopedia of Gardening.*
New York: Time-Life, 1972.

Crouch, Stanley. *Always in Pursuit: Fresh American Perspectives, 1995–1997.* New
York: Pantheon, 1998.

Cruse, Harold, et al. "The Alain Locke Symposium." *Harvard Advocate* 107.4 (1974):
9–28.

Dean, Blanche Evans. *Trees and Shrubs in the Heart of Dixie.* Birmingham, AL: Coxe, 1961.

Devlin, Paul. "Albert Murray at Ninety." *Antioch Review* 65.2 (2007): 256–65.

Dewey, John. *Art as Experience.* 1934. New York: Capricorn, 1958.

———. *Democracy and Education.* New York: Macmillan , 1916.

Dirr, Michael A. *Dirr's Trees and Shrubs for Warm Climates.* Portland, OR: Timber, 2002.

Edwards, Louis. "Albert Murray on Stage." *Conversations with Albert Murray.* Ed. Roberta S. Maguire. Jackson: U of Mississippi P, 1997. 78–93.

Ellison, Ralph. "The Art of Fiction." *Shadow and Act.* New York: Random House, 1953. 167–83.

———. *Invisible Man.* New York: Random House, c. 1952.

———. *Juneteenth.* Ed. John F. Callahan. New York: Random House, 1999.

Eversley, Shelly. *The Real Negro: The Question of Authenticity in Twentieth-Century African American Literature.* New York: Routledge, 2004.

Faulkner, William. *The Reivers: A Reminiscence.* New York: Random House, 1962.

Fauset, Jessie. *The Chinaberry Tree: A Novel of American Life.* 1931. New York: AMS, 1969.

Foreman, Anita Kathy, and Teresa Nance. "From Miscegenation to Multiculturalism: Perceptions and Stages of Interracial Relationship Development." *Journal of Black Studies* 29.4 (1999): 540–57.

Gebhard, Caroline. Personal videotaped interview with Louis A. "Mike" Rabb. Sept. 19, 2007.

Gelburd, Gail. "Bearden in Theory and Ritual: An Interview with Albert Murray." *Romare Bearden: Photomontage Projections, 1964.* New York: Harry Abrams / Whitney Museum of American Art, 1997. 53–60.

Gilman, Edward F., and Dennis G. Watson. "*Melia azedarach:* Chinaberry." Document ENH-565. Nov. 1993; rev. Apr. 2007. Environmental Horticulture Department, Florida Cooperative Extension Service, Institute of Food and Agricultural Sciences, University of Florida. <http://edis.ifas.ufl.edu/st406>.

Grant, Greg. "Chinaberry Trees." *Horticultural Update.* Sept. 1977. Extension Horticulture, Texas Agricultural Extension Service, Texas A & M University System. <http://aggie-horticulture.tamu.edu/extension/newsletters/hortupdate/hortupdate_archives/huwoct97.html>.

Hedrick, U. P. *A History of Horticulture in America to 1860.* 1950. Portland, OR: Timber, 1988.

Hudgins, Andrew. *Ecstatic in the Poison: New Poems.* Sewanee Writers' Series. Woodstock, NY: Overlook, 2003.

Hurston, Zora Neale. *Novels and Stories.* New York: Library of America, 1995.

Jones, Carolyn M. "Race and Intimacy: Albert Murray's *South to a Very Old Place.*" *South to a New Place: Region, Literature, Culture.* Ed. Suzanne W. Jones and Sharon Monteith. Baton Rouge: Louisiana State UP, 2002. 58–75.

Jones, Madison. *A Cry of Absence.* New York: Crown, 1971.

Kelder, Diane. *Stuart Davis: Art and Theory, 1920–1931.* New York: Pierpont Morgan Library, 2002.

Kennel, Sarah. "Bearden's Musée Imaginaire." *The Art of Romare Bearden.* Ed. Ruth Fine. New York: Harry Abrams / National Gallery of Art, 2003. 138–56.

Lamb, Brian. Interview with Albert Murray. *Booknotes* June 16, 1996. <http://www.booknotes.org/Transcript/?ProgramID=1308>.

Malraux, André. *The Voices of Silence.* Princeton: Princeton UP, 1990.

Mann, Thomas. Foreword. *Joseph and His Brothers.* Trans. H. T. Lowe-Porter. New York: Knopf, 1948.

———. *Joseph and His Brothers.* Vol. 1 of *Joseph and His Brothers.* Trans. H. T. Lowe-Porter. New York: Knopf, 1934.

———. *Joseph in Egypt.* Vol. 3 of *Joseph and His Brothers.* Trans. H. T. Lowe-Porter. New York: Knopf, 1938.

Mundt, Hannelore. *Understanding Thomas Mann.* Columbia: U of South Carolina P, 2004.

O'Meally, Robert. Interview with Albert Murray. Smithsonian Institution Jazz Oral History Program, New York. June 30, July 1, Aug. 8, Sept. 23, 1994.

Patton, Sharon. "Romare Bearden: Narrations." Catalog Essay. *Romare Bearden: Narrations.* Purchase, NY: SUNY Purchase / Neuberger Museum of Art, 2003. 4–15.

Pearson, Nathan W., Jr. *Goin' to Kansas City.* Urbana: U of Illinois P, 1987.

Pinsker, Sanford. "'The Bluesteel, Rawhide, Patent-Leather Implications of Fairy Tales': A Conversation with Albert Murray." *Georgia Review* 51.2 (1997): 205–21.

Powell, Richard J. "Art History and Black Memory: Toward a 'Blues Aesthetic.'" *The Jazz Cadence of American Culture.* Ed. Robert G. O' Meally. New York: Columbia UP, 1998. 180–95.

———. "Changing, Conjuring Reality." *Conjuring Bearden.* Ed. Richard J. Powell. Durham: Duke UP, 2006. 19–31.

Price, Richard, and Sally Price. *Romare Bearden: The Caribbean Dimension.* Philadelphia: U of Pennsylvania P, 2006.

Rampersad, Arnold. *Ralph Ellison: A Biography.* New York: Knopf, 2007.

Roberts, Dorothy. *Killing the Black Body: Race, Reproduction, and the Meaning of Liberty.* New York: Vintage, 1997.

Rourke, Constance. *American Humor: A Study in the National Character.* New York: Doubleday, 1931.

Rowell, Charles H. "'An All-Purpose, All-American Literary Intellectual': An Interview with Albert Murray." *Callaloo* 20.2 (1997): 399–414.

———. "Inscription at the City of Brass: An Interview with Romare Bearden." *Callaloo* 11.3 (1988): 428–46.

Scherman, Tony. "The Omni-Americans." *Conversations with Albert Murray.* Ed. Roberta S. Maguire. Jackson: U of Mississippi P, 1997. 122–36.

Schmutterer, H., ed. *The Neem Tree Azedirachta indica A. Juss. And Other Meliaceous Plants, Sources of Unique Natural Projects for Integrated Pest Management, Medicine, Industry and Other Purposes.* Weinheim, Germany: VCH Verlagsgesellschaft, 1995.

Schwartzman, Myron. "Of Mecklenburg, Memory, and the Blues: Romare Bearden's Collaboration with Albert Murray." *Bulletin of Reseach in the Humanities (Continuing the Journal of the New York Public Library)* 86.2 (1983): 140–67.

———. *Romare Bearden: His Life and Art.* New York: Harry Abrams, 1990.

Seymour, Gene. "Talking with Albert Murray: A Hero and the Blues." *Conversations with Albert Murray.* Ed. Roberta S. Maguire. Jackson: U of Mississippi P, 1997. 54–65.

Staples, Robert. *The Black Family.* Belmont, CA: Wadsworth, 1999.

Stowe, Harriet Beecher. *Uncle Tom's Cabin.* 1852. New York: Penguin, 1966.

Thometz, Kurt. "The Well Dressed Bibliophile: Interview with Albert Murray." Feb. 26, 2003. <http://colophon.com/privatelibrary/interviews/murray.html>.

Thompson, Mark Christian. *Black Fascisms.* Charlottesville: U of Virginia P, 2007.

Tompkins, Calvin. "Profiles: Putting Something over Something Else." *The Jazz Cadence of American Culture.* Ed. Robert G. O'Meally. New York: Columbia UP, 1998. 224–43.

Walsh, Lauren. Personal interview with Albert Murray. May 12, 2007.

Welty, Eudora. *The Collected Stories of Eudora Welty.* New York: Harcourt Brace and Jovanovich, 1980.

Wood, Joe. "The Soloist: Albert Murray's Blues People." *Conversations with Albert Murray.* Ed. Roberta S. Maguire. Jackson: U of Mississippi P, 1997. 94–109.

Contributors

BARBARA A. BAKER, director of the Women's Leadership Institute and associate professor at Auburn University, taught English at Tuskegee University in Alabama for eleven years and was a professional musician before entering academe. She is the author of *The Blues Aesthetic and the Making of American Identity* (2003) and several articles exploring musical manifestations in American literature.

GAIL BUCKLEY is Lena Horne's daughter and the author of several books, including *The Hornes: An American Family* (2002).

JOHN F. CALLAHAN is Morgan S. Odell Professor of Humanities at Lewis and Clark College. He is literary executor of Ralph Ellison's estate, and in that capacity edited *Juneteenth* (1999). He also coedited with Albert Murray *Trading Twelves: The Selected Letters of Ralph Ellison and Albert Murray* (2000).

PAUL DEVLIN, doctoral student at Stony Brook University, adjunct instructor at St. John's University in Queens, New York, and close personal friend of Albert Murray, has published recently in *Slate* and the *Antioch Review*. He is coediting with Murray an autobiography of drummer "Pap" Jo Jones.

ELIZABETH MAYER FIEDOREK has been an art dealer and photographer in New York City for twenty years. She owned a private art consulting business and an art gallery, and most recently was the director of the Twenty-fifth Street gallery location for PaceWildenstein in New York's Chelsea Art District.

CAROL FRIEDMAN is a widely published photographer known for her portraits of art and entertainment figures. She has designed and photographed hundreds of CD covers for jazz, classical, and soul artists. She served as chief photographer for Blue Note Records and vice president and creative director for Elektra Entertainment and Motown. Her book *The Jazz Pictures* (1999) is a retrospective of her jazz portraits.

HENRY LOUIS GATES JR. is Alphonse Fletcher University Professor at Harvard University, where he is director of the W. E. B. Du Bois Institute for African and African American Research. The critically acclaimed author of dozens of books, he is best known for his groundbreaking *The Signifying Monkey: A Theory of Afro-American Literary Criticism* (1988).

CAROLINE GEBHARD, professor of English at Tuskegee University, is coeditor of *Post-Bellum, Pre-Harlem: African American Literature and Culture, 1877–1919* (2006). The author of many essays on American literature, she is currently at work on a forthcoming book, *Invisible Legacy: The Women of Tuskegee, 1881–1981*.

ANNE-KATRIN GRAMBERG is the dean of the College of Liberal Arts at Auburn University. A native of Germany, she is the author of many books and articles on business and German, and she serves on the board of directors of the Alabama Germany partnership.

BERT HITCHCOCK, professor of English at Auburn University (retired), served as the Hargis Professor of American Literature and as head of the English department. He is the author of a book on Richard Malcolm Johnston and is the coeditor of four editions of the textbook anthology *American Short Stories*, published by Longman.

ROY HOFFMAN is the author of *Almost Family*, winner of the Lillian Smith Award for fiction, and *Back Home: Journeys through Mobile* (2001). A native of Mobile, he worked in New York City for twenty years as a journalist, speechwriter, editor, and teacher before returning south as writer-in-residence at the *Mobile Register*, where he is now on staff.

EUGENE HOLLEY JR. is a writer and radio producer. His work has appeared in *Black World Today, Down Beat, Ebony, Jet, Jazz Times, Hispanic,* the *New York Times Book Review,* the *Village Voice,* and *Vibe.* His radio work includes the National Public Radio series *Dizzy's Diamond* and Public Radio International's *Duke Ellington Centennial Radio Project.*

MICHAEL JAMES was the nephew of Duke Ellington, a dear friend and intellectual companion of Murray, and a frequent visitor to the Murray's Harlem home.

JAY LAMAR is the director of the Caroline Marshall Draughon Center for the Arts & Humanities at Auburn University and the coeditor of *The Remembered Gate: Memoirs by Alabama Writers* (2002).

ROBERTA S. MAGUIRE is associate professor of English at the University of Wisconsin, Oshkosh, where she directs the University Honors Program. The editor of *Conversations with Albert Murray* (1997), she has also published articles on Murray and other southern writers in *Southern Quarterly, Southern Literary Journal, Genre,* and *History of Southern Women's Literature.*

WYNTON MARSALIS, trumpeter and composer, is musical director of Jazz at Lincoln Center and author of *To a Young Jazz Musician* (2005). A protégé of Murray, he has won nine Grammys and a Pulitzer Prize for Music.

MICHELE MURRAY is Albert and Mozelle Murray's daughter. She was a professional dancer with the Alvin Ailey Company.

DON NOBLE, professor of English at the University of Alabama (retired) and adjunct professor of journalism, is host of the Alabama Public Television literary interview show *Bookmark* and editor of *Climbing Mt. Cheaha: A Collection of Stories by Emerging Alabama Writers* (2004).

SIDNEY OFFIT has written two novels, ten books for young readers, and *Memoir of a Bookie's Son* (2003). He was senior editor of *Intellectual Digest,* book editor of *Politics Today,* and contributing editor of *Baseball* magazine. For more than three decades he has served on the boards of the Authors Guild and PEN American Center as curator of the George Polk Journalism Awards.

SANFORD PINSKER, emeritus professor of humanities at Franklin and Marshall College, is the author or editor of twelve book-length studies and more than eight hundred articles, essays, editorials, and book reviews.

MAURICE POGUE, a doctoral student at Michigan State University and recipient of a University Enrichment Fellowship, was a UNCF/Mellon fellow while studying English at Tuskegee University. His first publication, "Sutpen the Half Human," was published by the *Mellon Mays Undergraduate Fellowship Journal*.

LOUIS A. "MIKE" RABB has been associated with Tuskegee University for fifty-four years, first as a student and later as an administrator of John Andrew Hospital and secretary to the university's board of trustees. At Tuskegee he met George Washington Carver, Robert Russa Moton, Ralph Ellison, and Albert Murray and maintained friendships with the latter two for many years.

GREG THOMAS, host of *Jazz It Up!*, an online jazz news and entertainment TV show, is a writer, jazz critic, and host of a radio talk show on WBAI in New York City. He contributes regularly to the interview series associated with the Jazz Museum in Harlem, and has authored numerous articles on jazz.

LAUREN WALSH earned a PhD in English and comparative literature, as well as BA and MA degrees, from Columbia University. She has studied in Germany and France and taught at Columbia, Eugene Lang College at the New School, and New York University. Her scholarly interests include the role of memory and history in twentieth-century literature from Woolf to Ellison to contemporary writers including Milan Kundera and the late W. G. Sebald.

Index

European influence, 27, 38, 47, 55, 70, 75, 76, 77, 80, 222, 224, 226, 228
European modernism, 75, 79, 85
European tradition, 75
existentialism, 27, 39, 63
extension, 58, 105, 135, 181, 182, 188

fairytales, 8, 13, 24, 93, 140, 179
fakelore, 167, 168, 214
Faulkner, William, 1, 15, 20, 34, 55, 63, 85, 123, 136, 140, 158, 183, 220, 228
Feeling and Form, 13
fiction, 13, 15, 16, 33, 44, 47, 54, 55, 57, 58, 59, 63, 70, 85, 88, 90, 91, 110, 120, 130, 131, 137, 139, 156, 183, 185, 213, 218; southern, 48
fictional writing, 19, 57, 116, 130, 138, 139, 149, 163, 192
Fiedorek, Elizabeth, 8, 221–22
filthlore, 124
fine art, 53, 56, 57, 63, 66, 73, 169, 221
folklore, 1, 16, 46, 57, 124, 164, 167, 168, 174, 214; of white supremacy, 1, 124, 164, 167, 214
folktale, 88, 93, 175
Foster, Luther M., 127
frames of acceptance and rejection, 132, 134
Freud, Sigmund, 1, 89, 192
Friedman, Carol, 8, 227–29
futility, 6, 134, 135

Garveyites, 16
Gates, Henry Louis, Jr., 3, 4, 8, 15–36, 54, 69, 81n1, 202–3, 209, 210
Gebhard, Caroline, 6, 114–29
geopolitics, 25
Gillepsie, Dizzie, 133

Giovanni, Nikki, 18

Hamilton, Gerald, 121, 122, 131, 158, 159, 217
Hampton Institute, 128
Hanscom Air Force Base, 148
Harlem, 3, 5, 20, 24, 72, 77, 78, 79, 82n6, 84, 137, 138, 139, 140, 199, 209, 210, 212, 216, 218, 225
Harper, Michael S., 31
Harper's Magazine, 47, 121, 157
Harris, Joel Chandler, 20, 175, 229
Hemingway, Ernest, 1, 6, 19, 20, 39, 48, 55, 63, 64, 65, 75, 85, 122, 123, 134, 135, 136, 139, 140, 141, 144, 192, 213, 225, 228
Henry, John, 46, 107
hero, 6, 8, 14, 22, 24, 33, 45, 46, 49, 53, 60, 61, 63, 89, 91, 94, 95, 96, 98, 110, 114, 117, 118, 119, 127n11, 131, 134, 140, 141, 142, 147, 163, 170, 172, 192, 193, 194, 195
Hero and the Blues, The, 53, 56, 57, 59, 60, 64, 76, 84, 85, 87, 96, 99, 100n2, 101n9, 111, 158, 159, 170, 193
Hero: A Study in Tradition, Myth, and Drama, The, 22
heroic action, 5, 23, 53, 57, 60, 61, 67, 92, 131, 132, 161, 170, 171, 172
heroic artist, 5, 70
heroic literature, 33
heroism, 22, 28, 213
Highness, Royal, 147
Hitchcock, Bert, 7, 179–90
Hoffman, Roy, 6, 138–46
Holley, Eugene, 8, 223–26
Hollis Burke Frissell Library, 158, 161
Homer, 20, 34, 225

Malcolm X, 18, 21

Malraux, André, 17, 20, 29, 64, 73, 75–77, 85, 152, 192, 228

Mann, Thomas, 5, 15, 17, 20, 24, 29, 65, 75, 84–100, 123, 129n19, 139, 140, 200, 225, 226, 228

Man's Fate, 20, 57, 228. *See also* Malraux, André

Marsalis, Wynton, 3, 5, 8, 20, 29, 34, 143, 199, 202, 203, 205, 218, 221, 223, 224. *See also* protégé

Marshall, Little Buddy, 94, 97, 105, 106, 109

McCray, Deljean, 94

McMillan, Terry, 21

McPherson, James Alan, 33–34

messianic view, 16

metaphor, 4, 13, 52, 55, 61, 63, 92, 115, 128n16, 130, 131, 132, 136, 156, 157, 160, 161, 162, 168, 169, 170, 188, 194

Metcalf, Lexin, 107, 108, 192

military, 25, 42, 43, 123, 136, 137

Miss Tee, 109, 122

Mitchell and Ruff: An American Profile in Jazz, 78

Mobile, AL, 23, 92, 193

Mobile County Training School, 1, 117, 121, 137, 141, 144, 159

modernism, 6, 16, 24, 77, 79, 80, 85, 125

modernist, 64, 70, 73, 74, 75

Morris, Willie, 26, 32, 47, 143, 157

Morrison, Toni, 21, 34, 213

Moynihan Report, 24

mulatto, 7, 55, 58, 99, 108, 165, 166, 169, 171, 172; aesthetic, 55, 56; American, 7, 55, 56, 164, 169, 173, 176; culture, 53, 56, 166

Mumford, Lewis, 35

Murray, Albert: Alabamian, 14, 52, 140, 209; anthropological relationship, 32; autobiographical elements in writings, 34, 62, 67, 127n, 130, 136, 193, 202; Cosmos Murray, 4, 52–67, 211, 223; cultural critic, 15–16, 36, 123, 193; use of cultural background in writings, 98; cultural presumption, 27, 203; elaborations, 1, 20, 73; hero culture, 6, 22, 70; integrationist, 16, 26, 105, 120, 124, 127n, 168, 219; influences on, 64, 85, 129n, 102; literary relationships, 32, 39, 43; literary aesthetics, 70; literary techniques, 113, 121; nonfiction, 22, 70, 130, 139, 156, 218; panegyrics, 22; protégés, 20, 202, 217, 218; trope, 87, 121, 165, 169, 174. *See also* Ellison, Ralph

Murray, Michele, 7, 43, 147–54

Murray, Mozelle, 24, 43, 45, 62

myth, 6, 35, 73, 85, 88, 93, 94, 125

mythic, 6, 22, 31, 33, 39, 46, 54, 87, 88, 89, 91, 93, 94, 98, 100n9

mythmaker, 99

mythologies, 5, 88. *See also* Brer Rabbit

National Book Award, 45

Neal, Larry, 18, 26, 28

Negro, 18, 22, 25, 27, 38, 41, 43, 48, 54, 55, 56, 59, 60, 65, 74, 78, 79, 80, 91, 127n9, 141, 144, 165, 167, 177, 183, 184, 191, 200, 214, 224; culture, 16; idiom, 17

Neruda, Pablo, 34

new black vanguard, 16

New York City, 3, 4, 6, 8, 15, 20, 24, 25, 27, 30, 31, 33, 41, 42, 47, 61, 71, 72, 73, 74, 83n15, 125n2, 138, 142, 143, 144, 151, 152, 153, 157, 176, 203, 209, 211, 221, 225

Noble, Don, 6, 60, 130–37